MW00988895

Thor Heyerdahl
Voyages of the Sun

The
Kon-Tiki Museum
Archive

atelier éditions

A note on language
Quoted material has been reproduced according to original sources and not changed to reflect contemporary usage.

HUMBOLDT CURRENT
KON-TIKI EXPEDITION
RA & RA II EXPEDITIONS
TIGRIS EXPEDITION
LARVIK
FATU HIVA
RAPA NUI (EASTER ISLAND)
BELLA COOLA VALLEY
REPUBLIC OF MALDIVES
TÚCUME
GALÁPAGOS ISLANDS
COLLA MICHERI
NEW
HIVA OA
NUKU HIVA
KON-TIKI EXPEDITION
RAROIA
TAHITI
RAPA ITI
PITCAIRN
HUMBOLDT CURRENT
PACIFIC OCEAN

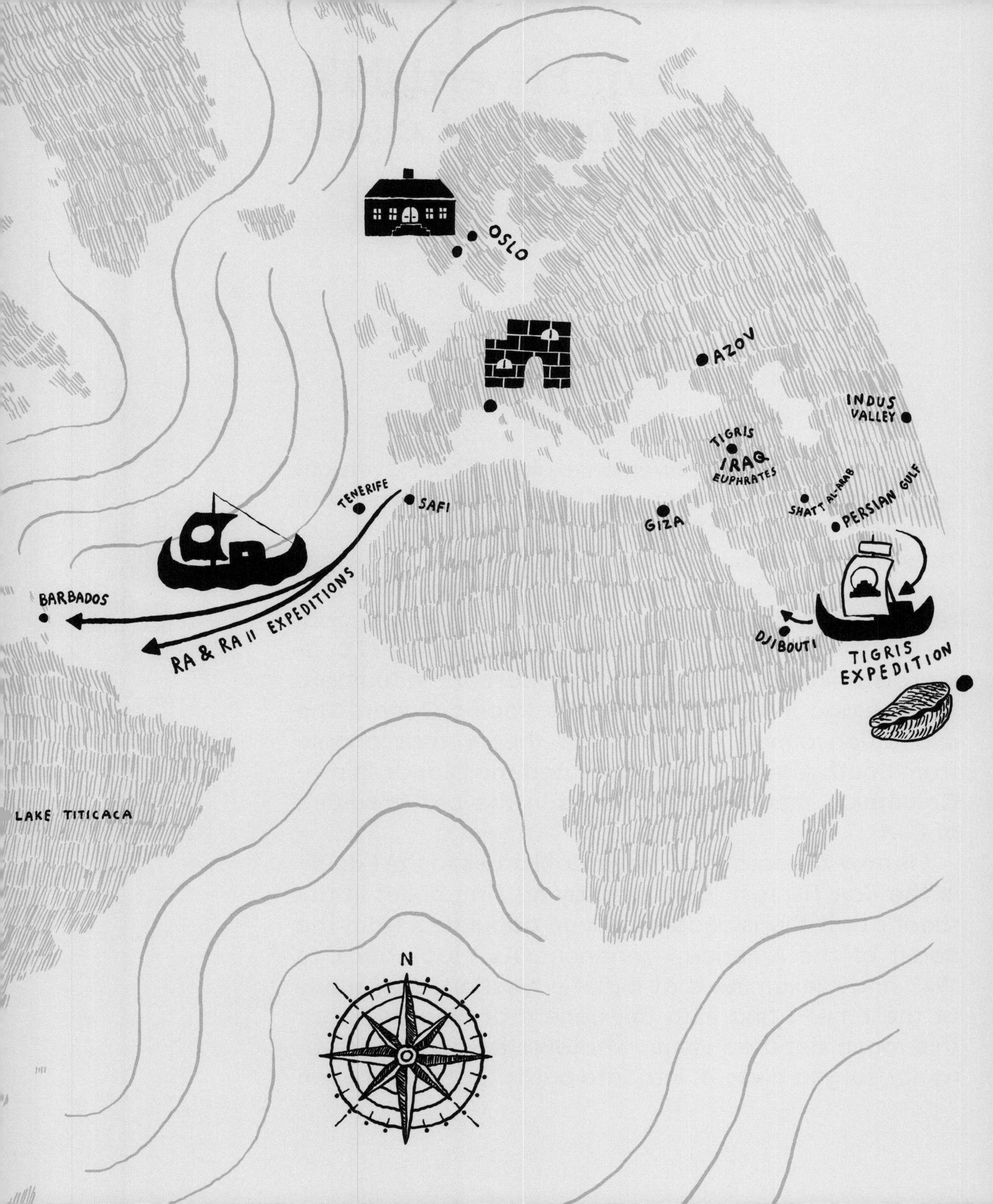
OSLO
AZOV
INDUS VALLEY
TIGRIS
IRAQ
EUPHRATES
SHATT AL-ARAB
PERSIAN GULF
TENERIFE
SAFI
GIZA
BARBADOS
RA & RA II EXPEDITIONS
DJIBOUTI
TIGRIS EXPEDITION
LAKE TITICACA
N

Thor Heyerdahl's Polynesian Legacy

Sonia Haoa Cardinali
Archaeologist

On 28 April 1947, the Norwegian explorer Thor Heyerdahl set sail, along with a crew of five intrepid sailors, from the Port of Callao in Peru in the direction of Polynesia. They made the journey on a raft of balsa logs constructed using the authentic ancestral materials and techniques of the indigenous people of Lake Titicaca. It took them 101 days to travel the 4,350-mile (7,000-km) distance to the atoll of Raroia, part of the Tuamotu Archipelago in the middle of the Pacific Ocean. The expedition aimed to prove the theory that people from South America had populated the islands in pre-Columbian times, as recounted in the oral tradition of Peru.

It is now 75 years since Heyerdahl crossed the Pacific in the *Kon-Tiki* raft, propelled by his firm belief in the theory that the islands had been populated from the coast of the American continent. As I look back to 1947 and reexamine that belief—questioned by many at the time—I find with the benefit of hindsight that this much debated issue, whatever its academic veracity, forged diverse, intricate paths that would open the way for the scientific examination of everything he put forward as an object of study.

To my mind, Heyerdahl is the most experienced, daring, courageous, and thoughtful explorer the modern world has seen. His intellectual curiosity knew no limits. For his scholarly interest in all matters archaeological, anthropological, sociological, linguistic, geographical, biological, botanical, and cultural, among others; for his sharp intuition; for his passion for unveiling ancient mysteries; and for the tremendous humility he showed in his encounters with every land and its people, I believe that his contribution to contemporary science is unparalleled. Heyerdahl had an enthusiastic interest in all sciences, and, if we are to tackle contemporary issues, such as climate change and pollution, his inclusive way of looking at the world is a lesson to us today.

Each one of his journeys contributed to the further identification of the islands and other enclaves around the Tuamotu Archipelago, with all that it entailed. In doing so, with his broad vision, he has managed to highlight the heterotopia within each of these spaces. As an indigenous person of what was possibly his most studied island, I have no qualms in acknowledging that it was he who put Rapa Nui on the world map.

Once established as the focus of growing interest to researchers the world over, Rapa Nui—or Easter Island as it is often known—which at the time relied on only subsistence agriculture and precarious artisanal fishing, began to benefit from a whole movement of pioneering travelers. This gave rise to the first attempts at tourism, which helped to sustain a minimal local economy and spurred the development of the inhabitants' own tourist initiatives, assisting the visitors' in their countless forays to wonder at, observe, discover, study, and learn about the island and, in particular, its distinctive statues.

Over the decades, Heyerdahl's many generous gestures toward the Rapa Nui people have faded from memory, and so I wish to remind my people of the significant contributions the explorer made to what we have become: generous gestures, such as the donation of around $5,000 to the community—a sum of money that amounted to a veritable fortune at that time—which was used to fund, among other things, the building of the church and to purchase the first vehicle to travel on the island.

Confronted with what was clearly our dire need, Heyerdahl showed no hesitation in buying old handcrafted pieces to take back with him as artifacts. Many of these had been recently manufactured and forcibly aged so that they could be sold or exchanged for the utensils, tools, clothing, or food the explorer brought with him. Aware of the harsh reality of island life, moved by the local population's inability to access goods, and extremely supportive of them, he would accept every single piece he was offered with a knowing nod, aware that they were not all genuine antiquities.

His contribution to Rapa Nui's heritage is probably most significant in material terms and most important from a historical perspective. It was always his most fervent wish that the pieces he bought from the indigenous people would be returned to the island at some point, never intending to appropriate the objects but instead to research them more completely.

Nor was he possessive or selfish in regard to his findings. Instead, he drew many other scientists to the island through the years, laying the foundations for the historical reinterpretation of events that had taken place over the centuries concerning the extremely developed people that first inhabited the island, one that could almost be considered a civilization in its own right.

The Rapanui might have been recognized as such, had the island's extreme isolation not prevented the territorial conquest of other peoples, who could have assimilated their culture. Nevertheless, they possessed technology, their own language, writing, architecture, engineering, and other markers of development and social organization that are evidence of a multifaceted cohesion, in particular, in regard to the statues that have survived close to 1,000 years.

To me, Heyerdahl represents the most important scientific point of reference in relation to Pacific cultures, given that his theory, accurate or not, continues to attract academic interest and research, whether to refute or defend it. Any discussion of Polynesian migration must explore his theories, because it is impossible to ignore his contribution. He made people engage with this subject—whether that be to prove or disprove his assertions.

A couple of decades after his first visit to Rapa Nui, the Canadian scientific expedition METEI (Medical Expedition to Easter Island) carried out medical examinations among the population, giving rise to many other initiatives of genetic interest. For the most part, these initiatives attempted—through the study of vegetal and other species—to trace the migratory route of the Rapanui ancestors from Southeast Asia eastward, across Oceania some 3,000 years ago, before settling on Rapa Nui a little under 2,000 years later.

As ancient navigators who seem to easily interpret the movement of tides, currents, birds, the moon, and the stars, the Polynesian people have a deep-rooted connection to the natural world. For this reason, I am personally inclined to assert that we originated from the West and not from South America.

It is well known that on large continental landmasses, navigation usually ran in parallel to the coast, from where the terrestrial landscape could be inspected and contact could be made with other peoples, creating commercial links and leading to the exchange of goods and materials of mutual interest, or simply to the conquest of new lands. Although straying away from safe, visible coastlands on uncertain, dangerous routes would have been less common, we cannot entirely rule out the possibility of contact between these groups.

Nevertheless, I should make clear that the conclusions I draw now—with all the technological tools at my disposal today enabling me to do so—could not have been reached in the middle of the last century, when those tools were not available. Thor Heyerdahl's daring theories and expeditions set the stage for all subsequent inquiry, resulting in an unparalleled legacy and references to him in every book on this subject.

He was a man with a broad vision and transparent intentions. From him, I learned how to look beyond the obvious, keep an open mind, and be a scientist that leaves space for other possibilities rather than maintaining narrow or inflexible points of view. Cherishing freedom of thought as he did, he never imposed a particular way of looking at things on me, and instead celebrated our differences. Nor did I ever feel any pressure other than to think and analyze things for myself and come to my own conclusions. His aim was one of understanding and not ownership, implying the rejection of many privileges and comforts in favor of advancing scientific progress. He believed that the sea belonged to everyone, and that by gathering diverse teams of people with differing viewpoints, we could tackle questions more broadly and more effectively.

I feel nothing but gratitude toward him. I hold on to the memory of the hard work involved whenever he would invite me to one of his excavations, either on Rapa Nui or in another corner of the world. He managed to make the leap from a small island in Polynesia to a region of South America, from research in a part of Canada to a study in the Mediterranean, because he, more than any other explorer I know of, had a truly Universal Mind.

Prologue

White Shadows in the Southern Seas

Fatu Hiva, 1937

Gathered around the seashore's stone hearth, enveloped by gentle twilight, two young, earnest, golden-sunbathed Norwegian beachcombers listened fascinated as an Island elder, Teite Tua Kipote, leant meditatively forward. "Tiki, the god of mankind, who lives in heaven, created the earth,"[1] Teite Tua declared. After creating water, Tiki had then created fish, birds, mammals, fruits, and humankind. Gazing upward at the heavens, and across the luminous Pacific Ocean, the two listened enraptured as the island elder elaborated. "Tiki … was both a god and a chief. Tiki … brought my ancestors to these islands on which we live. Before that we lived in a great land far beyond the sea."[2] Latterly married and now honeymooning, 23-year-old Thor Heyerdahl, abandoning University of Oslo geography and zoology classes, and his wife, 20-year-old fellow student Liv Coucheron Torp, had themselves voyaged from lands far beyond the ocean. They had journeyed forth on Christmas Day 1936 (having married just the day before), first by railroad from Oslo to Marseille, then onward upon a French cargo-passenger ship, *Commissaire Ramel*, across the Mediterranean Sea and North Atlantic Ocean, down through the Panama Canal, far across the long-daydreamed-for South Pacific Ocean to paradisiacal Tahiti. And onward, finally, to Fatu Hiva, a verdant South Pacific island within the isolated Marquesas archipelago. Lying some 1,000 miles (1,610 km) northeast of Tahiti, and 3,000 miles (4,828 km) west of Mexico, Fatu Hiva, then reachable only via intermittent visits from coconut-trade vessels, today remains one of the most isolated archipelagos on Earth. Heyerdahl and Liv had departed Oslo that December beneath the aegis of a zoological expedition organized independently by Heyerdahl, supported by his influential zoology professors, Dr. Kristine Bonnevie and Dr. Hjalmar Broch, and financed by Heyerdahl's somewhat reluctant father. Ostensibly, Heyerdahl was to gather zoological specimens, document the apparently decaying vestiges of an ancient Polynesian culture, and analyze the Marquesas Islands' species' origins, migratory cycles, and subsequent evolutions within isolated populations; research similar, in fact, to British biologist and naturalist Charles Darwin's transformative evolution research conducted on the Galápagos Islands. Heyerdahl also sought ethnological artifacts, antique and contemporary,

Previous page: Thor Heyerdahl and his wife, Liv, on Fatu Hiva.

the sale of which would finance, he hoped, additional zoological expeditions.

Truthfully, however, Heyerdahl and Liv sought most to return to an Elysian, nature-centered, self-sufficient, isolated island existence, unencumbered by the multitudinous amenities, social obligations, and disquieting political developments of modern Western Europe. Fearful of war's imminence and deeply disillusioned by contemporary life's artificial separation from nature, Heyerdahl sincerely believed that returning to a "natural state" of existence analogous to that of the first hominid—who, they believed, had plausibly originated from the parallel tropics of Java—would restore for them that long-neglected symbiosis between nature and civilization.

Heyerdahl, fascinated by Teite Tua's revelation of Tiki's universe creation mythology, and the journey of the islands' ancestors from a vast land beyond the sea, remained unable to sleep that transformative evening, the soughing Pacific Ocean evoking Tiki's Polynesian island landfall millennia ago. Descending at last into contemplative sleep, he was immediately struck by the extraordinary resemblances between Fatu Hiva's enigmatic stone monoliths, lost in the depths of the island's jungles, and the giant statues erected by the ancient civilizations of South America. Were the two practices, cultures, and geographies somehow entwined? From whence had come these unknown people, he wondered, drowsing now beneath somnolent visions of imaginative conjecture.

Heyerdahl's Norwegian Boyhood

Larvik, Norway, 1914–1933 Oslo, Norway, 1933–1936

Thor Heyerdahl's experimental voyage toward what he forecast as unsullied, unexplored nature found gestation in an adventurous boyhood. An only child, Heyerdahl was born on 6 October 1914 to master brewer Thor Heyerdahl (1869–1957) and museum association director Alison Lyng (1873–1965), in the tranquil harborside village of Larvik, at the Oslo Fjord's mouth. Number 7 Steingata, the Heyerdahls' majestic wooden residence, commanded panoramas across the water and contained innumerable antiquities and works of art—traditional Norwegian folk-culture artifacts and works by contemporary practitioners. Alison's long-held fascination with Charles Darwin's radical theory of evolution, which she first encountered as an adolescent after a year-long sojourn to England, and the natural sciences (exercised in marked contrast to her husband's traditional Christian faith), nourished Heyerdahl's nascent fascination with zoology, and catalyzed his sustained attempts to reconcile Christian faith with empirical scientific rationale. Heyerdahl's mother raised her young son in a rather sheltered fashion, and he remained a largely solitary child, drawn to illustrations of exotic flora and fauna, endlessly dreaming of far-flung lands beyond picturesque Larvik's sedate horizons. Deeply entranced by the natural world, yet possessed by an intractable fear of water after nearly drowning beneath the ice of a nearby lake, and a corresponding inability to swim, despite his father's patient labors, Heyerdahl, a precocious reader, eagerly devoured Henry Neville Hutchinson's (et al) 1902 encyclopaedic work, *The Living Races of Mankind,* H. G. Wells' 1920 *The Outline of History,* and Arthur E. Brehm's 1895 work, *Brehm's Life of Animals,* among many other books containing evocative illustrations of Polynesia, anthropological theory, and prehistoric biology, all helping to catalyze the young boy's exploratory mind and engender a fascination with humankind's history in the tropics. At the age of 12, Heyerdahl constructed an admirable zoological museum, the Animal House, within a disused warehouse belonging to his father, replicating 16th-century *kunstkammer* cabinets of zoological curiosities and containing insects, fish, and reptiles, all preserved within mason jars of formaldehyde, alongside unusual mementos from his father's regular travels abroad. Heyerdahl's Animal House, frequently visited by his schoolfriends and teachers, and characterized by his taxonomizing of disparate natural elements together, anticipated his subsequent interdisciplinary theoretical paradigms.

⇝

Heyerdahl spent each summer's vacations with his mother at an isolated summer cabin at Hornsjø, high above Lillehammer and Lake Mjøsa, overlooking undulating mountain plateaux enshrouded with heather, juniper, and birch, deep, forest-enveloped valleys and the snow-covered Jotunheimen and Rondane Alps. Adolescent Heyerdahl meditatively wandered the open moorlands that lay above Hornsjø and the lake-suffused, glacier-riven countryside, cross-country skiing and camping beneath the alpine heavens. Such formative expeditions were encouraged by further adventures with an amicable woodsman, Ola Bjørneby, around the isolated Asta Valley near Hornsjø, high above the pine-enshrouded Gudbrandsdalen and Østerdalen Valleys in eastern Norway. Heyerdahl first met Bjørneby one summer, when he and his mother were hiking together and came upon the man's cabin. A once-wealthy sawmill proprietor's son, with the evaporation of the family fortune, Ola had sought sanctuary in the wilderness, inhabiting a spartan farmhouse and possessing only life's necessities, hunting and fishing in near-ascetic solitude. Bjørneby's hermetic existence was, in the mind of young Heyerdahl, near-utopian, calling to mind the instinctive and less "civilized" heroes of his youth, among them Tarzan. He was captivated by the healthful radiance and simplicity of the introverted Norwegian woodsman, and in adolescence, he and Bjørneby would pass enormously influential days together, of "summer, light and liberty,"[1] the elder mountain dweller imparting enduring lessons in woodcraft, wilderness observation, and all-season self-sufficiency—as well as instilling in him an enduring belief that "theory and practice are two vastly different things."[2]

Heyerdahl was often accompanied on his forest excursions by his dear friend, ideological confidant, and fellow detractor of modern Western civilization's notions of progress, Erik Hesselberg. As youths, Heyerdahl and Hesselberg passed their time together cross-country skiing and, as they matured into young adults, such excursions developed into more demanding mountain expeditions. The duo, regularly accompanied by Heyerdahl's cousin Gunnar Nissen and always by his faithful Greenland husky, Kazan, explored, often for several weeks and with minimal provisions, Norway's mountainous, highly remote Rondane and Jotunheimen regions, evading Oslo's unnavigable metropolitan demands for the majestic revelations offered by Mother Nature. Financing such journeys with articles authored for various newspapers, with accompanying photographs, the two adolescents spent their time constructing snow shelters among Norway's highest summits and glaciers, traversing formidable passes and assembling winter camps high above the picturesque valley panoramas. Amidst the cloud-wreathed summits and glacier-cleaved valleys, silenced beech forests, snow-suffocated plateaus, and immaculate blue heavens, Heyerdahl frequently experienced transcendental peace on Earth.

Heyerdahl's archetypal Scandinavian adolescence unfolded within a post-discovery age, one characterized by the widely held assumption that hardly any of the world remained unexplored—a somewhat disdainful, questionably Eurocentric conviction he vehemently rejected. Instead, he was absorbed by popular accounts of the daring, heroic age of Arctic and Antarctic explorations undertaken by fellow Norwegian explorers such as Fridtjof Nansen, Otto Sverdrup, and Roald Amundsen, and devoured popular children's tales of adventure, including the Norwegian Robinson Crusoe, *Haakon Haakonsen,* by Oluf Wilhelm Falck-Ytter; the weekly magazine *Allers,* which contained stories of exploration, history, and science; and perhaps most importantly, Walter Booth's boy's adventure comic *Rob the Rover,* within which the eponymous Rob, accompanied by an old fisherman, Daniel True—who first encounters orphaned Rob, senseless and adrift at sea upon a raft—voyages about the world's oceans in search of lost treasures. Rob's journey even takes him to Easter Island, and once treasure is discovered and securely ensconced in a museum, the young boy becomes an indefatigable adventurer. Such daring tales kindled young Heyerdahl's adventuresome spirit and foreshadowed the remarkable journeys he would later undertake. Other favorites included American adventure writer James Oliver Curwood's *Kazan,* about a wolf-husky who travels to the Canadian wilderness and from which Heyerdahl's own faithful hound derived his name.

Young Heyerdahl wished also to journey to Africa, where his mother's half-brother Jacob Matheson then resided, inspired by the valiant exploits of famed Scottish Christian missionary and explorer, David Livingstone. Heyerdahl wrote in a school essay that he wished to return with a "suitcase stuffed with hunting trophies and photographs."[3] Captivated by tales of isolated cultures discovered within his mother's extensive library, and entranced by popular films such as 1925's *The Lost World,* and *Simba: King of the Beasts*—a documentary by two Swedish naturalists—Heyerdahl resolved to someday become a celebrated explorer himself.

Daydreaming of adventure and undiscovered lands, Heyerdahl became gradually disillusioned with modern civilization. "I took to the forests, the mountains, and the open seashore whenever I could," he wrote, reflecting the famous words of celebrated 19th-century American poet, Henry David Thoreau, "and became skeptical toward … a civilization designed to take man further from this environment."[4] Analogizing modern European civilization to an asphyxiating, 20th-century "Tower of Babel," he declared that society "serves no purpose but to complicate existence."[5] Having been born at the outset of World War I, even as a boy he was sorrowfully cognizant of humanity's capacity for inconceivable destruction. Distrustful of the preceding generation, with their ceaseless moral, political, and theological disagreements, and the international escalation of armaments, he wondered whether humankind's endeavor to artificially civilize Earth while advancing increasingly sophisticated warfare against one another would eventually assure complete biological annihilation. Characterizing himself as an inmate "calmly preparing to jump off a train that was on the wrong tracks,"[6] Heyerdahl, believing that Western civilization would either collapse, or catalyze another devastating war, became instead fascinated by humanity's common origin and began to consider an escape to a land—and in some ways, a time—in which such natural beginnings could be explored, even perhaps revived. In 1933, at the age of 19, Heyerdahl enrolled at the University of Oslo, where he studied geography and zoology. Infatuated by now with ancient "unspoiled" civilizations, he began to augment his prescribed curriculum with additional scholarship, undertaking analyses of Polynesian archaeology and anthropology. Such extracurricular activities were enthusiastically conducted within the world's then-largest private collection of books and scientific papers examining the South Seas, an extraordinary archive assembled by an affluent Norwegian wine merchant, Bjarne Kroepelien. Kroepelien had himself resided on Tahiti from 1917 until the death of his wife, Tuimata "Amelie" Teraiefa Teriierooiterai, daughter of a Papeeno chief, Teriieroo, from Spanish influenza brought about his return to Norway in 1919. Kroepelien, while surely amassing an extraordinary material research resource, was nevertheless another European male in an extensive lineage of Eurocentric explorers who traveled to the region, voyeuristically appraising the indigenous peoples' practices and culture, regularly becoming romantically involved with (often much younger) island girls. Such expatriates included, notoriously, the French post-impressionist artist Paul Gauguin, employing notions of cultural relativism to sanction such questionable endeavors.

Rather ironically, perhaps, Kroepelien the outsider, pursuing unsullied nature emancipated from the shackles of modern civilization, should lose his wife to a plague imported from Western civilization—though, while this is the generally accepted version of events, Liv claimed in letters years later that Tuimata had in fact lived, and that Kroepelien visited her many years later. Their union appeared to be a happy one, however, the couple producing a son during their years together and Kroepelien being adopted as a son by Tuimata's chieftain father. The Norwegian also obtained the Legion of Honor for his work aiding the disease-ravaged islands. Kroepelien would immortalize his transformative Polynesian experiences within an elegiac 1944 memoir, *Tuimata*. As an older man, Kroepelien enthusiastically welcomed Heyerdahl's inquiries regarding Polynesian life, initiated several introductions to Tahitian contacts, and wholeheartedly encouraged Heyerdahl's desire to journey to the islands himself. These resources and relationship, combined with Heyerdahl's zoological education, nascent fascination with Polynesia, and a now-inescapable disillusionment with modern civilization, invariably coalesced into an indefatigable desire to undertake an extraordinary Pacific expedition of his own.

⟿

Liv Coucheron Torp was, in 1933, an enchanting 17-year-old high-school girl from the seaside town of Brevik, with voluminous blonde tresses, and "damned intelligent eyes."[7] She and Heyerdahl first encountered one another on 28 May at a school's end graduation ceremony held at a picturesque restaurant, Kronprinsen, set on a pier in Stavern. While Heyerdahl's schoolfriends danced joyously, liberated at last from interminable schooldays, he gazed meditatively over the obsidian fjord's waters, lost in deepest reverie. Unannounced, Torp, a schoolfriend's companion, had appeared and Heyerdahl, long bashful with women —"magical, not real human beings"[8]—became immediately transfixed. Impassioned conversation followed, first light-hearted and then philosophical, Heyerdahl's quixotic notion of returning to nature capturing the young woman's imagination. Later, when asked if she would go with him, she replied, "then it would have to be all the way."[9] However, that fall the young Heyerdahl left for university and another year would elapse before Heyerdahl and Torp were reunited, in fall 1934, when both were attending the University of Oslo. Immediately infatuated with one another, Torp accompanied Heyerdahl across the alpine meadows and summits of Hornsjø, wandering and camping together, enveloped by the rapturous incandescence only an adolescent love affair imparts. Heyerdahl again inquired of Torp whether she would accompany him upon what he hoped would be a transcendental voyage to the South Pacific, forsaking Western civilization in order to return to an elementary, self-sustaining state of paradisiacal nature. Torp acquiesced to Heyerdahl's proposition, and they began extensive preparations including physical acclimation within nearby forests, and extensive reading on the South Seas, including American author Frederick O'Brien's enormously successful 1919 travelogue of French Polynesia exploration, *White Shadows in the South Seas.* Heyerdahl and Torp were to become members of that vast, often conceivably problematic lineage of European castaways who ventured from the distant shores of Western civilization, questing for earthly paradises wholly emancipated from modernity.

After some deliberation, the young couple resolved to voyage to Polynesia's isolated Marquesas archipelago. They wished to make their home on Fatu Hiva, understood then as an island that held archaeological evidence indicating the origins of the first settlers of the archipelago. That intention was frustrated by the colonial French government, which at that time forbade European visitors from spending longer than 24 hours on the island. Fortunately, an introduction by Bjarne Kroepelien to Chief Teriieroo proved indispensable, and the two young Norwegian castaways were afforded permission to remain. Fatu Hiva itself remained emblematic of Heyerdahl and Torp's naturalistic island idyll—a largely uninhabited yet effortlessly habitable, fecund, and unclaimed "free port of refuge from the iron grip of civilization,"[10] within the sunshine-suffused, saline turquoise of the South Pacific. Examining "the colorful map of the South Seas," they had, "for the thousandth time ... sailed around on the vast ocean [seeking] a single virgin speck among the thousands of islands and atolls."[11] Fatu Hiva, a beautiful, mountainous island, once cannibalistic, largely unpopulated, and unscathed by modern civilization, exemplified an environment within which two heedless —and enormously fortunate, the voyage being largely financed by Heyerdahl's father—Norwegian explorers could enact an extraordinary, practical application of a rather romantic notion, where "man and woman, could resume the life abandoned by our ancestors."[12] While the two voluntary castaways made preparations for their voyage, and Heyerdahl in particular had survived under comparable ascetic conditions for limited periods in the Norwegian Alps, theirs would be an excessively optimistic and idealistic attitude—disquietingly approaching dismissive concepts of the "noble savage"— which would eventually prove the explorers' downfall.

In December 1936, however, Heyerdahl remained enamoured by elysian notions of returning to untrammeled lands inhabited by innocent children of paradise, among whom he, disillusioned Adam, and Torp, acquiescent Eve, would reside in joyous symbiosis with nature. Aided by influential Professor Bonnevie, Norway's first female professor and first female member of the Norwegian Academy of Science and Letters, and by Professor Broch, a zoologist and conservationist, on Christmas Day, Heyerdahl and Liv—now Liv Heyerdahl—journeyed westward at last, bound for Fatu Hiva, abandoning Western civilization, and attempting to recreate that elementary yet beatific existence long forgotten by modernity.

Thor Heyerdahl with his mother, Alison, outside their house on Steingata 7, Larvik, Norway.

Top: Thor Heyerdahl and Kazan, a Samoyed, trekking in Norway, 1934–36.

Bottom: Liv and Thor Heyerdahl camping in the mountains above Lillehammer during the summer of 1936.

Revelation

Tahiti, Fatu Hiva, and Hiva Oa, 1936–1937

Jubilantly singing Tahiti's tender celebration song, *E mauruuru a vau* (poetically translated as "happy am I" or "farewell for just a while"), after six weeks of first-class passage from Oslo, Heyerdahl and Liv alighted at Arcadian Papeete on Tahiti, the island capital of French Polynesia and the entrance to "our lost Garden of Eden."[1] After several days of ecstatic exploration, wandering among the Polynesian town's cornucopia of fragrant copra (dried coconut kernels from which coconut oil is extracted) warehouses and colonial bureaux, picturesque wooden bungalows, iron church spires, Chinese merchants' stores (and the restaurant "Too Fat"), and kaleidoscopic marketplaces, the two young wayfarers, capitvated as they were, remained eager nevertheless to evade the civilized town. Heyerdahl and Liv headed 10 miles (16 km) eastward to the banana plant, coconut palm, and papaya tree-enshrouded valley of Papenoo, welcomed as celebrated guests of Supreme Chief Teriieroo (father of Tuimata, Bjarne Kroepelien's long-deceased wife), the chief's wife Faufau, and their many children. Herculean Chief Teriieroo, vast and embracing, was a "pureblooded Polynesian of the clearly vanishing type."[2] Heyerdahl admiringly observed the chief's preservation of traditional Tahitian practices; the chief himself was wholly unaware of Heyerdahl's unconscious preoccupation with salvage ethnography. Teriieroo and Faufau generously accommodated the two young travelers at Papenoo, where they spent several weeks exploring, acquainting themselves with traditional Polynesian fare gathered from the surrounding jungle, waters, and coconut palms, and learning, in Heyerdahl's case, to competently swim, as well as to acquire some proficiency in the local language, constructing hearths and fashioning tools. After an immense farewell banquet held in Heyerdahl and Liv's honor, during which they were adopted by Teriieroo as Terai Mateata Tane and Terai Mateata Vahine (Mr. and Mrs. Blue Sky), they eventually boarded a diminutive, two-masted white copra schooner, *Tereora,* commanded by an eccentric and dissuasive Englishman, Captain Brander, who believed the experiment both quixotic and futile, and a Tahitian trading master, the affable Théodore, bound for Fatu Hiva. A demanding voyage of several weeks during which the two Norwegians—housed on *Tereora's* deck amidst cacophonous livestock, ample sacks of aromatic copra, trading merchandise, provisions, and melodious travelers—visited several atolls and two Marquesas islands, Nuku Hiva and Hiva Oa, both dismissed as unsuitable for Heyerdahl and Liv's experiment. Encountering enormous shoals of dolphins, fish, and seabirds, and interrogating the relative deficiencies and advantages of modern civilization with Captain Brander, himself a long-time Polynesia resident and disillusioned émigré who never went ashore, after temperate days spent beneath the Pacific sunshine expectantly gazing from the deck, binoculars at hand, hypnotically examining each isolated island, at last Fatu Hiva's formidable, mountainous silhouette appeared upon the horizon. Wading ashore at the expansive Omoa Valley, on Fatu Hiva's spectacularly beautiful southern seashore on 18 March 1937, Heyerdahl and Liv, encumbered by two large, impractical valises, a small tent (intended only for use until they could establish a permanent shelter), 16 boxes of botanical-collection equipment, mountains of field notebooks, glass vials, formaldehyde and ether, and other indispensable equipment —conceding also the addition of an iron cooking pot and a long machete, two implements insisted upon by Chief Teriieroo as essential to island subsistence—bid farewell to the *Tereora*'s lifeboat as the rowboat retreated over the tumultuous surf, "alone on an unknown boulder beach."[3] Enveloped by an immense solitude, castaways upon what both imagined was a largely uncontactable, scarcely populated tropical island, Heyerdahl and Liv, each inhaling a fortifying breath and exchanging courageous laughter, gazed about the tropical landscape, and wandered into their long-desired seclusion from the modern world.

Omoa Valley, however, was not uninhabited. Islanders, silently observing as the two explorers wandered inland from the seashore, gradually revealed themselves among the coconut palms.[4] Hesitation gave forth to irresistible fascination when Liv's white Norwegian flesh was determined authentic by an inquiring old woman. And before long, Heyerdahl and Liv were surrounded by islanders, many of whom suffered from painful diseases such as elephantiasis, tuberculosis, and leprosy. The pair were led to a nearby village within which lay a central clearing umbrellaed by an enormous banyan tree. There, they were received by a Swiss-Polynesian settler, William Grelet, the recalcitrant proprietor of the village's general store, at the windows and threshold of which gathered silent spectators. Grelet, Heyerdahl wrote, determined he and Liv "the strangest creatures that had ever come ashore, but he understood our plan." An enthusiastic hunter deeply knowledgeable of the Omoa Valley's landscape, Grelet revealed by kerosene lamplight that evening that they "should find what we wanted, in the interior of the island, where the natives rarely went and where abandoned gardens were engulfed by jungle growth."[5] Grelet assisted the young couple late into the evening by composing a dictionary of words translated into the local dialect. By dawn, Heyerdahl and Liv began wandering inland upon an ancient royal pathway, guided by gentle Ioane, Grelet's Marquesan brother-in-law, journeying deeper into the tropical valley, "a luxurious lost garden." Enveloped at last by the near-impenetrable jungle foliage, Heyerdahl reflected they were Adam and Eve, expelled not from the Garden of Eden, but rather returning to such. As they were absorbed beneath the young coconut palms and lianas and into the pulsating ecosystem of birds, insects, mammals, and reptiles, each passing hour became a euphoric dream finally realized. Gradually they ascended higher into the valley, hacking away with their machetes at the foliage, following the valley's clear whispering river. Then, abandoning the river path after several hours, Heyerdahl, Liv, and Ioane eventually reached a wilderness of enormous trees and foliage, among which, scattered beneath the undergrowth, were several artificial terraces, masterfully constructed from colossal boulder-stones and enshrouded with verdant moss. Pausing before one of the many plateaus, replete with a spring of clear, cold, potable water, Ioane indicated that this was once the royal plateau where the island's last queen, his grandmother, had resided long before. While the overgrown "impenetrable chaos of foliage" obscured views of the valley below, on the terrace itself grew coconut palms, breadfruit trees, colossal-leafed bananas, taro plants, and "the largest lemon tree we had ever seen, loaded like a Christmas tree with golden fruits."[6] Heyerdahl and Liv were immediately enamored, agreeing to settle on the royal plateau for a modest annual sum payable to both Ioane and the village chief. They bid farewell to their affable guide and he vanished back into the undergrowth. Soon after, evening came, shadows lengthened, and darkness fell upon the jungle; Heyerdahl and Liv, now "as happy as children," built a fire, and baked breadfruit and *fei* (Polynesian banana) beneath the colossal leaves, before retiring elated beneath the welcoming canvas of their diminutive tent: "The mosquito was the only devil in our Paradise."[7]

After three laborious days clearing away the royal plateau's thickest jungle carapace with calloused hands and a cutthroat machete, and discovering innumerable stone adzes, gouges, pounders, hammer stones, a king's stone chair, and a beautiful wooden bowl, all artifacts from the royal household, the plateau became habitable at last. Afforded nourishing sunlight, gentle breezes, and expansive panoramas of the palm-enshrouded Omoa Valley below and the summits and palisades of the adjacent, scarlet-earthed mountains, Heyerdahl and Liv, having removed many strata of decaying vegetation, now began construction of an enormous leaf and cut-bough shelter—which Ioane immediately dismissed as readily penetrable by insects, wild horses, and tropical rainfall. Instead, he offered his assistance with the construction of a habitable shelter. "In Robinson Crusoe fashion, we ate from huge glittering mother-of-pearl shells and drank from cups of coconut shell,"[8] Heyerdahl wrote of the celebratory supper that accompanied the completion of his and Liv's traditional 6 by 12-foot (1.8 x 3.6-m) jungle residence, constructed with plaited palm leaves, hibiscus-bark rope, and bamboo-boughs, which they had erected over several days with Ioane's learned assistance and the practiced labor of several island villagers, all frequently interrupted with celebratory feasting, entertaining performances, and long siestas beneath the cooling jungle canopy. Eventually, however, Ioane and the villagers returned to the island's seashore with much of the contents of Heyerdahl and Liv's suitcases, long a source of fascination to island inhabitants largely unaccustomed to Western implements and apparel, leaving the two alone at last. "A new life started the day the village visitors had finished helping us build our home and left with their rewards," Heyerdahl noted. "Peace reigned in the valley."[9]

On Fatu Hiva, time evaporated, assuming new dimensions: "When marked by the sun, the birds … time never ran away."[10] The days, divinely long, were suffused by revelatory perceptive, auditory, and olfactory experiences. Enveloped by the luxuriant, undomesticated universe of the Omoa Valley, Heyerdahl and Liv became symbiotically entwined with the tropical jungle's multitudinous flora and fauna, all breathtakingly beautiful. "Our sense of perception seemed to be tuned into a different and clearer reception," he observed, "and we smelt, saw, and listened to everything around us as if we were tiny children witnessing nothing but miracles."[11] Heyerdahl noticed that the wide variety of vegetation distributed across Fatu Hiva was dictated by the Tauaouoho mountain range's fracturing of the westerly trade winds' thick, eastern-originating clouds, which in turn dispersed the tropical rainfall. This observation of Fatu Hiva's east to west ecosystem orientation would eventually go on to effect his most profound revelation about the original direction of Polynesia's settlement.

Surrounded by superabundant natural wonders, Heyerdahl and Liv spent their days in transfixed exploration among shaded valleys and near-impenetrable liana-suffused tropical jungle, across golden savannas, and over nearby mountainsides. The young castaways felt themselves "survivors of a forgotten catastrophe"[12] as they feasted on inexhaustible supplies of bananas, plantains and papayas, cassava and taro tubers, oranges, lemons, pineapples, green coconuts, and dark river crustaceans, all accompanied by fresh spring water, young coconut milk, sugarcane-suffused lemonade, and orange leaf tea. Indeed, at first Heyerdahl and Liv had not intended to hunt, practice animal husbandry or consume anything non-indigenous to the island, and even attempted to live only upon the plentiful fruits that grew around them. Unfortunately, malnutrition saw off that one optimistic endeavor, the pair resorting to animal proteins after a time, such as freshwater crayfish.

Spending beguiling days exploring the area, Heyerdahl and Liv discovered decaying vestiges of long-lost indigenous peoples: yet more gleaming stone adzes, turtle shell and human bone figures, fractured craniums and long-decayed bones, large animistic sculptures, sacrificial altars, and ingenious cavern mausoleums decorated with petroglyphs illustrating benevolent spirits, or containing demonic stone gargoyles prohibiting entry. In the summer of 1937, Heyerdahl and Liv contracted a grave disease the islanders called *fe-fe,* which resulted in dangerous abscesses forming across their lower limbs. Natural remedies proving ineffective, they were forced to travel to Hiva Oa, and abhorred civilization, to obtain treatment, eventually staying six weeks until the castaways' wounds healed at last.

On Hiva Oa, they also found colossal, carved, red-stone monoliths, grotesque figures with enormous eyes, expansive abdomens, and diabolical visages. These remarkable monoliths, some containing elaborate reliefs of fish, turtles, sun symbols, large eye-ornaments, and crescent-shaped vessels, were strangely reminiscent in aesthetic, proportion, and artisanship of ancient South American sculptures Heyerdahl had examined before. The proportions of a head about a third of the size of the body and arms clasped across the body called immediately to mind not only Mayan sculptures, but also those from San Agustín in Colombia, and, he would later realize, those from Tiahuanaco in Bolivia. These similarities suggested enigmatic origins far beyond the islands' shores.

"Who had carved these eyes and the peculiar vessel?" Heyerdahl wondered. "Why did no two scientists share the same theory about the whereabouts of the former Polynesian homeland," despite general scientific consensus among migration scholars then that Asia remained the direction "from where the canoes of the old Marquesans would have had to travel more than one third of the way around the world against all prevailing winds and currents?"[13] Nevertheless, archaeologists and anthropologists had long surmised that Polynesia and South America, separated by some 4,000 miles (6,437 km) of the Pacific Ocean, remained impossibly distant for any pre-European contact.

Ahead of Heyerdahl's 1937 Marquesan archipelago journey, two other archaeological expeditions had occurred. German physician Karl von den Steinen was, in 1897, commissioned by the Ethnological Museum of Berlin to undertake an expedition to the South Sea Islands. Voyaging by ship from San Francisco to Nuku Hiva, the largest of the Marquesas, von den Steinen spent six months traveling from island to island conducting empirical research on material culture and genealogies, gathering and translating the myths of several indigenous groups while also collecting ethnological artifacts. In 1925, von den Steinen published the first of three extensive volumes, *Die Marquesaner und ihre Kunst*, on Marquesan history and culture. Von den Steinen later observed that he was "perhaps half a year too late," as the indigenous culture had already begun to disappear.

American anthropologist Ralph Linton participated in the 1920–22 Bayard Dominick expedition, initiated by the Bernice P. Bishop Museum of Honolulu, Hawaii, which despatched four working parties to gather anthropological and archaeological data across the Marquesas Islands, several other Polynesian island groups, and Hawaii. Linton, confounded by negligible ceramic artifacts and frustrated by near-impenetrable vegetation enshrouding prospective archaeological sites, oriented himself toward ethnological research into Marquesan art, crafts, and material culture. While on the Marquesas archipelago, he undertook a surface-survey, gathered artifacts for the Bishop Museum and acquired knowledge of traditional Marquesan wood carving from the *tuhungas*, or master craftsmen. Linton's subsequent, expansive survey, *Ethnology of Polynesia and Micronesia*, was published in 1926, while he served as Assistant Curator of the North American Indian Collections at the Field Museum of Natural History in Chicago.

Despite such exhaustive fieldwork, Heyerdahl nevertheless claimed that no "significant" archaeological expeditions had explored Fatu Hiva, but rather only superficial ethnological research—examinations of character variances between various island populations—had occurred. The scarlet hue of the islanders' hair, for example, had been the basis for much discussion and speculation, attributed variously to intentional bleaching, the natural bleaching effect of sunlight and sea water, or intermixing with the colonizers. To Heyerdahl, such idiosyncratic phenomena suggested the possibility of the arrival of numerous varied settlers before the European explorers. Increasingly unsatisfied by scholars' migration hypotheses and anthropological theory, he remained perplexed by the idiosyncratic artifacts he had found. Heyerdahl began speculating upon the origins of these archaeological discoveries and their mysterious creators. Moreover, he began to postulate specifically on how ancient Polynesian argonauts had discovered these remote Pacific islands, long beforethe mythopoeic voyages of Western European explorers such as Christopher Columbus and Captain James Cook. Heyerdahl himself became fascinated by discovering the ancient sea routes of Polynesian voyagers, an intractable enigma to scholars, rather than "the itinerary of irrational coleopters and gastropods." [14] Originally tasked with analyzing "the emigration of living creatures to Polynesia," Heyerdahl observed that "no migratory species was more intriguing than man himself." [15]

While residing upon Fatu Hiva, Heyerdahl and Liv's infrequent open-ocean voyages within vessels of colonial European construction prompted Heyerdahl to wonder why the island ancestors had long abandoned the construction of buoyant, seaworthy rafts in favor of fragile crafts with wooden-planked hulls.

Ancient oceanic cultures, as attested to by archaeological record and mythological narrative, were seafaring peoples and adept ocean navigators, capable of voyaging far beyond sight of their inhabited lands. They possessed large and small canoes of which they had great capacity for fishing, sailing, and traversing interisland distances for economic and social intentions. These sailors had, for thousands of years, frequently conducted vast exploration voyages, seeking sources of desirous commodities such as feathers, or workable stones with which to construct effective adzes. Marquesan islanders in particular were deliberate voyagers, "land-seekers," adeptly organizing large fleets bountifully stocked with provisions, animals, and young plants, and successfully transporting hundreds of migrants between South Pacific islands. Discovery voyages within double canoes were conducted across great distances, some over 1,400 miles (2,253 km), skillfully identifying various islands while employing astral bodies as a navigational means. Additionally, Polynesian sailors possessed an extensive body of knowledge on prevailing wind systems, star movements, wave features, and methods of committing these physical attributes and voyage routes to memory. However, with escalating 18th-century engagement with European sailors, missionaries, merchants and explorers, contraction of diseases, exponential increase in foreign shipping, and devastating civil wars, traditional canoe-making ceased; remaining island populations inherited European vessels, construction methods and outrigger canoes.

At the time of Heyerdahl's residence on Fatu Hiva, much of this knowledge was lost; the enduring anthropological-theoretical assumption was that indigenous peoples voyaged exclusively along continental and island coastlines, drawn by the currents, and were incapable of open-ocean navigation. Amplified by the idiosyncratic archaeological discoveries he had discovered within the archipelago's moss-threaded jungles, and having experienced the "westward-moving elements of the Pacific," Heyerdahl began to interrogate accepted anthropological and migratory theory.[16] How was Polynesia originally discovered and settled, when scholars categorically dismissed South America's coastal civilizations as the first ancestors of the island's present inhabitants? Who constructed the megalithic monuments found there? Was the subsequent wave of Polynesia's seafaring settlers originally from Malaya and the west, as many scholars insisted? Why was South America, a continent vastly more accessible to the Pacific Ocean's archipelagos than Asia, of no consideration in determining the origins of these voyaging islanders? Perhaps, despite scholars' somewhat ethnocentric rejection of the possibility of pre-European contact between South America and Polynesia, contact had in fact once occurred? Polynesian mythology long encompassed tales of an industrious ancestral people with fair skin and lightened hair who inhabited these islands when the present inhabitants made landfall centuries ago. Heyerdahl was well aware that analogous mythologies are found in Aztec and Inca ancestral belief systems, as are remarkably similar stone-carved monoliths, appearing along Columbian, Ecuadorian, and Peruvian Pacific coastlines as well as on Rapa Nui and the Marquesas archipelago.

Not long after Heyerdahl began to contemplate these nascent theories, he was introduced by Terai, an affable male nurse from Tahiti who had ministered to his and Liv's infected limbs, to an eccentric Norwegian auto-didact, Henry Lie, on Hiva Oa, who by extraordinary coincidence was known by Heyerdahl's mother. As an adolescent, around 1907, Lie had originally arrived in the Marquesas as a deck-hand upon an old sailing vessel. Dissatisfied by the tumultuous life aboard the ship, captained by a quarrelsome drunkard, Lie had escaped into the jungle wilderness after being commanded ashore to obtain potable water. He then labored on copra schooners before marrying a local woman and producing a son, Aletti. Later widowed and remarried, Lie eventually established a copra trading business in the vast Puamau Valley, as well as a general store, assembling an extraordinary collection of books and periodicals. Welcomed into Lie's idiosyncratic bungalow, Heyerdahl and Liv passed an agreeable evening together with Lie, forming an unexpected isle of Norwegian company within the vast isolation of Polynesia.

At dawn the next day, Heyerdahl and Aletti wandered inland together, deeper into the valley, before Heyerdahl was struck by the most extraordinary sight. "Suddenly we saw them. The giants. They stared at us from the thickets with round eyes as big as life belts and grotesque mouths drawn out in diabolical grins wide enough to swallow a human body." Larger "than gorillas and nearly twice the height of a man," the inevitable question crossed Heyerdahl's mind: who had constructed these colossal red-stone monuments, and how?[17] He and Aletti uncovered several more of the remarkable statues, many in various states of disrepair, abdomens, limbs and decapitated heads scattered chaotically beneath the undergrowth, alongside long-degraded terraces and walls. It was evidently a temple site, where cannibal festivities had supposedly once occurred before the Hawaiian missionary, James Kekela, attempted to convert the island's inhabitants to Christianity in the mid-19th century. Karl von den Steinen, Ralph Linton, and English lexicographer F.W. Christian had visited the Puamau Valley's stone colossi in 1896, 1920, and 1894 respectively. Questioning the island's inhabitants regarding the sculptures' arcane origins, all three discovered nearly nothing was known of them, except that the sculptures had existed when island ancestors originally settled on Hiva Oa and expelled the first inhabitants, of whom nothing was known, away into the mountains, where legend held they were eventually absorbed into the Naiki tribe. Heyerdahl was transfixed by the tale. Who were these masterful sculptors? Where had they originally appeared from, and evaporated to? Why had they constructed these colossi? "My introduction to the Puamau stone giants ... was to guide my destiny for many eventful years to come," he wrote. That introduction "set me asail on rafts, led me into continental jungles, and made me excavate Easter Island monuments as high as buildings of several stories. All in an effort to solve a mystery that puzzled me from the day I began to suspect that an enterprising people with the habit of creating stone colossi had reached the eastern headland of Hiva Oa before the Polynesian fishermen arrived. The Polynesians' ... bent was generally to the sea, to the warpath, and to wood carving. These stone monuments," he suspected, "have a different story to tell."[18]

That evening, by kerosene lantern light, Lie presented Heyerdahl with several illustrated books, which contained comparable mythologies of eastward-originating peoples, ancestral genealogies, and near-identical colossal stone monoliths that appeared both across coastal South America and throughout Polynesia. Heyerdahl was reminded once more of the enduring belief throughout Polynesia, from Rapa Nui to Samoa, New Zealand, and Hawaii, that another people, characterized as fair-skinned, auburn-haired, and claiming descent from the sun god, had once inhabited the islands before the arrival of the present population's ancestors. Who inhabited Polynesia first, Heyerdahl wondered, when South America lay 4,000 miles (6,437 km) away, and Indonesia over 7,000? That same evening, an unnamed, diminutive old French beachcomber possessing an enormous mustache appeared, a dear friend of Lie's. He also remained fascinated by the remarkable similarities between Puamau Valley's red-stone colossi and those unearthed across South America, enthusiastically revealing illustrations of near-identical colossi discovered at San Agustín, Columbia, in the northern Andes.[i] An astounded Heyerdahl knew large stone figurative sculptures were scattered across

i Unfortunately, Heyerdahl never gives this source, so we do not know which specific statue it was an illustration of. He later connected this to Tiahuanaco, Bolivia.

Opposite: Gazing at a miracle of nature, off in the distance and visible only as a white speck, the natural tunnel of Tehavahinenau—which goes right through the mountain—can be seen from certain spots around the island. In prehistoric times, the inhabitants had cut a rough path to the tunnel and used it as one of the only means of access between the eastern and western half of the island. Today, the path is no more and the inaccessible hole, according to the locals, is filled with human bones.

the South American continent, from the Andes down to Tiahuanaco at Lake Titicaca, and eventually the Pacific coastline. Aymara people informed Spanish conquistadors that such colossi were constructed not by their ancestors, but rather, in remarkable parallel with Polynesian mythology, by fair-skinned peoples who claimed descent from the sun god and eventually embarked upon balsa-wood rafts and evaporated westward into the Pacific Ocean. Heyerdahl, confronted with such undeniable parallels, yet knowledgeable of prevailing scholarship which had long held that Polynesia was originally settled from Asia and Indonesia, wondered how one could possibly deny so many resemblances? And, drowsing now on Lie's iron bed, he wondered whether Polynesia's first argonauts had in fact originated from South America. "Dreams are like seeds,"[19] he wrote of his nocturnal meditations in Lie's Norwegian bungalow, and required conscientious nourishment. Eager to undertake archaeological excavations upon Fatu Hiva and Hiva Oa, Heyerdahl "carried a secret dream of challenging the dogma that seemed to have blocked all unbiased research in Polynesia: the unproven axiom that only aboriginal voyagers from Asia sailing across the ocean could have reached Polynesia."[20] He wrote home to his new parents-in-law, Andreas Torp and Anna Henningine Coucheron Torp, revealing that "The plans are, after staying home for a few years, to arrange a new and larger expedition down here that manages to bring back larger archaeological, osteological, geological, botanical and zoological finds. For Fatu Hiva is a valuable island."[21]

Orthodox Polynesian scholars, Heyerdahl believed, dogmatically imagined the Pacific possessed only "a western shoreline. To the east there was an impenetrable abyss. It was as if America had not yet been placed on the map by Columbus."[22]

GAZING AT A MIRACLE OF NATURE. OFF IN THE DISTANCE AND VISIBLE ONLY AS A WHITE SPECK (BELOW THE ARROW) CAN BE SEEN FROM CERTAIN SPOTS ON THE ISLAND. THE NATURAL TUNNEL OF TEHAVAHINENAU WHICH GOES RIGHT THROUGH THE MOUNTAIN IN PREHISTORIC TIMES THE NATIVES HAD CUT A ROUGH PATH TO THE TUNNEL AND USED IT AS ONE OF THE ONLY MEANS OF ACCESS BETWEEN THE EASTERN AND WESTERN HALF OF THE ISLAND. TODAY. THE PATH IS NO MORE AND THE INACCESSIBLE HOLE ACCORDING TO THE NATIVES IS FILLED WITH HUMAN BONES.

Opposite (top): Tahiti was the closest they could get to Fatu Hiva with a passenger ticket. In those days, Tahiti had only one regular call a month, when a French steamer arrived after six weeks of ocean travel. On this island, they had to wait until a copra schooner could take them northward to the isolated Marquesas Islands, near the equator.

Opposite (bottom): The Marquesas Islands finally rose from the Pacific. As the rugged mountains of one island in this group sank into the sea, others rose in front of them, and they were able to visit most of them before the little schooner made a special call at Fatu Hiva, where they had asked to be let off.

Top: Their Ouia home was set beside the beach and raised on poles to proect against wild boars. The peak above them was the first land sighted by Europeans in Polynesia, when the Mendaña expedition sailed from Peru in 1595. Before then, aboriginal people had planted South American pineapples, which now grew wild nearby.

Bottom: The valleys of Fatu Hiva were all surrounded by the steep walls of extinct craters. Erosion had opened all of them toward the sea. Dense jungle crept up from the valley bottom wherever it could get a foothold. The flora of the interior highlands varied from impenetrable rain forest to semidry savanna with grass and ferns.

Opposite (left): With a spy on their heels, they visited an old burial ground to study and collect ancient Polynesian skulls. Their Polynesian shaddower kept watch over them all the time, but when Thor went farther away, he followed him, so Liv was left alone and able to fill a hemp sack with specimens for anthropological studies.

Opposite (right): Statue in the Puamau Valley. The unknown Frenchman (see page 35) is sitting on the outstretched legs of a swimming monster, which is resting on a pedestal that extends from the belly into the ground. In the entire Pacific hemisphere, there is nothing similar to this sculpture, which closely follows the prone statues of San Agustín in all its aesthetic ideas. Had the unidentified artists on this island come with the winds and currents from South America?

Left: With a shrieking piglet in her arms, Liv finds rest and shade from the tropical heat in a cave as we flee up the steep rock face out of the Ouia Valley, Fatu Hiva.

Right: Back to nature: Running below their cabin in Omoa was a fresh mountain stream with natural swimming pools shaded by palms and tropical vegetation. Delicious shrimp could be caught in this clear water and provided a welcome addition to their fruitarian diet.

Hypothesis

Beyond the Empire of the Sun

Fatu Hiva, 1937

Gathered about a driftwood hearth, beneath the Pacific's twilight, Teite Tua, the Fatu Hivan elder who had visited and befriended Heyerdahl and Liv in their Omoa Valley hut, patiently answered Heyerdahl's questions regarding the origins of the ancestral Polynesian god, Tiki, in a combination of French and Heyerdahl's rudimentary Marquesan. "From *Te-Fiti,* the east,"[1] Teite Tua replied, gazing contemplatively out from the hearth they lay gathered about, eastward below the horizon and toward where the sun rises, *"i te tihena oumati,"* where faraway South America lay. "Tiki, he was both god and chief," he declared. "Tiki who brought my ancestors to these islands," from a vast land "beyond the sea."[2] Where had these ancient, fair-complexioned argonauts originated from? Heyerdahl was astounded, and yet Teite Tua's disclosure paralleled that of several other indigenous island elders. As the flames rose over the soughing eastern trade winds, delicate palm fronds caressed the twilight's shadows, and the cacophonous Pacific Ocean broke over the island's eastern seashore, Teite Tua continued. He spoke of Tiki leading his ancestors, millennia before, westward to the Marquesas archipelago. Voyaging unimaginable distances across the Pacific from a mythical eastern land, *Fiti-Nui,* Teite Tua's ancestors settled across these Polynesian island idylls, just as Eastern voyagers and European explorers would thousands of years later. However, 4,300 uninterrupted ocean miles lay between coastal South America and the Marquesas archipelago. How exactly had Teite Tua's intrepid forefathers successfully navigated such a journey? What compulsion had sent them westward? And, supposedly lacking seaworthy vessels, modern navigational equipment, and established ocean routes, how had they voyaged across such unimaginably vast distances? "For the first time," Heyerdahl wrote, "I really started to wonder whether these islands could have been reached first by one of the many different cultures that had succeeded each other before the Inca dynasty in ancient Peru. All kinds of physical types were realistically represented in the ceramic art of pre-Inca Peru. … All the Inca traditions stressed that their main god, Viracocha, and the people who followed him into the Pacific were white,"[3] a tradition also maintained within Polynesian mythology. Heyerdahl later discovered the complete Incan name for the departed god-king was in fact Con-Tici-Viracocha, known throughout his reign at Tiahuanaco (present-day Bolivia) simply as Tici, Ticci, or Tiki.

Past and present entwined within Heyerdahl's rapidly speculating mind as Teite Tua recalled the mythopoeic voyages of Fatu Hiva's ancestors. He felt now that these tales, rather than long-dismissed, fantastical mythologies, were in fact elaborate chronologies of Polynesia's intrepid forefathers, and the genesis of all indigenous Pacific habitation. The stone hearth's embers faded away at last beneath the heavens as Teite Tua ended a sorrowful composition, played on a hand-carved bamboo flute. Heyerdahl found himself deeply contemplative. "I sat and marveled at this sea which never stopped proclaiming that it came this way, rolling in from the east, from the east, from the east … ."[4] Descending into haunted sleep that temperate island evening, Heyerdahl began to gestate upon Teite Tua's remarkable hearthside tales, Liv's observation of the ocean's ceaseless eastward landfall, all he had discussed with Henry Lie, and the undeniable resemblances between Hiva Oa's colossal stone monoliths and those of South America, wondering whether, and how, such extraordinary migration across the vast expanses of the Pacific Ocean had conceivably occurred.

"Fatu Hiva is in the midst of a floating river," Heyerdahl daydreamed later, enveloped by ocean and air, while "Peru had two major rivers … the Amazon, which flows eastward through the green jungles of Peru, and the Humboldt Current, which flows westward through the blue Pacific Ocean."[5] Perhaps these seawater passages entwined continental South America and the isolated archipelagos of Polynesia? "I had begun to look at the Pacific Ocean … with other eyes," he wrote—the vast ocean, rather than an impediment, becoming a source of ready transportation between Polynesia and South America. "Why would the great, truly great civilizations of Peru continue for centuries and millenniums to navigate their unprotected Pacific shore in balsa log rafts and totora reed boats if these peculiar kinds of watercraft were not seaworthy?"[6] And what of all the other parallels Heyerdahl discovered between Polynesia and South America, such as the widespread practice of trepanning, and identical botanical species, including the coconut, papaya, pineapple, sweet potato, and tomato, which several botanists already believed were cultivated in the Marquesas islands from species originally introduced from South America? American botanist F.B.M. Brown himself had identified one variety of pineapple as proof of contact: "Although it appears that the main stream of Polynesian immigration came from the west, just the opposite direction from which the indigenous flora came, undoubtedly some intercourse may have occurred between the natives of the American continent and those of the Marquesas."[7] Heyerdahl's interdisciplinary ruminations would galvanize, with time, into an inexorable epistemological obsession. "I had not the faintest idea," he later wrote, "that I was to come back to Polynesia with five friends sailing with me from Peru on an Inca-type balsa raft."[8]

Over the following days, Heyerdahl and Liv prepared to leave Fatu Hiva. Although their 15-month peregrination had been a constructive and enlightening one in many respects, eventually they succumbed to the innumerable difficulties of island habitation. Having wished to withdraw themselves wholly "from our artificial life,"[9] Heyerdahl and Liv had sought independence from civilization's aid—from animal husbandry, hunting, and omnivorous sustenance, from everything, in fact, except nature's virgin cornucopia and divine munificence. Unimaginably idealistic, Heyerdahl's problematic notion of emulating the "primitive" lives of "noble savages," yet remaining isolated from the island's inhabitants and somewhat uneducated regarding fundamental Polynesian cultural mores, such as gift-exchange systems, betrays an unconscious ethnocentrism and diminishing exoticism then emblematic of much of Western anthropological and ideological theory. Heyerdahl would eventually recognize, and attempt to reconcile such myopic, equally contemptuous yet admiring conceptions of indigenous peoples.

That failure therefore could be seen as cultural rather than a case of practical idealism. Although they should well have been better prepared for climate, humidity, and disease, Heyerdahl and Liv's downfall was downfall occurred from less obvious quarters. They wished to live alone, as in the Garden of Eden, but withdrawing completely from the island community in such a fashion was deemed unimaginably offensive. In such circumstances, disastrous rumors readily proliferated, encouraged by the French Catholic priest, Père Victorin, who believed them to be Protestant missionaries—a suspicion not helped by the introductory letter Bjarne Kroepelien had written to Chief Teriieroo, father of his late wife Tuimata. As a protestant himself, he introduced Heyerdahl in turn to the Protestant community on Fatu Hiva—unfortunately only three individuals among a majority of Catholic inhabitants.

Heyerdahl and Liv's more joyous experiences occurred when their encounters with the island population were successful, amicable, and mutually enriching. Community, seemingly, even if tainted by the mores of civilization, remains necessary for all Earth's inhabitants.

Days later, as he gazed into the ocean's "endless dimensions and permanence" while awaiting the return of the white-sailed schooner, Heyerdahl contemplated. "There was something beyond human comprehension about its immeasurable size … how could I know that the endless Pacific … would shrivel to quite comprehensible dimensions in my mind …?"[10] He gazed to the heavens. "How strange, with this endless myriad of stars to choose from, that the Polynesians, on all their far-flung islands in both hemispheres, should start their new year the first day the insignificant Pleiades appear above the horizon. Just as people did on the coast of Peru and among some ancient Mediterranean civilizations."[11] Heyerdahl's meditations would, with time, eventually evolve into an extraordinary voyage of discovery.

Opposite (top): Liv Heyerdahl on top of the mountain range above the valley of Omoa, Fatu Hiva, Marquesas Islands.

Opposite (bottom): Liv Heyerdahl picking mother-of-pear shells on a beach on Takaroa, Tuamotu Islands.

Top: Cave dwellers waiting for a ship. The last weeks were spent hiding on a lonely beach, keeping a constant lookout for a ship that could take them away from Fatu Hiva. Apart from a few pineapples brought in secrecy by Tioti at night, their diet was the seafood collected by hand among the rocks and a few coconuts from a couple of palms growing by the beach.

Bottom: Stone head in the Puamau Valley of Hiva Oa on the site of I'ipona me'ae, probably representing Ta'aroa, with fishlike eyes.

Resolution

Assembling an Archetype

Norway, New York, and Canada 1938–1947

"You're wrong, absolutely wrong," insisted the eminent American anthropologist Dr. Herbert Spinden, sitting across from Heyerdahl in his regal, well-appointed vitrine- and book-lined bureau at the Brooklyn Museum in the late summer of 1946.[1] "You can't treat ethnographic problems as a sort of detective mystery!"[2] That intractable ethnographic problem—from whence had come the first Polynesian island inhabitants?—had plagued Heyerdahl from the very hour he his wife, Liv Heyerdahl, had sailed away from the paradisiacal Marquesan island of Fatu Hiva in late November 1937.

Returning to Norway in February 1938, Heyerdahl and Liv initially resided in a cabin, Svippopp, near Lillehammer, close to where Heyerdahl himself had passed much of his boyhood, and where they were to have their first child, Thor Jr., that same year. Fascinated by the inexplicable question of Polynesia's island inhabitants' arcane origins and consumed by identifying the equally enigmatic sun-god Tiki, Heyerdahl began investigating Polynesia's cultural past and ocean migration phenomena, undertaking exhaustive, independent scholarship within Oslo University's Library.

Numerous scholars, Heyerdahl declared, had offered equally numerous theories, frequently disproved by subsequent research as to the Polynesians' homeland: "Malaya, India, China, Japan, Arabia, Egypt, the Caucasus, Atlantis, even Germany and Norway" had all then been ventured.[3] And, where scientific inquiry ceased, imaginative hypotheses appeared: Rapa Nui and the islands of Polynesia were in fact the remaining vestiges of a fantastical, now-submerged, continent. Heyerdahl, however, remained unconvinced, particularly by inconclusive hypotheses in prevailing scholarship which held that, despite enormous ocean distances, Polynesia's inhabitants had originally voyaged southeastward from Asia and Indonesia.

Encountering research which equally sustained and negated his intuitive conjecture that antecedent Polynesians migrated from the Pacific coastlines of South America, Heyerdahl began amassing evidence regarding the Polynesian question from every field, including archaeology, anthropology, botany, ethnography, geography, linguistics, and oceanography. Heyerdahl's research continued to draw him away from the Old World, where scholars had long sought the origins of Polynesia's inhabitants, and toward the New World, and the pre-Incan civilizations of South America. "I found in Peru surprising traces in culture, mythology, and language," he wrote, "which impelled me to identify … the origin of the Polynesian tribal god Tiki."[4] On reading of the Incan legend of the Peruvian sun-king, Viracocha, originally known as Kon-Tiki, the near-annihilation of his followers by Chief Cari of the Coquimbo Valley, his miraculous escape to the Pacific coast, and eventual disappearance to the west, Heyerdahl became convinced[5] that "the white chief-god Sun-Tiki, whom the Incas declared that their forefathers had banished from Peru on to the Pacific, was identical to the white chief-god Tiki, son of the sun, whom the inhabitants of all the eastern Pacific islands hailed as the original founder of their race and that Polynesia was first settled by peoples voyaging westward from South America, not from the Indian subcontinent and Southeast Asia, as conventional theories propounded." Heyerdahl speculated that these argonauts, aided by the westward-oscillating, temperate Humboldt Current, were gradually dispersed throughout the Pacific archipelagos over the succeeding centuries. Enduring evidence of such long-forgotten ancestors was illustrated by the near-identical linguistic, mythological, cultivational, astronomical, and cultural practices among the Pacific's various island inhabitants, as well as by the presence of certain cultivated plants such as the pineapple, sweet potato, *Ipomoea batatas*, the bottle-gourd, *Lagenaria vulgaris*, and the coconut palm, *Cocos nucifera*. "My deductions seemed simple," he would later declare. "Certain cultivated plants had been brought from South America to Polynesia by pre-European people."[6]

In the summer of 1938, Heyerdahl had a chance encounter with Iver Fougner, a Norwegian school teacher and onetime Indian Agent with the Bella Coola Indian Agency. Fougner was the brother of a neighbor in Lillehammer from whom Heyerdahl and his family purchased their daily milk. Fougner happened to be visiting from Canada, and after hearing Heyerdahl giving an educational lecture on Norwegian radio, he shared with him photographs of extraordinary artifacts from indigenous peoples living in the Bella Coola Valley, British Columbia. Heyerdahl began to hypothesize that perhaps a distant relationship existed between Polynesia and coastal Pacific Northwest indigenous peoples, and that two independent migrations had conceivably occurred from the New World to Polynesia—the first in which a people originating from a pre-Incan culture (those related to Kon-Tiki) voyaged upon the Humboldt Current westward from South America and modern-day Peru. In the second, another people voyaged from Indonesia on the Japan Current to coastal North America before journeying with the trade winds through Hawaii, southeastward to Polynesia. That theory both disputed and in part aligned with the widely held assumption by most scholars that the current inhabitants had come from the West.

Questions regarding these two independent waves of Polynesian migration now became Heyerdahl's obsession, drawing himself and Liv to Canada's west coast to study the Kwakiutl First Nation in the Bella Coola Valley and consult archaeological collections in museums in Victoria, Seattle, and Vancouver, just as the Second World War descended upon Europe. Engaging eminent scholars on Northwest Coast cultures, Heyerdahl was introduced to an enormous variety of theories regarding the origins and development of Pacific Northwest Coast indigenous peoples; however, none of these substantiated his hypothesis of Polynesian migration routes originating from, and encompassing both South America and Asia. Nevertheless, after journeying through the Bella Coola Valley with local guides, and spending time with Kwakiutl First Nation peoples—interrupted only by the birth of his second son, Bjørn, in 1940—Heyerdahl became convinced of his disruptive theory by his observations of petroglyphs and implements employed in the region that ostensibly possessed resemblances to those he had seen in the Marquesas archipelago. He believed the second wave of Polynesian settlers had migrated from Asia to North America and then onward to the islands of the south Pacific Ocean. Heyerdahl's unorthodox hypothesis, unwittingly recounted to a *Vancouver Sun* newspaper reporter, and subsequently appearing in *The New York Times*, drew immediate criticism from several eminent scholars, including the celebrated American anthropologist Margaret Mead. Nevertheless, Heyerdahl remained devoted to his unconventional research on Polynesia, and in May 1941 his first article regarding the subject, "Did Polynesian Culture Originate in America?" was published in *International Science*, no doubt helped somewhat by his unintentional observations to that *Vancouver Sun* news reporter. "Did Polynesian Culture Originate in America?" was the first presentation of Heyerdahl's Pacific migration theory before an international scientific community, and although the article's reception is now unknown, its publication surely catalyzed his continued study.

In summer 1942, Heyerdahl enlisted with the Norwegian army, disrupting his life's work for several years. During the war's course, he was successively promoted from private to lieutenant, training with special forces units both in Canada and later England (where he also trained as an undercover agent), appearing on the Norwegian frontier near Kirkenes in various missions alongside Russian forces to drive German troops south out of Norway. All the while, the would-be scholar-turned-serviceman undertook several labors to sustain his young kinfolk, Liv, Thor Jr., and Bjørn. For example, in May of 1942 he engaged American archaeologist Ralph Linton to sell his expansive Marquesas artifact collection to Dr. Herbert Spinden, curator of the Brooklyn Museum, for the negligible sum of $1,000. Unbeknownst then to Heyerdahl, Spinden would later prove unexpectedly instrumental in assuring Heyerdahl's unorthodox Pacific migration theory achieved international recognition.

Simultaneously, Heyerdahl sought to advance his studies wherever possible, utilizing every opportunity during leave from service to conduct further research. During one such time, Heyerdahl visited Stonehenge, a megalithic monument on Salisbury Plain in Wiltshire, southern England. Illustrating his propensity to draw inspiration and connection between seemingly disparate geographies and peoples, he wrote afterwards in a letter to Liv: "We, conceited mediocres, think that only we exist, that only our time period matters. We are like horses with blinders. Man's wisdom is pathetic and miserably egocentric. It has always been thus, between individuals, between nations, between races, between eras… Place the sun and any Pius in all his golden splendour side-by-side, and try and tell me that they were heathens any more than we are in 1944!"[7]

In late summer 1945, after the war's end, Heyerdahl returned home to Norway to reunite with Liv, Thor Jr., and Bjørn, and to begin assembling his voluminous Polynesian migration research into a new manuscript, developed from Heyerdahl's first article, published in 1941. In June 1946, he journeyed once more to New York City to conduct additional Polynesia research, aided by Dr. Spinden and the Brooklyn Museum. Heyerdahl's manuscript, now titled "Polynesia and America: A Study of Prehistoric Relations," combined his original research with that undertaken with the Kwakiutl peoples in British Columbia, his study of Central and South American mythologies of Kon-Tiki Viracocha, and of course his experiences and research in the Marquesas. Desiring validation from the international scientific community and publication of his theory, Heyerdahl sought reviews of *Polynesia and America* from anthropology professor Fay-Cooper Cole at Chicago University, anthropologist Ruth Benedict at Columbia University, and Charles Marius Barbeau at the National Museum of Canada, all of whom, while praising his undeniably innovative research and imaginative postulation, nevertheless resoundingly rejected Heyerdahl's Polynesian migration hypothesis.

Heyerdahl visited Dr. Spinden again in an attempt to persuade him but, bemused and dismissive of Heyerdahl's emphatic insistence that present-day Polynesians may have originated from South America, Spinden stated, "We know for certain that none of the peoples of South America got over to the islands of the Pacific. … The answer's simple enough. They couldn't get there. They had no boats!"

"They had rafts," Heyerdahl hesitatingly objected, "balsa-wood rafts." Dr. Spinden remained unconvinced, steadfastly refusing to read Heyerdahl's enormous manuscript, which lay unopened upon his desk. Quietly he dismissed the impassioned Norwegian, suggesting, "Well, you can try a trip from Peru to the Pacific islands on a balsa-wood raft."[8] And, returning the voluminous manuscript, he dismissed Heyerdahl.

Heyerdahl recognized that his unconventional migration theory would never obtain widespread acceptance on account of the vast expanses of Pacific Ocean separating South America and Polynesia. In a quixotic decision that would commit his name and hypothesis to posterity, Heyerdahl now declared, "I'm so sure that the Indians crossed the Pacific on their rafts that I'm willing to build a raft of the same kind myself and cross the sea just to prove that it's possible."[9] The nascent explorer's inability to obtain a publisher for his unconventional theory throughout those years of research became in fact the catalyst for the extraordinary voyage which would propel him into meteoritic celebrity and assure his reputation as one of the most renowned explorers of the 20th century.

Opposite (top): On a ship from Norway to Canada in 1939. Thor Heyerdahl Jr. on a bunch of bananas, probably in Panama.

Opposite (bottom): Princess Astrid, Prince Harald, and Princess Maud of Norway with the Heyerdahl family's bear, Peik, in Canada. The bear lived with the family over the winter, sleeping in bed with the children.

Top: Thor Heyerdahl is ready for military service. No information is available about where or when.

Top: Liv Heyerdahl, Bjørn (Bamse) Heyerdahl, Thor Heyerdahl Jr. and Thor Heyerdahl in Canada during World War II, just before Heyerdahl left to join the Norwegian Armed forces in England. These photographs were later used in war propaganda, as they showed a young Norwegian couple.

Opposite: Herman Watzinger and Thor Heyerdahl (second and third from left) planning the Kon-Tiki expedition with the Danish polar explorer Peter Freuchen (right) and an unidentified Scottish member, at the Explorers Club in New York (see page 69). Unfortunate ethnocentric parallels once drawn between non-European peoples and primates are illustrated by proximate photographs of an indigenous individual and a chimpanzee that can be seen to the right.

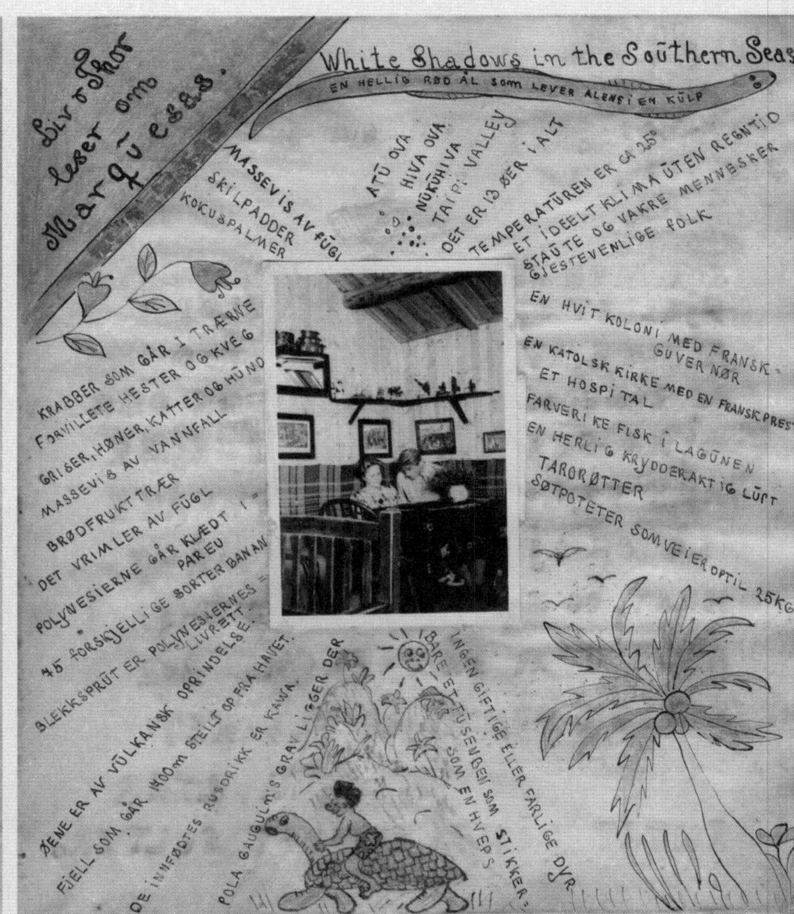

Left: A page from Thor and Liv Heyerdahl's diary detailing their relationship and trip to Fatu Hiva in 1936–37. Thor Heyerdahl owned a Samoyed called Kazan, after a popular novel by James Oliver Curwood, published in 1914.

Right: A page from Thor and Liv Heyerdahl's diary detailing their relationship and trip to Fatu Hiva in 1936-37. Here, they plan the trip, probably to Hiva Oa, Marquesas, at the Heyerdahl family cottage near Lillehammer in the summer of 1936.

Opposite: Drawing by Thor Heyerdahl from his and Liv's journal, showing cut and engraved stones forming the entrance to a communal grave in the Hanavavae Valley, Fatu Hiva. The title reads "Drawing of the red-stone roof of the burial chamber. The length of the stone blocks 210 cm; The height of the stone blocks 60–70 cm; The width of the stone blocks c.20 cm."

SKISSE OVER

GRAVKAMMERETS RØDE STENTAK

HELLENES LENGDE 210 cm.
" BREDDE 60-70 cm.
" TYKKELSE ca 20 cm.

THE
LIVING RACES
OF MANKIND

KORALL-ØER I TUAMOTUGRUPPEN
TIL MARQUESAS
AHE
MANIHI
TAKAROA
TAKAPOTO
MATAHIVA
RANGIROA
ARUTUA
TIKEI
TIKAHAU
APATAKI
ARATIKA
MAKATEA
KAUKURA
KAUEHI
RARAKA
TOAU
NIAU
FAKARAVA
TIL MARQUESAS MED "TEREORA"
FAAITE
TAHANE
TETIAROA
ANAA
MOOREA
TAHITI
MEHETIA
VI ER ALLE SMÅ MORMONER
MEN DER SKAL ENNU VÆRE EN VAKLENDE SJEL PÅ TAKAROA

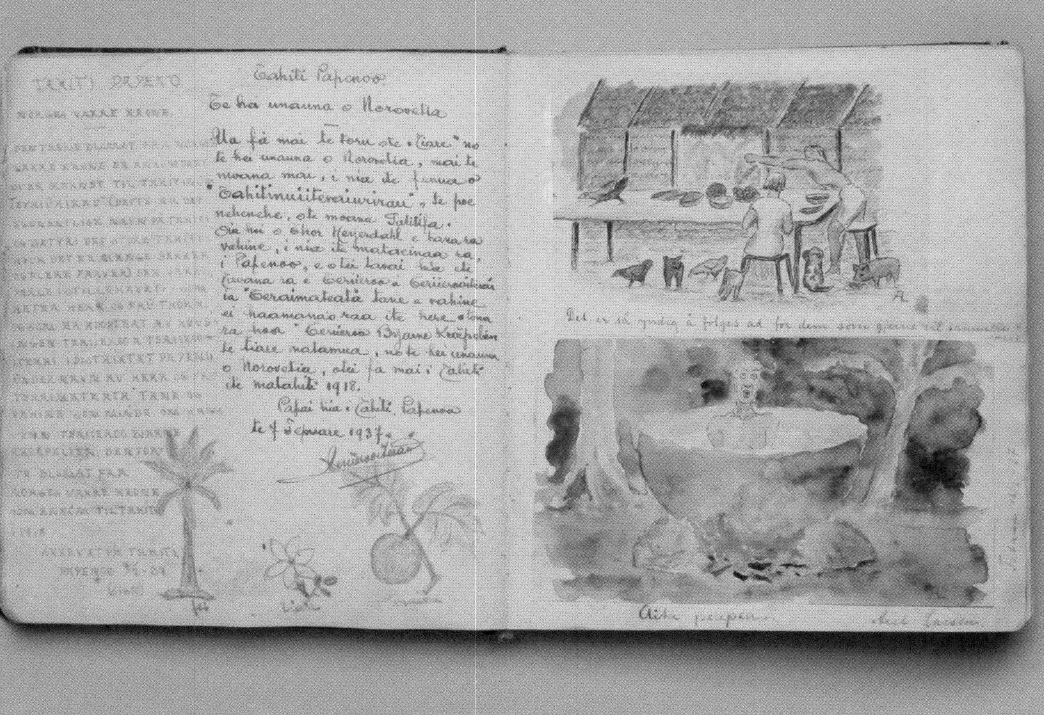

Tahiti Papenoo
Aita peapea

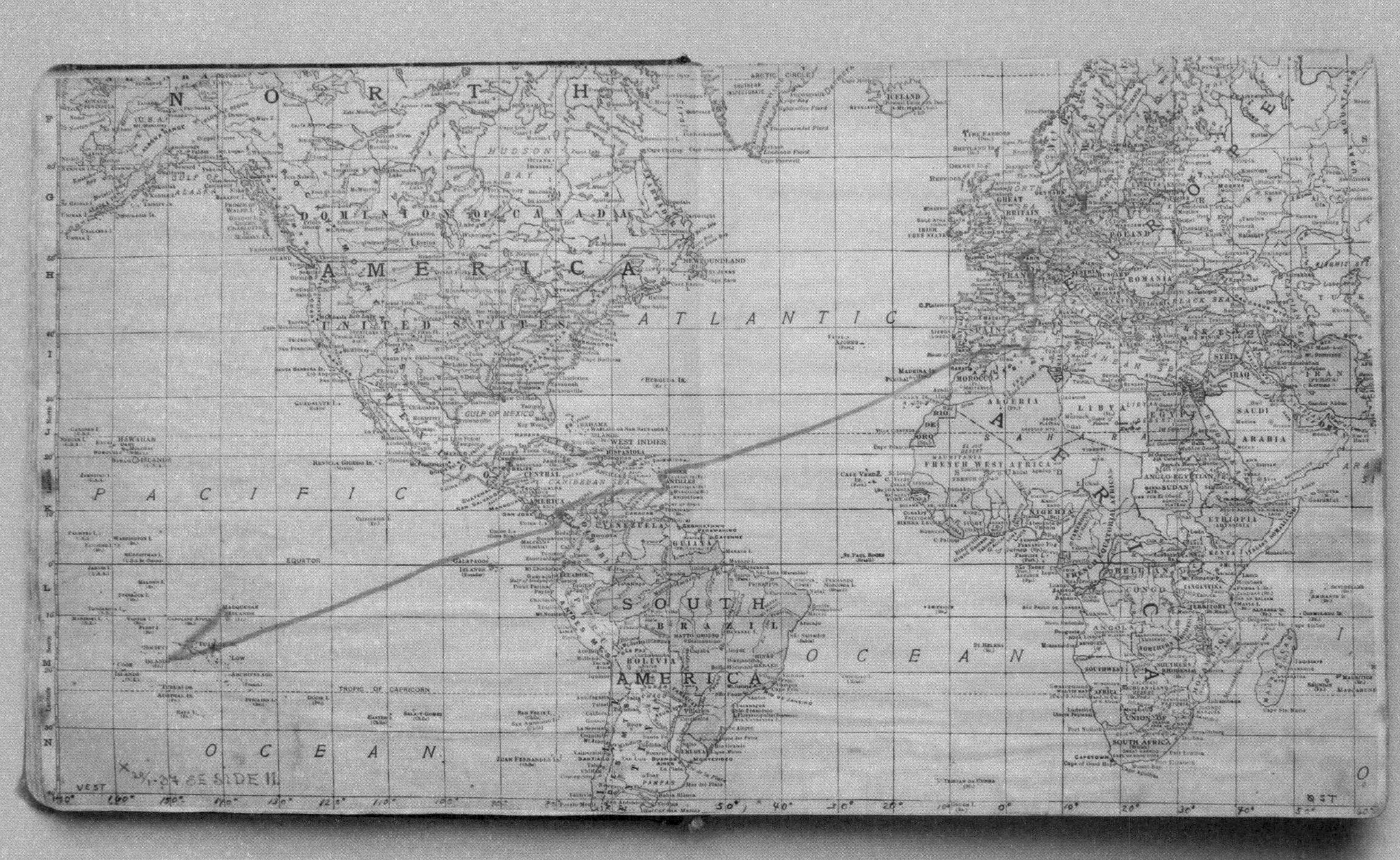
NORTH AMERICA
DOMINION OF CANADA
HUDSON BAY
UNITED STATES
GULF OF MEXICO
WEST INDIES
ATLANTIC OCEAN
PACIFIC OCEAN
EQUATOR
TROPIC OF CAPRICORN
SOUTH AMERICA
BRAZIL
BOLIVIA
EUROPE
AFRICA
ALGERIA
LIBYA
SAHARA
FRENCH WEST AFRICA
ARABIA
IRAQ
ICELAND
ARCTIC CIRCLE

Previous spread (left): *The Living Races of Mankind,* published by Hutchinson & Co. (1902). Being confined mostly to his house to avoid the Spanish flu, a five-year-old Thor Heyerdahl was mesmerized by the maps and photos and he fell in love with Polynesian culture.

Opposite and previous spread (right): A notebook belonging to Liv and Thor Heyerdahl. It was a gift from Liv's mother and became the young couple's note- and "cottage" book in December 1936, when they set out on a journey to Fatu Hiva, one of the Marquesas Islands, to return to nature. With rhyming texts, colorful drawings, and pasted photographs, the notebook tells the story of how Liv and Thor met each other and became a couple as well as documenting preparations for the trip and their exotic adventure.

Overleaf: The Kon-Tiki raft on a short test voyage in Callao harbour prior to the start of the expedition. At the back you can see a carpenter from the Peruvian Navy working to finish things off.

1947

Kon-Tiki Expedition

“Well, you can try a trip from Peru to the Pacific islands on a balsa-wood raft.”

Dismissed by the academic community and unable to promulgate his unorthodox migration theory before a general audience, Heyerdahl resolved to undertake a remarkable, treacherous experiment, voyaging across the Pacific Ocean from coastal Peru to Polynesia. Drawing upon several illustrations of balsa-wood rafts authored by European explorers of Pacific-coastal South America, and the observations revealed by numerous sailors Heyerdahl encountered at the Norwegian Sailors' Home in Brooklyn where he was then residing, he, who had never sailed before, contrived nevertheless to construct a vessel in exactly the same fashion as the ancient South Americans—square-sailed, with five centerboards (retractable keels) and a long steering oar positioned at the stern.

Heyerdahl first consulted with several knowledgeable Norwegian sea captains regarding his voyage. One captain in particular, Wilhelm Eitrem, although immensely skeptical of the endeavor, believed such a voyage was indeed possible. Emboldened by such optimism and believing an expedition would interest potential supporters much more than an unpublished manuscript, in November 1946 Heyerdahl visited New York City's venerable Explorers Club. In "an atmosphere of lion-hunting, mountaineering, and polar life" within an interior reminiscent of a luxury, world-voyaging yacht, members of the club—including Heyerdahl—assembled for supper or evocative lectures among "trophies of hippopotamus and deer, big-game rifles, tusks, war drums and spears, Indian carpets, idols and model ships, flags, photographs, and maps."[1] That evening, a presentation was delivered by one Colonel Haskin of the U.S. Air Force Material Command, during which Haskin demonstrated several new military inventions of potential aid to scientific expeditions. He also generously offered any of the club's members the use of such innovative new equipment for any forthcoming expedition they may undertake. As good fortune would ensure, Heyerdahl's Pacific Ocean expedition gained substantial equipment that very same evening.

Several days later, while breakfasting at the Norwegian Sailors' Home, Heyerdahl enlisted the expedition's first member: Herman Watzinger, an engineering student from Trondheim, central Norway, who was then studying thermodynamics and who Heyerdahl enlisted largely on the strength of the man's character and enthusiasm. (Watzinger would eventually become second-in-command during Heyerdahl's remarkable Kon-Tiki expedition.) Having secured their engagement, Heyerdahl and Watzinger visited The Explorers Club together and met with celebrated Danish polar explorer Peter Freuchen, who was himself well acquainted with raft travel down the vast rivers of Siberia and off the Arctic coastline, and who became an enthusiastic supporter of the expedition. Now wholeheartedly committed to the enterprise, Watzinger resigned from his position as a refrigeration engineer and he and Heyerdahl set about sourcing additional expedition members and sufficient supplies for four proposed months at sea. Joining the expedition now were Knut Haugland and Torstein Raaby, who had both served alongside Heyerdahl as wireless operators in the Norwegian Army. Next came Heyerdahl's boyhood friend Erik Hesselberg, a painter and experienced sailor. "Am going to cross Pacific on a wooden raft to support a theory that the South Sea islands were peopled from Peru," Heyerdahl wrote to all three. "Will you come? I guarantee nothing but a free trip to Peru and the South Sea islands and back ... Reply at once."[2] Haugland, Raaby, and Hesselberg all immediately agreed. Sourcing equipment for the unorthodox expedition proved relatively achievable. In December 1946, Heyerdahl contacted former colleagues in the British armed forces, and decorated Norwegian war hero Captain Bjørn Rørholt, who had served alongside Raaby. Rørholt proved instrumental in aiding the expedition. Also crucial to these stages was Gerd Vold Hurum, then head of encryption at the Norwegian Embassy in Washington, who Heyerdahl had recruited as the expedition's secretary and project director. Vold Hurum was the unofficial seventh member of the team and the only woman. She was instrumental to the preparations and diplomatic relationships beforehand, and through contacting the Pentagon and the United States Army, secured field equipment, including sunscreen, water-resistant sleeping bags, matches, and expedition boots. Primus stoves, kitchen utensils, floating knives and water kegs, as well as field service rations, including 684 boxes of pineapple, were also procured from the United States War Department—along with their much-needed endorsement. The expedition was also supplied with four radios, which were to be operated by Raaby and Haugland. The two radio operators were to make frequent reports to the North American Newspaper Alliance, and supply regular articles to editor Peter Celliers. Over the succeeding months, support for Heyerdahl's remarkable expedition expanded. Rørholt and Norwegian journalist Egil Tresselt, engaged with the foreign minister in the Norwegian wartime government, also assisted Heyerdahl in obtaining support from United Nations' delegates from Ecuador and Peru, while letters of support to the presidents of Ecuador and Chile were authored by a Chilean amateur archaeologist and UN assistant secretary Dr. Benjamin Cohen. In addition, Norwegian ambassador Wilhelm von Munthe af Morgenstierne lent the expedition invaluable support with a personal loan of $2,000 and the provision of office space and assistants.

In January 1947, Heyerdahl and Watzinger boarded an airplane bound for Ecuador's tropical port city of Guayaquil. Descending over the equator and through "milk-white clouds," the verdant, subtropical jungles of South America now appeared; the two Norwegians entered an "atmosphere of a hothouse to meet chattering Southerners in tropical clothes ... our shirts sticking to our backs like wet paper ... We had reached the country where the balsa tree grows and were to buy timber to build our raft."[3] However, large balsa-wood trees, they discovered, were available only from Ecuador's jungle interior, not from harborside Guayaquil. In desperation, time being of the essence before gales drew northward from Antarctica and hurricane season began in Polynesia, Heyerdahl and Watzinger boarded a cargo plane for the nation's altitudinous capital, Quito, situated 9,000 feet (2,740 m) above sea level upon the Andean Plateau, with the intention of journeying over the mountains and subtropical jungle to Quevedo, where the balsa tree plantations lay. Aided by the American military attaché, the two intrepid Norwegians embarked upon a perilous two-day journey by military jeep, directed by one well-armed Captain, Agurto Alexis Alvarez, through *bandidos*-infested territory. The party traveled "over sun-smitten slopes without a bush or tree and down into valleys of desert sand and cactus," ascending over snowfields to 12,000 feet, before descending back into "the sea of jungle" far below,[4] inundated by a temperate tropical deluge, then finally crossing the Quevedo River by balsa-wood raft—Heyerdahl's' maiden voyage by raft.

→>>>

Don Frederico, the balsa plantation's proprietor, was well acquainted with balsa-wood rafts, recalling that they were once sailed along the Peruvian coastline by indigenous people intending to sell fish at Guayaquil. He led Heyerdahl and Watzinger to an enormous tree, some 3 feet (900 cm) thick. "In Polynesian style we christened the tree … Ku, after a Polynesian deity of American origin," Heyerdahl wrote, before Ku was laboriously felled over several long hours, eventually accompanied by Kane, Kama, Ilo, Mauri, Ra, Rangi, Papa, Taranga, Kura, Kukara and Hiti—"twelve mighty balsas, all christened in honor of Polynesian legendary figures whose names had once been borne with Tiki over the sea from Peru."[5] Heyerdahl, Watzinger and two local laborers then fashioned the 12 balsa-wood logs together into two rafts with durable lianas, complete with steering oars. Launching the rafts upon the river, the party sailed downstream back toward Guayaquil, with Heyerdahl, and Watzinger transferring to a paddle steamer just outside the city. Watzinger then accompanied Ku, Kane, Kama, Ilo, Mauri, Ra, Rangi, Papa, Taranga, Kura, Kukara, and Hiti's labored passage to Peru by coasting steamship, while Heyerdahl boarded yet another airplane, bound now for Lima, "where a faithful copy of the Indians' old-time vessels"[6] was to be constructed at Callao Bay. Afforded an audience with President Bustamante y Rivero, on account of an introduction by helpful Dr. Cohen, Heyerdahl succeeded in securing a section of Callao Bay's naval dockyard, access to naval workshops, equipment, storage, the use of a dry dock, and several naval personnel.

Rather serendipitously, a Swedish-Finnish scientific expedition was then due to be conducted among the indigenous people of the Amazon jungles, and two of the Swedish members of that party had just arrived, by canoe, in Quito. One of the pair, Bengt Danielsson, an anthropologist from Uppsala University, was completely fascinated by Heyerdahl's balsa-wood raft expedition across the Pacific Ocean, and and sought him out. "I've come to ask if I may come with you on the raft," Danielsson inquired. "I'm interested in the migration theory." Heyerdahl, knowing nothing of Danielsson "except that he was a scientist and that he had come straight out of the depths of the jungle," was somewhat apprehensive, but acquiesced: "If a solitary Swede had the pluck to go out on a raft with five Norwegians, he could not be squeamish."[7] Danielsson became Heyerdahl's sixth expedition member, and the only member able to speak Spanish.

Heyerdahl's expedition members—Watzinger, Haugland, Raaby, Hesselberg, Danielsson, and Heyerdahl himself—assembled in Lima on 14 March 1947, as well as Gerd Vold Hurum, who was to lead the expedition from land, transmitting information to and from the voyage's members onboard the raft, including news of home. "No two of these men had met before, and they were all of entirely different types," Heyerdahl wrote of the new sailors. It was a recruitment practice that would characterize all his subsequent expeditions. Recognizing that the six members had several weeks onboard for tiring of one another's tales, Heyerdahl acknowledged that "no storm clouds with low pressure and gusty weather held greater menace for us than the danger of psychological cloudburst among six men shut up together for months on a drifting raft."

Construction now began of the traditional balsa-wood raft (or *pae-pae*) in the naval dockyard at Callao Bay. Supervised by Watzinger and assisted by 20 Peruvian sailors, the nine vast and deeply grooved balsa-wood logs from the Quevedo forest were lashed together with 300 stout lengths of thick hemp rope, then reinforced crosswise with additional balsa-wood lengths. A 19-foot (5.8-m) steering oar, housed within a thick block of balsa-wood, was installed at the stern and a deck of split bamboo lengths was laid over the balsa-wood logs, which was then overlain with braided bamboo reed matting. An open cabin constructed of bamboo canes and plaited bamboo reeds was erected near the raft's center. Forward of the cabin, two masts cut from mangrove wood "as hard as iron"[8] were lashed together. A yard made from double-strength bamboo stems was then bound to the mast, upon which an enormous rectangular sail was hauled. Fir plank centerboards, a fixture of all Incan balsa-wood rafts, were interspersed among the balsa-wood logs, to assist with navigation. "The whole construction was a faithful copy of the old vessels in Peru and Ecuador," Heyerdahl wrote, with neither nails, nor iron stakes, nor wire rope employed. Despite the expedition's enormous enthusiasm for the balsa-wood raft, several foreign naval experts, diplomats, ambassadors, admirals, captains, and sailors, assembling at Callao Bay, pessimistically questioned the vessel's seaworthiness. "Your mother and father will be very grieved when they hear of your death," one fatalistic ambassador quietly informed Heyerdahl. Assailed by such disheartening assessments, Heyerdahl repeatedly questioned himself as to the expedition's safety. An enduring conviction, however, galvanized his belief in the voyage's success. "I knew all the time in my heart that a prehistoric civilization had been spread from Peru and across to the islands at a time when rafts like ours were the only vessels on that coast," he wrote. "If balsa wood had floated and lashings held for Kon-Tiki in AD 500, they would do the same for us now if we blindly made our raft an exact copy of his."[9]

Before sailing forth into the Pacific Ocean, provisions for six men for four months were assembled onboard: military rations, 250 gallons of drinking water, large wicker baskets containing coconuts, bananas, and other fresh fruits and vegetables, including sweet potatoes and gourds from Peru, just like those possessed by the argonauts' ancient predecessors. Wireless radio equipment, scientific instruments, primus stoves and camera film, as well as the six members' personal effects, including drawing paper, books, Hesselberg's guitar, and a latterly gifted green parrot, Lorita, were all stowed within the raft's diminutive bamboo cabin. Christened *Kon-Tiki* by Vold Hurum with a coconut struck ceremoniously over the bow, the raft's bamboo yard arm was hauled up, and the vast rectangular sail shaken open. Emblazoned triumphantly across the sail was a scarlet illustration of the sun-king, Kon-Tiki, drawn by Hesselberg from a statue discovered within the pre-

Colombian city of Tiahuanaco, western Bolivia. On 27 April 1947, Heyerdahl's expedition assembled on deck before an ecstatic quayside audience of fascinated spectators, excited journalists, various national ambassadors, government ministers, naval representatives, and Peruvian President José Luis Bustamante y Rivero himself. Later that afternoon, after much celebratory fanfare, the hulking *Kon-Tiki* was drawn away from Callao Bay's sanctuary by the naval tugboat, *Guardian Rios,* which overnight ferried her 50 nautical miles (92 km) northwest into the Pacific Ocean. After a ceremonious farewell to the 35 sailors of the *Guardian Rios* on 29 April, the towropes were cast away, and the *Kon-Tiki* was at last alone. The expedition's members glanced about themselves with expressions of anticipation and exhilaration, and some relief for having left the press behind. As the steady southeasterly trade wind rose, *Kon-Tiki's* sail triumphantly expanded, "bent forward like a swelling breast, with *Kon-Tiki's* head bursting with pugnacity … We shouted westward ho! and hauled on sheets and ropes. The steering oar was put into the water" as the vessel gradually gathered momentum yard by arduous yard. Absorbed by the rapidly flowing, Antarctic-fed Humboldt Current, the raft continued on, the crew rapidly learning how to steer and captain *Kon-Tiki,* with significant difficulty, as they went. "The water was green and cold and everywhere about us; the jagged mountains of Peru had vanished into the dense cloud banks astern," Heyerdahl wrote.[10] His prototypical yet ancient balsa-wood raft voyaged laboriously northwestward, into the incandescent Pacific sunset.

→⫽⫽

Ominously carried north toward the Equator and the Galápagos Islands, where treacherous ocean countercurrents oscillated, *Kon-Tiki's* anxious crew fought the elements to stay on their westward, Polynesia-bound course. Mercifully, after several days at sea, and now covering 55–60 nautical miles (100–110 km) each day, their unorthodox vessel was embraced first by the Humboldt Current and then the South Equatorial Current, drawing *Kon-Tiki* away from the coastal current and eventually setting the grateful expedition on their intended west-north-westward journey. "We were now so accustomed to having the sea dancing round us that we took no account of it," Heyerdahl wrote. "What did it matter if we danced around a bit with a thousand fathoms of water under us, so long as we and the raft were always on top?"[11] *Kon-Tiki's* balsa-wood logs remained largely impenetrable by seawater, and despite the constant pressure and motion between the vessel's innumerable joints, the hemp ropes nevertheless held. They happened upon abundant shoals of tuna, dolphins, sea turtles and sardines, and gleaming deluges of flying fish, which they caught and eagerly devoured. "When at last we came out into the blue water where the sea rolled majestically by, sunlit and serene, ruffled by gusts of wind," Heyerdahl wrote, "we could see [the flying fish] glittering like a rain of projectiles which shot from the water and flew in straight till their power of flight was exhausted and they vanished beneath the surface."[12] *Kon-Tiki's* argonauts gradually sailed across the vast expanses of the Pacific Ocean and Polynesia's scattered archipelagos. Intermittently captivated by phosphorescent plankton, and the equally incandescent stars of the dark tropical heavens, or startled by the inquisitive glances of enormous, motionless squid with "devilish green eyes shining in the dark like phosphorous," Heyerdahl's sailors achieved, with each passing hour, symbiotic equilibrium between themselves, *Kon-Tiki,* various marine life, the fathomless ocean, ceaseless sunshine, and cerulean horizon. On 24 May, the party encountered an enormous whale shark. The leviathan swam placidly back and forth beneath the raft, possessing a body longer than the raft itself. All six expedition members grasped insufficient hand harpoons in anticipation as the shark encircled the raft ever closer; only when Hesselberg violently struck the animal's head was the *Kon-Tiki* liberated from her inquisitive pursuer.

Enveloped by the South Equatorial Current and now voyaging due westward, Heyerdahl's balsa-wood raft was just 400 nautical miles south of the Galápagos Islands, the large eponymous sea turtles visiting the crew occasionally. Indolent days passed peaceably by; the expedition "saw no sign either of a ship or of drifting remains to show that there were other people in the world. The whole sea was ours, and, with all the gates of the horizon open, real peace and freedom were wafted down from the firmament itself." Saline air, and "all the blue purity that surrounded us, had washed and cleansed both body and soul. To us on the raft the great problems of civilized man appeared false and illusory—like perverted products of the human mind. Only the elements mattered." No longer a fearsome, destructive enemy, the elements, Heyerdahl wrote, "had become a reliable friend which steadily and surely helped us onward."[13]

"When Kon-Tiki sailed from the coast of Peru after his defeat by Lake Titicaca," Heyerdahl hypothesized, the sun-king could have possessed two objectives, either "to follow the sun itself ... in the hope of finding a new and more peaceful country" or "to sail his rafts up the coast of South America in order to found a new kingdom out of reach of his persecutors." Either objective, Heyerdahl believed, saw Kon-Tiki "fall an easy prey to the southeast trade wind and the Humboldt Current," propelling any sun-worshipper's voyage, including Kon-Tiki, directly toward the sunset.[14]

→>>>>

After 45 days at sea and 2,000 miles (3,220 km) from coastal South America, on 12 June Heyerdahl's expedition advanced over the 108th latitude, and were now halfway to Polynesia. Accompanied in these deeper waters by schools of obsidian-blue whales, octopuses whose pensive eyes glistened beneath them in the dark, and zebra-striped pilot fish, Heyerdahl wrote, "waves and fish, sun and stars came and went."[15] The crew regularly submerged themselves in a rudimentary diving basket to observe the ocean's majesty from within. "When we looked down into the bottomless depths of the sea, where it is eternal black night, the night appeared to us a brilliant light blue on account of the refracted rays of the sun."[16] Astoundingly, fish could be seen with unimaginable clarity, many fathoms down into the very depths of the Pacific Ocean. The days passed quietly by and all six argonauts developed an extraordinary intimacy with the ocean, and an enduring respect for the ancient peoples who lived in symbiosis with the ever-metamorphosing waters. Despite enormous advancements in marine science, saline estimations, and Latin nomenclature for various species, "the picture the primitive peoples had" of the oceans, Heyerdahl believed, nevertheless remained "a truer one than ours."[17]

Navigating by the constellations, Heyerdahl also naturally contemplated the extraordinary navigational capacities of Polynesia's seafarers. Deeply knowledgeable of the constellations, planets, the equator, the northern and southern tropics, and the earth's shape, Polynesian sailors, navigating with extraordinary accuracy aided by gourd-etched charts, maps, and north-south star readings, had "explored and brought under their sway… the whole of the sea nearest to America."[18] Once more he speculated that the Polynesian sailors had obtained "their vast astronomical knowledge and their calendar" from the "old vanished civilized race … who had taught Aztecs, Mayas, and Incas their amazing culture in America."[19] Kon-Tiki knew the stars when he set sail upon the Pacific Ocean.

Sea turtles, swordfish, and frigatebirds, synonymous with land's proximity, all began to appear, but land itself did not. Rapa Nui and the Galápagos Islands were the nearest landmasses now, more than 500 miles (800 km) away. Onboard *Kon-Tiki,* such enormous distances remained abstract to Heyerdahl's sailors, "for the horizon glided along with us unnoticed as we moved and our own floating world remained always the same—a circle flung up to the vault of the sky with the raft itself as center, while the same stars rolled on over us night after night."[20] That immense isolation, however, could occasionally prove disconcerting to the argonauts, particularly when viewing the balsa-wood raft from an inflatable dinghy tethered to *Kon-Tiki* herself. "The sea curved away under us as blue upon blue as the sky above, and where they met all the blue flowed together and become one," Heyerdahl wrote. "It almost seemed as if we were suspended in space. All our world was empty and blue; there was no fixed point in it but the tropical sun, golden and warm."[21] Returning to *Kon-Tiki* from the dinghy offered an illusory sense of consoling homecoming, and unassailable equilibrium. Sailing beneath the tropical heavens, enveloped by the stars with which Polynesian seafarers so expertly navigated, Heyerdahl's sailors experienced a profound emancipation. "Whether (the year) was 1947 BC or AD suddenly became of no significance," Heyerdahl wrote. "We lived, and that we felt with alert intensity. We realized that life had been full for men before the technical age … richer in many ways than the life of modern man. Time and evolution somehow ceased to exist," he observed, harkening back to those very same beliefs that had first compelled he and Liv to seek out Eden on Fatu Hiva. "All that was real and all that mattered were the same today as they had always been and would always be. We were swallowed up in the absolute common measure of history—endless unbroken darkness under a swarm of stars."[22]

Heyerdahl, contemplating *Kon-Tiki's* southwestward progress while writing away in the raft's diminutive basket-woven cabin, conjured visions of horizon-vast, balsa-wood flotillas captained by fabled Sapa Inca (emperor) Topa Inca Yupanqui, who supposedly voyaged across the Pacific Ocean from coastal Ecuador in circa 1480, questing for new conquerable islands, and eventually discovering the Galápagos Island archipelago. Yupanqui eventually returned to South America, but, Heyerdahl believed, those who voyaged under the aegis of Kon-Tiki never returned, the sun-god's seafarers instead permanently settling in Polynesia. Heyerdahl contemplated Mexican, Peruvian, and Central American mythologies and archaeological representations which recalled "wandering teachers … of an early civilized race from across the Atlantic,"[23] who, journeying upon the westward-streaming ocean currents and trade winds, from the Canary Islands to the Gulf of Mexico, inhabited vast swathes of South America before enigmatically vanishing, archaeologically and culturally, in Peru. And yet, elements from those same people's culture had equally enigmatically appeared in Polynesia, upon so-called Easter Island, known by the Polynesians as Rapa Nui, meaning "large Rapa"—that strange island, the eastward-lying center of Polynesian civilization Heyerdahl had long remained fascinated by, and toward which *Kon-Tiki* now sailed southward. Why did Rapa Nui, the "insignificant little island [that] is dry and barren" and furthest from Asia, from whence its settlers supposedly came, bear the "deepest traces of civilization"?[24] Heyerdahl remained certain that the ocean, and the island's proximity to Peru, was essential—much in the same way that civilizations had appeared in South America, despite the inhospitable desert and jungle landscape and with an absence of any archaeological material illustrating a gradual development of such high civilizations, suggesting they were somewhat spontaneously established where Atlantic Ocean currents collide with the South American continent.

Expanding his musings, Heyerdahl's thoughts turned now to Rapa Nui's colossal stone heads. How were such statues originally carved, transported, and erected? What was their significance and what mechanical knowledge had the statues' long-deceased master sculptors once possessed? Answers to Rapa Nui's insoluble mystery, Heyerdahl contemplated from *Kon-Tiki's* deck, may also be found eastward across the Pacific Ocean. Heyerdahl speculated that *Kon-Tiki's* seafaring ancestors from Peru had in fact constructed the hundreds (today known to be over 1,000) of enormous stone figures, or *moai,* found across Rapa Nui. Polynesian mythology recalls the discovery of the island, known also as *Te Pito te Henua,* "Navel of the World," and the stone-carved sphere, or "golden navel," found upon the island's eastern seashore, symbolizing, Heyerdahl believed, both the various islands' birthplace, and an umbilical connection to ancestral South America. Fascinated by these tales, Heyerdahl had intended to land *Kon-Tiki* on Rapa Nui, or failing that, the Marquesas. Rapa Nui remains unimaginably remote, almost inaccessible, however, and *Kon-Tiki* would not reach the island in 1947—indeed, Heyerdahl himself would not arrive at Rapa Nui until 1955.

On 4 July, *Kon-Tiki* was assailed by a devastating maelstrom, an encounter Heyerdahl compared to an altitudinous squall: "the wilds in a storm, up on the highest mountain plateaus ... the raft glided up and down over the smoking waste of sea."[25] After the worst of the storm had passed, a near-fatal disaster was mercifully averted. Herman Watzinger, diving overboard in an attempt to save Torstein Raaby's displaced sleeping bag, was saved by Knut Haugland's extraordinary courage, who dived into the ocean to rescue him. "Man overboard!" the expedition members cried, trying to launch the raft's rubber lifeboat, the distance between Watzinger and *Kon-Tiki* increasing with each elapsing second. Haugland leaped into the convulsing ocean, clutching a lifebelt, and swam desperately for Watzinger. He eventually reached the fatigued seafarer, and both expedition members were hauled back by Heyerdahl, Hesselberg, Raaby, and Danielsson, saving the two from drowning—and from the dark creature that drew Raaby's sleeping bag away into the depths of the ocean. With the sky now leaden above, and winds increasing to gale force, another cacophonous squall struck the *Kon-Tiki.* Several days passed within which the weather vacillated between full storm and light gale: "The sea dug up into wide valleys filled with the smoke from foaming gray-blue seas," Heyerdahl wrote. On the fifth day, the heavens were cleaved apart, and "the malignant, black cloud cover gave place to the victorious blue sky as the storm passed on."[26] *Kon-Tiki,* unbroken but nevertheless significantly weakened by palisades of Pacific Ocean fury, continued sailing westward, toward the Marquesas and Tuamotu archipelagos. By now, the crew were being visited by flocks of inquisitive frigate birds and dolphins, species of flying fish Heyerdahl recognized from fishing expeditions in Fatu Hiva, and a motionless column of cumulonimbus cloud, signaling land's proximity, despite Polynesia remaining around 1,000 nautical miles away. *Kon-Tiki* was ostensibly still on course to land upon the Marquesas archipelago, an end destination that would lengthen the voyage by several weeks. Unimaginably fatigued and desiring home, however, one evening Torstein Raaby altered *Kon-Tiki*'s course. Drawn first toward Fatu Hiva, then the Tuamotu archipelago, *Kon-Tiki* voyaged southwest into the sunset, accompanied by the "deafening clamor" of thousands of seabirds, all heralding land ahead.

"Land! An island! We devoured it greedily with our eyes," Heyerdahl wrote on 30 July of sighting Puka-Puka, the outermost western island of the Puka Puka, an island on the far western edge of the Tuamotu archipelago. Imbued with "a warm, quiet satisfaction at having actually reached Polynesia," *Kon-Tiki's* elated sailors, unable to reach the island on account of the strong ocean and tidal currents that surround the archipelago, nevertheless experienced "a faint momentary disappointment at having to submit helplessly to seeing the island lie there like a mirage while we continued our eternal drift across the sea westward."[27] Puka-Puka gradually evaporated beyond the horizon, frigate birds disappeared, dolphins grew fewer, and *Kon-Tiki* continued her voyage unaccompanied. Once again sighting clouds, which signaled the islands of Angatau and Fangahina, for three days Heyerdahl's raft sailed westward. "Land ahead!" Torstein triumphantly declared at dawn on 3 August, having sighted Angatau. Immediately *Kon-Tiki's* six expedition members scrambled across the raft's deck, rapidly hoisting Norwegian, French, American, British, Peruvian, Swedish, and Explorers Club flags into the fresh trade wind. Zigzagging along Angatau's length, Hesselberg tacking back and forth against the powerful tidal currents, the elysian island, the white seabirds sailing peacefully about the palm trees, the verdant waters, the gentle sand beaches, the cacophonous shore waves, and the devastating scarlet reef that frustrated *Kon-Tiki's* landing ashore nevertheless left an indelible impression, never to be effaced from the memories of Heyerdahl's jubilant argonauts. "We should never see a more genuine South Sea island," he wrote. "Landing or no landing, we had nonetheless reached Polynesia; the expanse of sea lay behind us for all time."[28] Euphoria enveloped *Kon-Tiki.* "Ninety-seven days. Arrived in Polynesia. There would be a feast in the village that evening,"[29] Heyerdahl joyously wrote. Haugland, recognizing that strong winds were frustrating all efforts to land, leaped overboard and managed to clamber ashore. However, unable to secure assistance from the island population, he finally returned and the expedition, exhausted by several hours of battle against the Pacific Ocean's currents and trade winds, conceded defeat. With all hope evaporating, *Kon-Tiki* gradually drifted westward, away from Angatau's sanctuary. Three days passed, as *Kon-Tiki* drifted further west without sighting any land, sailing directly toward the ominous, 50-mile (80-km) long Takume and Raroia coral reefs which would almost certainly shipwreck the raft, should she be cast against them. Now almost 100 days at sea, and with *Kon-Tiki* drifting diagonally, drawn northward toward Raroia's thorned palisades, all six expedition members began "preparation for our inevitable wreck on the coral reef. Every man learned what he had to do when the moment came; each one of us knew where his own limited sphere of responsibility lay."[30]

"With mixed feelings ... we saw the blue Pacific being ruthlessly torn up and hurled into the air all along the horizon ahead of us," Heyerdahl wrote. "I knew what awaited us; I had visited the Tuamotu [archipelago] before, and had stood safe on land looking out over the immense spectacle in the east, where the surf from the open Pacific broke in over the reef."[31] Preparations for the voyage's end were made onboard the raft; with sail down and centerboards cast away, *Kon-Tiki* lay completely sideways, "entirely at the mercy of wind and sea." Anxious hour succeeded anxious hour as the raft drifted "helplessly sideways, step after step, in toward the reef." "Very close now," Heyerdahl wrote at 9.50 a.m. on 7 August, his final entry within *Kon-Tiki's* logbook. "Only a few hundred yards or so away. All clear. All in good spirits; it looks bad, but we shall make it!"[32]

Deep troughs between the cascading waves saw *Kon-Tiki* swung violently upward, higher and higher, all expedition members ordered to remain grasping the raft, come what may. "Hold on, never mind about the cargo, hold on!" came Heyerdahl's command as the raft was enveloped by the ocean, the anchor rope now cut, all six sailors poised in expectation of the final, inevitable assault against Raroia's coral reef. "A sea rose straight up under (the raft), and we felt the *Kon-Tiki* being lifted up in the air," Heyerdahl wrote. "The great moment had come; we were riding on the wave back at breathless speed, our ramshackle craft creaking and groaning as she quivered under us. The excitement made one's blood boil." Heyerdahl manically thundered orders into the maelstrom, Ulysses lashed to the mast before the temptation of the sirens, drawing enthusiastic beams from the other expedition members as the raft sailed before the wild seas: "*Kon-Tiki's* baptism of fire; all must and would go well."[33]

Elation, however, gave forth almost immediately to desperation as wave after wave cascaded over the raft, submerging the besieged craft entirely, and nearly drawing the sailors into the merciless seas. Dashed against the coral reef, *Kon-Tiki,* "our pleasant world," was shattered into an unrecognizable mass; the bamboo cabin crushed "like a house of cards," the hardwood mast, starboard side, "broken like a match," projecting askew over the treacherous reef, the steering oar "smashed to splinters," and the bow's splashboards "broken like cigar boxes." The entire deck "was torn up and pasted like wet paper against the forward wall of the cabin, along with boxes, cans, canvas, and other cargo." Drawn "out of the witches' kitchen," back and forth within the tumultuous backwash against the scarlet Raroia reef, Heyerdahl's hopes of all six expedition members' survival ebbed away. Miraculously, however, Raaby appeared among the waves, then Haugland, Hesselberg, Watzinger, and Danielsson. Battered yet triumphant, all six clambered onto the reef, salvaging as much as they could from *Kon-Tiki,* shipwrecked deep across the reef. “Anemones and corals gave the whole reef the appearance of a rock garden covered with mosses and cactus and fossilized plants, red and green and yellow and white,” Heyerdahl wrote. Within the reef, “a half-submerged fortress wall,” lay an island, with palm crowns rising into the heavens and enveloped by “snow-white sandy beaches … a green basket of flowers … a concentrated paradise.” Toward that elysian island *Kon-Tiki's* exhausted sailors now labored, enveloped by a surreal sense of elation, gratitude, and inexplicable disbelief.[34]

“I shall never forget that wade across the reef toward the heavenly palm island,”[35] Heyerdahl wrote on 7 August after 101 days at sea. “I was completely overwhelmed.” The exhausted, jubuilant expedition collapsed gratefully upon the seashore of Raroia Island, among coconut palms and luxuriant foliage “thickly covered with snow-white blossoms … so sweet and seductive I felt quite faint.” “I sank down on my knees,” he wrote, “and thrust my fingers deep down into the dry, warm sand. The voyage was over. We were all alive.” Despite unimaginable tribulations, Heyerdahl's argonauts had successfully voyaged 4,300 nautical miles (7,963 km) from Peru, across the Pacific Ocean to Polynesia —a distance equal to that between Chicago and Moscow. “We had drifted automatically a fifth of the way around the globe … I don't think any of us will ever forget the wonderful feeling of stepping on warm dry sand and walking on solid ground.”[36] The exhausted sailors slashed open fresh young coconuts with machetes and gratefully devoured “the most delicious refreshing drink in the world—sweet, cold milk from young and seedless palm fruit.”[37] Luxuriating upon the dry sands of the island, *Kon-Tiki's* elated argonauts gazed insouciantly at the clouds sailing west above the palm crowns, no longer pursuing the same winds across the Pacific Ocean, and undeniably now in Polynesia.

After transmitting the intact expedition's position to Gerd Vold Hurum (via an amateur Californian radio operator named Harold Kempel) and reassuring her that they no longer required rescuing, the crew passed several days upon the island, and began considering how exactly they would journey on to Tahiti. Remarkably, however, on day two, Polynesian outrigger canoes with enormous white sails appeared, and *Kon-Tiki's* expedition members were soon exchanging exhilarated salutations with several islanders. Received the very next day by the island's chief, Tepiuraiarii Teriifaatau, both he and the island's fascinated inhabitants were astounded by Heyerdahl's extraordinary vessel, shipwrecked still across Raroia's coral reef.

“Pae-pae!” they excitedly exclaimed. “The Tiki isn't a boat, she's a *pae-pae,”* declared Chief Teriifaatau inquisitively, admiring the raft's construction, and revealing that *pae-paes* no longer existed upon Raroia, but were known to the oldest men of the village. The *Kon-Tiki's* sailors were welcomed at the village meetinghouse, accompanied by the entire village's ecstatic rendition of the *Marseillaise,* an unexpected, enduring aspect of French colonialism. They were then offered an enormous feast of roasted suckling pigs, chickens, roasted ducks, fresh lobsters and fish, breadfruit, papaya, and coconut milk. With garlands of luxuriant flowers wreathed about each sailor, all gorged themselves upon the feast as traditional hula songs were sung, and young women danced about the feast-

ing table. And as the evening progressed, gradually all six expedition members found themselves dancing equally ecstatically among the village inhabitants, collapsing only with dawn. Heyerdahl's argonauts were subsequently adopted as honorary citizens of Raroia, and received Polynesian names: for Heyerdahl, *Varoa Tikaroa,* Tikaroa's Spirit, King Tikaroa, Raroia island's very first king; Herman, *Tupuhoe-Itetahua* and Bengt, *Topakino,* two ancestor heroes who had destroyed a sea leviathan at the reef's entrance; Torstein, *Maroake,* the name of another village king; Eric, *Tane-Matarau* and Knut, *Tefaunui,* two fabled ancestor sea navigators. Several days later, a cordial welcome from Tahiti's governor was transmitted to the expedition by wireless radio. *Tamara,* the Tahitian government schooner, was despatched to Raroia Island to transport *Kon-Tiki's* sailors and the raft's now-rescued remnants to Tahiti. After a sorrowful farewell from all Rairoa island's 127 gracious inhabitants, the party sailed for Tahiti. Disembarking at Papeete, Heyerdahl's triumphant sailors were joyously welcomed by fascinated spectators drawn by the announcement of the remarkable *pae-pae's* voyage from South America. Welcomed once more with garlands of Tahitian wildflowers, among the celebratory spectators, Heyerdahl sought a long-awaited figure.

"Terai Mateata!" declared Heyerdahl's old friend Chief Teriieroo among the ecstatic cacophony of celebrations at Papeete. "Your *pae-pae* has in truth brought blue sky (terai mateata) to Tahiti, for now we know where our fathers came from."[38] Indolent days on Tahiti duly passed, *Kon-Tiki's* sailors bathing in lagoons beneath sunbathed palms, and wandering about the jungle-enveloped mountains, awaiting the arrival of the colossal Norwegian steamer, *Thor I,* from Samoa, to transport the expedition to the United States, then onward to Oslo. As the argonauts drew away on Sunday, 14 September 1947, Tahiti gradually disappeared beneath the palms and into the Pacific Ocean. Heyerdahl's expedition members gazed contemplatively from the ship's deck at the retreating island, *Kon-Tiki* herself now stowed safely alongside them. "Waves were breaking out on the blue sea," Heyerdahl wrote. "We could no longer reach down to them. We were defying Nature now. We were on our way to the twentieth century which lay so far, far away."[39]

⇝

"My migration theory, as such, was not necessarily proved by the successful outcome of the Kon-Tiki expedition," Heyerdahl acknowledged, once again on dry land. But his extraordinary experimental voyage onboard *Kon-Tiki* demonstrated practicable experiment emancipated from scholarly detachment, and emblematized an archetype for what would become many subsequent, theory-illustrating voyages. Nevertheless, Heyerdahl believed the expedition proved "the South American balsa raft possesses qualities not previously known to scientists of our time, and that the Pacific islands are located well inside the range of prehistoric craft from Peru. Primitive people are capable of undertaking immense voyages over the open ocean" aided by the trade winds and westward-oscillating equatorial currents, a westward orientation "never changed, in all the history of mankind."[40]

Heyerdahl's Kon-Tiki expedition was an enormous success, and he was immediately enveloped by meteoric celebrity, aided by the November 1948 publication of his expedition travelogue, the internationally best-selling *The Kon-Tiki Expedition,* which has been translated into 71 languages. By 1950, he was conducting numerous lecture tours and his *Kon-Tiki* film was released (and received an Oscar for best documentary in 1951). 1950 was also the year in which the inauguration of the Kon-Tiki Museum in Oslo occurred. Despite such monumental achievements, however, his migration theory remained divisive.[i]

Although Heyerdahl's publications were largely directed toward a lay readership—from whom he garnered widespread recognition and admiration—Heyerdahl nevertheless still desired validation from the academic community. Many believed his theory ethnocentric, suggesting the Polynesians were descended from a sagacious, white-complexioned race, or that such an unorthodox theory was impossible due to the ancient people's lack of seafaring knowledge and ability. While Heyerdahl's *Kon-Tiki* voyage had proved that drift voyaging was indeed feasible, to most, the archaeological and linguistic evidence suggested a west-to-east migration. Heyerdahl experienced dismissal from several famed experts, including American archaeologist Ralph Linton and perhaps most notably New Zealand scholar Sir Peter Buck (later Te Rangi Hiroa), who had some years previously already declared that an east-to-west migration theory was improbable: "since the South American Indians had neither the vessels nor the navigating ability to cross the ocean space between their shores and the nearest Polynesian islands."[41]

Heyerdahl's victorious expedition, ostensibly a defiant response to Professor Herbert Spinden's categorical dismissal of his westward Pacific migration theory in 1946, had sought to substantiate, through a practicable, publicity-garnering experiment, an alternative paradigm for the Polynesians' origin, which he had been dogmatically pursuing for over 10 years. While remarkably successful in capturing the public's imagination, he had nevertheless failed once again to convince his academic peers. In response to sustained criticism, Heyerdahl argued that his migration theory could not be completely appraised through popular travelogue alone. He, therefore, incorporated his previous academic works into a new, expanded book: *American Indians in the Pacific: The Theory Behind the Kon-Tiki Expedition,* which was published in 1952 in Oslo, London, and Stockholm.

Substantiating Heyerdahl's two decades of independent scholarship upon Pacific migration theory, *American Indians in the Pacific,* expressly written for an academic readership, became a leviathan of onerous length, with much of the migration theory Heyerdahl superficially introduced readers to within his engaging *Kon-Tiki* travelogue. First was an assertion that Stone Age peoples originally populated Polynesia's archipelago, with Heyerdahl proposing that "the neolithic ancestors of the recent Maori-Polynesian seafarers have dwelt, without metal, pottery, loom, or monetary system, somewhere along this northern Asiatic-American route, to push down upon Hawaii at the beginning of our millennium."[42] Moreover, he again suggested that Polynesians were first descended from a fair-complexioned race originating in the New World and arriving in two successive waves, which Heyerdahl substantiated through physical characteristics, in opposition to the linguistic similarities that other scholars use to connect Polynesians to a Malay origin. He also attempted to prove that the voyagers who populated the islands must have arrived relatively recently, because Polynesian culture is homogenous across the islands, as well as restated the numerous parallels of art, culture, and botany that exist between Polynesia and South America. "If our assumption is correct," he wrote, "and Peru supplied Polynesia with its earliest inhabitants, while the original island culture was later overrun by the arrival of war canoes from Northwestern America, this mingling of cultures on the islands ought to have left behind it a certain definite stratification. This tallies to an astonishing degree with actual conditions in Polynesia."[43]

American Indians in the Pacific was Heyerdahl's attempt to finally ensnare the attention of the international scientific community and obtain academia's recognition and validation. However, reviews remained mixed. While his theories were readily discussed and welcomed as valid areas of research, many of his detractors focused on multidisciplinary Heyerdahl's inability to truly master any one of the several scientific fields he synthesized together to support his theory. Although enthusiastic, detractors found him selective and often in error. For example, in a review from 1954, curator emeritus of anthropology at the American Museum of Natural History, Gordon Ekholm, stated: "An extraordinary amount and variety of anthropological, historical, and geographical evidence has been gathered together by Heyerdahl to validate this thesis of Polynesian origins. His attempt to bring the findings of diverse disciplines into focus on a major problem is a commendable procedure, but in many ways he has allowed his enthusiasm for his 'theory' to cloud his judgment of conflicting evidence."[44] Similarly, Ralph Linton, a long-time detractor, wrote: "The author's unquenchable enthusiasm for his theories is evident on every page. Again and again the 'possibility' cited in one paragraph becomes a 'probability' in the next and an established fact half a page later."[45] Ekholm, did, however, praise various aspects of Heyerdahl's work, specifically those relating to South American vessels.

Noticeably absent from most contemporaneous reviews is any condemnation of the racial dimension of Heyerdahl's hypothesis. Specifically, the suggestion of Polynesia's settlers originating from a fair, superior race (albeit not European) and the corresponding emphasis upon questionable physiological attributes. While that variety of ethnocentrism was somewhat acceptable at the time, modern anthropological discourse recognizes these elements as a deficiency in much of Heyerdahl's meritorious research and imaginative hypothesizing.

Conversely, *American Indians in the Pacific* was, in several ways, a success. Although many scholars may have dismissed Heyerdahl's hypothesis, his theory nevertheless catalyzed a sustained dialogue regarding a migration theory that would endure for several decades —despite the fact that some sought to maintain that dialogue with the intention of illustrating Heyerdahl's fallibility. The intrepid Norwegian's magnetism, celebrity, and engaging hypothesis would prove vital to the study of Polynesia and to migration study in many other geographies. Furthermore, Heyerdahl's explorations did not cease with *Kon-Tiki*—that expedition was just the beginning of his practicable experiment endeavors. And notwithstanding such sustained detraction, Heyerdahl was encouraged by many. For example, in 1953 anthropologist Professor Edward Norbeck declared, "I do not think the author's theories are so violently in opposition to general anthropological opinion as he appears to believe … I view this work as a contribution and wish [the] author good speed in his present venture in the Galápagos Islands."[46]

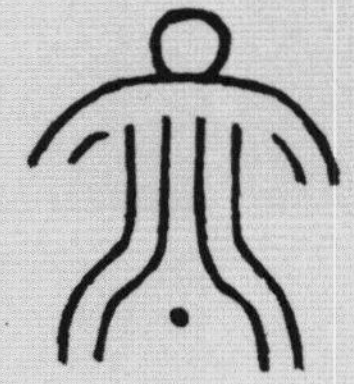

i Unfortunately, Heyerdahl's personal relationships were not so successful, and his relationship with Liv had by now become strained. Despite helping to organise the expedition early on, including securing a loan of $3,000 from the shipping agent Thomas Olsen, Heyerdahl felt that she no longer supported his endeavour—or him. Indeed, when Liv finally touched down in Lima on 5 October 1947, she shunned his embrace in front of cameras—a humiliation that Heyerdahl would not forget, and which would mark the beginning of the end for the pair's marriage.

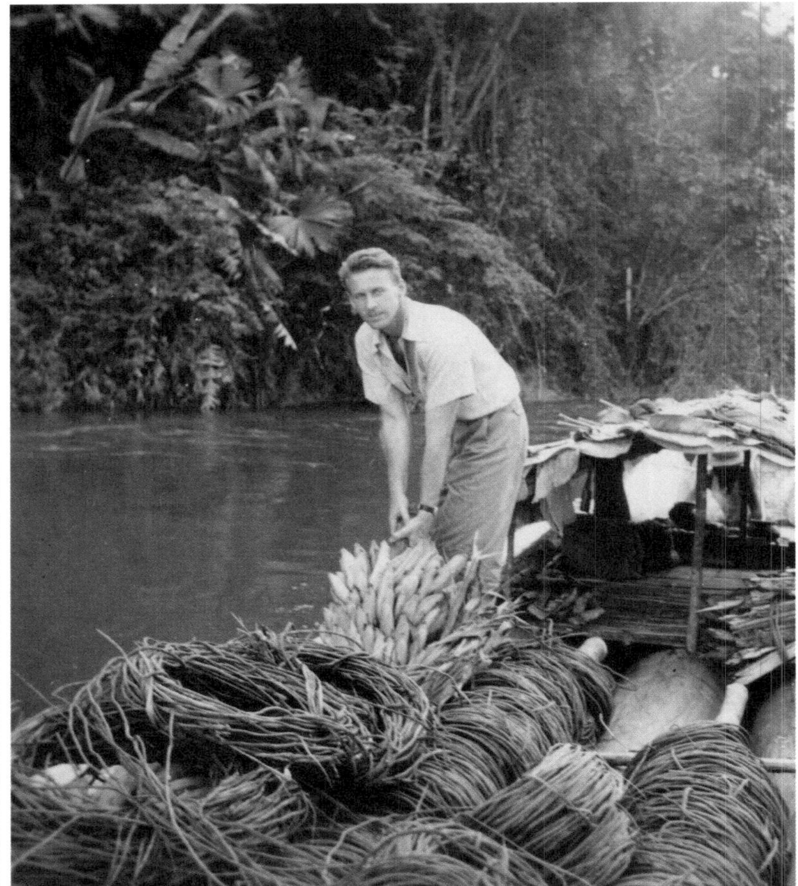

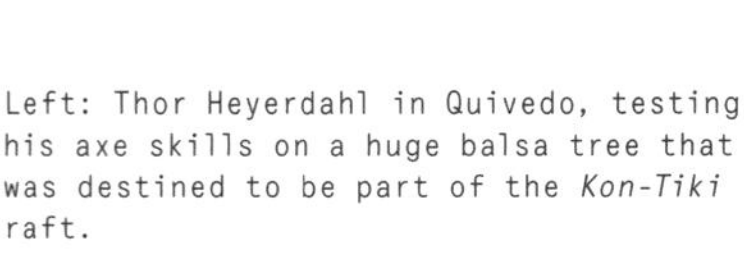

Left: Thor Heyerdahl in Quivedo, testing his axe skills on a huge balsa tree that was destined to be part of the *Kon-Tiki* raft.

Right: Thor Heyerdahl sailing on a makeshift balsa-log raft down the Palenque River, Ecuador.

Bottom right: The Ecuadorian Altiplano, enroute from Quito to Quivedo, to find balsa logs for the *Kon-Tiki* raft.

Opposite: Meeting local indigenous people on the road between Quito and Quivedo. Thor Heyerdahl and the driver, a captain in the Ecuadorian engineer troops, Jose Alejandro Agurto Alvarez, can be seen in military uniforms.

Opposite: The *Kon-Tiki* raft at the Callao Yacht Club just prior to departure.

Below: Erik Hesselberg and a Peruvian carpenter preparing the base for the rudder.

Opposite:
Erik Hesselberg and Herman Watzinger onboard the *Kon-Tiki* under sail.

Bottom:
Herman Watzinger measuring wind speed during the *Kon-Tiki* voyage.

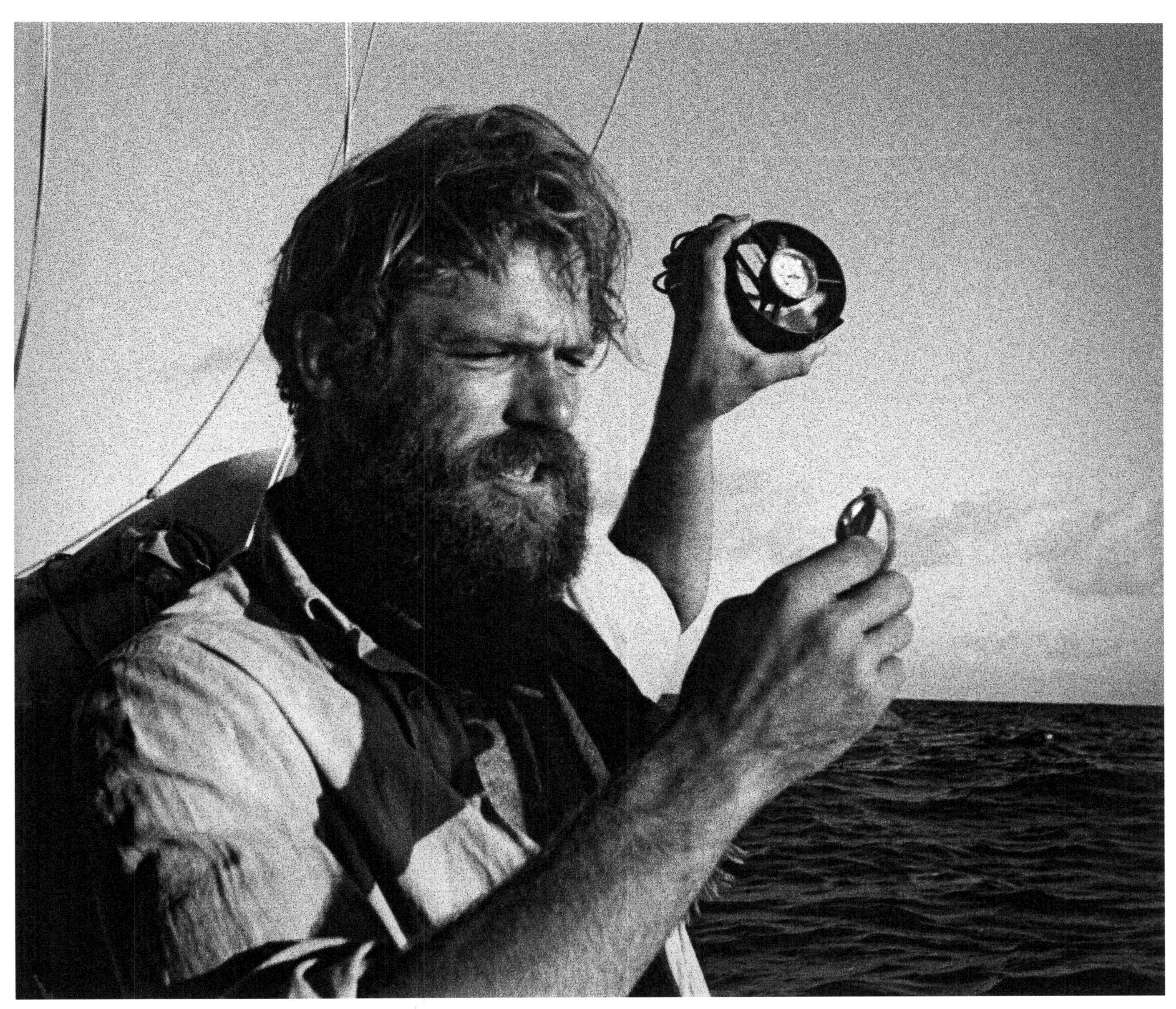

Bottom: Two sharks curious about the *Kon-Tiki* raft.

Opposite: Erik Hesselberg playing guitar and singing for Torstein Raaby.

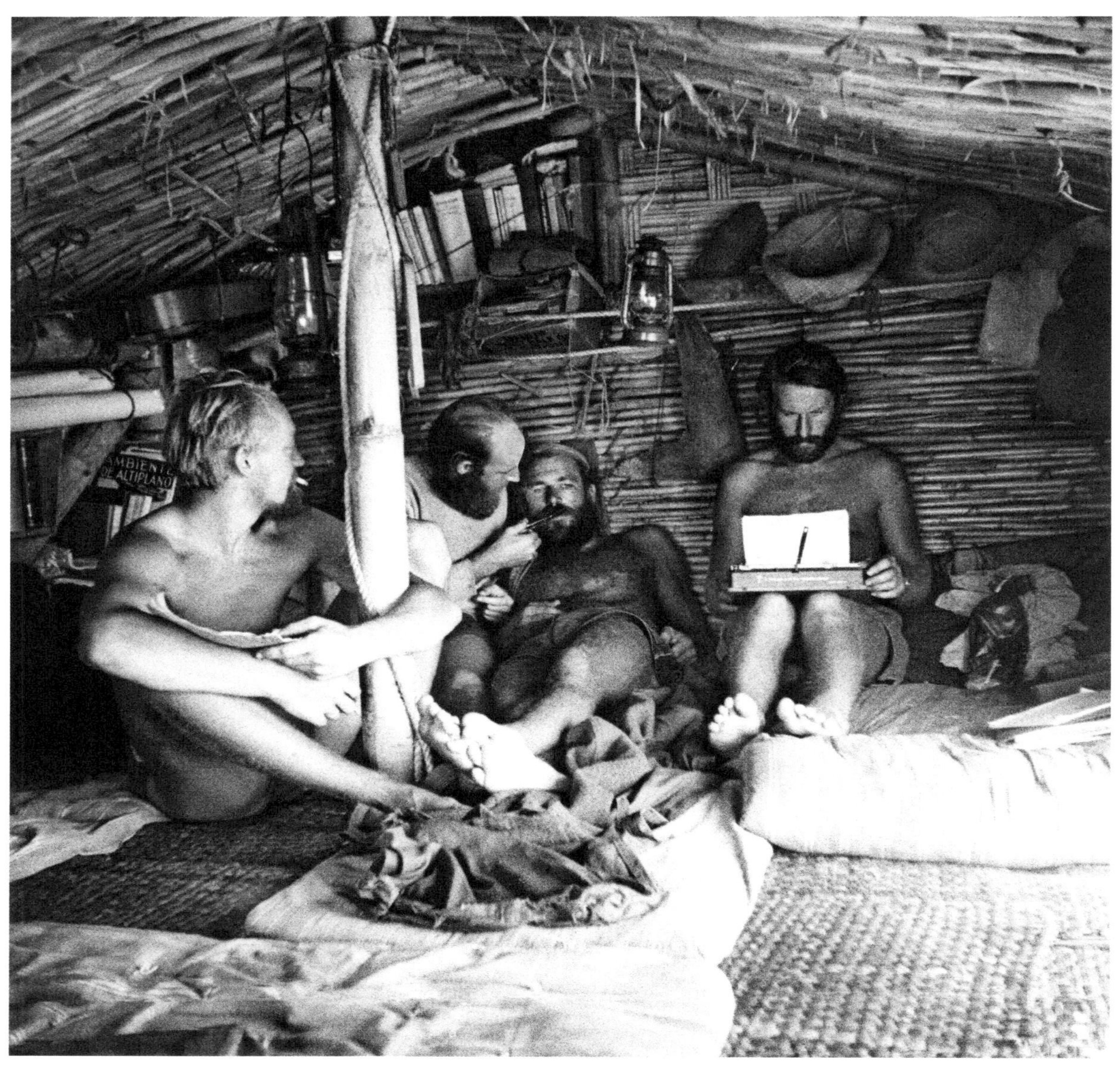

Bengt Danielsson cutting Herman Watzinger's beard while Torstein Raaby (smoking) is watching and Thor Heyerdahl is writing one of his articles, inside the small hut on the *Kon-Tiki* raft.

Opposite: Thor Heyerdahl at the top of the *Kon-Tiki* raft's mast, looking for land.

A whale passing the *Kon-Tiki* raft.

Opposite:
Thor Heyerdahl shows how to catch a shark with your hands.

Opposite (top left): Thor Heyerdahl with a resident of Raroia, Tuamotu Islands

Opposite (bottom left): Erik Hesselberg, the navigator, plotting in the expedition's final position on the map.

Opposite (bottom right): The stranded *Kon-Tiki* raft at Raroia reef.

Top left: Erik Hesselberg taking their last position at the *Kon-Tiki* islet on Raroia.

Top right: Two local men trying to drag the *Kon-Tiki* raft to the main village on Raroia, Tuamotu Islands.

Bottom right: Thor Heyerdahl showing off his coconut-climbing skills.

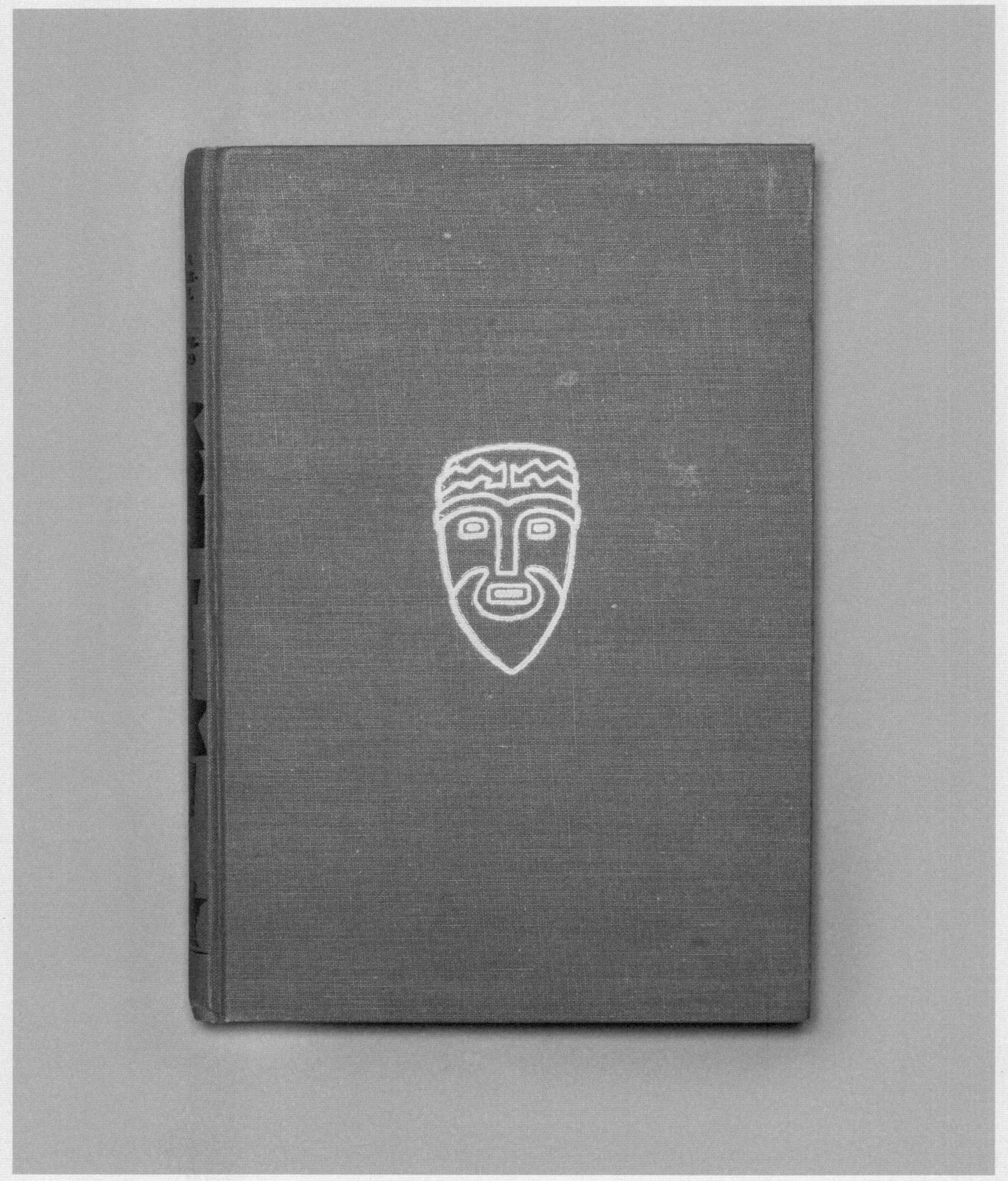

Opposite and below:
Kon-Tiki: Across the Pacific by Raft (1950) was a best seller around the world. It spent a year on the New York Times Best Seller list for nonfiction, and the first print run in the US and Soviet Union was 200,000 books. Today, the book is translated into 84 different languages. The book in the photograph is *Pengembaraan Kon-Tiki*, a Malaysian translation, printed in Kualalumpur in 1963.

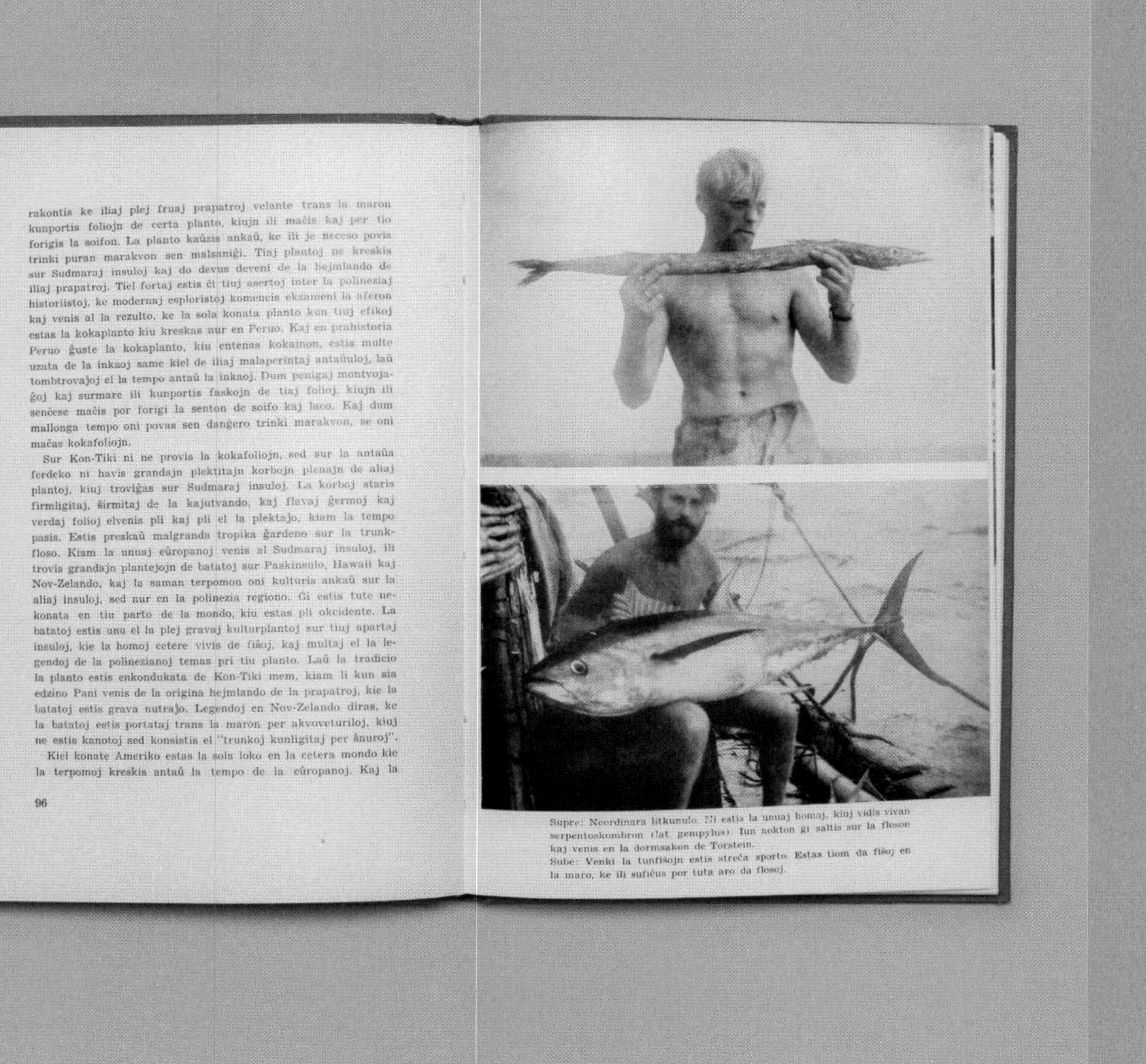

rakontis ke iliaj plej fruaj prapatroj velante trans la maron kunportis foliojn de certa planto, kiujn ili maĉis kaj per tio forigis la soifon. La planto kaŭzis ankaŭ, ke ili je neceso povis trinki puran marakvon sen malsaniĝi. Tiaj plantoj ne kreskis sur Sudmaraj insuloj kaj do devus deveni de la hejmlando de iliaj prapatroj. Tiel fortaj estis ĉi tiuj asertoj inter la polineziaj historiistoj, ke modernaj esploristoj komencis ekzameni la aferon kaj venis al la rezulto, ke la sola konata planto kun tiuj efikoj estas la kokaplanto kiu kreskas nur en Peruo. Kaj en prahistoria Peruo ĝuste la kokaplanto, kiu entenas kokainon, estis multe uzata de la inkaoj same kiel de iliaj malaperintaj antaŭuloj, laŭ tombtrovaĵoj el la tempo antaŭ la inkaoj. Dum penigaj montvojaĝoj kaj surmare ili kunportis faskojn de tiaj folioj, kiujn ili senĉese maĉis por forigi la senton de soifo kaj laco. Kaj dum mallonga tempo oni povas sen danĝero trinki marakvon, se oni maĉas kokafoliojn.

Sur Kon-Tiki ni ne provis la kokafoliojn, sed sur la antaŭa ferdeko ni havis grandajn plektitajn korbojn plenajn de aliaj plantoj, kiuj troviĝas sur Sudmaraj insuloj. La korboj staris firmligitaj, ŝirmitaj de la kajutvando, kaj flavaj ĝermoj kaj verdaj folioj elvenis pli kaj pli el la plektaĵo, kiam la tempo pasis. Estis preskaŭ malgranda tropika ĝardeno sur la trunkfloso. Kiam la unuaj eŭropanoj venis al Sudmaraj insuloj, ili trovis grandajn plantejojn de batatoj sur Paskinsulo, Hawaii kaj Nov-Zelando, kaj la saman terpomon oni kulturis ankaŭ sur la aliaj insuloj, sed nur en la polinezia regiono. Ĝi estis tute nekonata en tiu parto de la mondo, kiu estas pli okcidente. La batatoj estis unu el la plej gravaj kulturplantoj sur tiuj apartaj insuloj, kie la homoj cetere vivis de fiŝoj, kaj multaj el la legendoj de la polinezianoj temas pri tiu planto. Laŭ la tradicio la planto estis enkondukata de Kon-Tiki mem, kiam li kun sia edzino Pani venis de la origina hejmlando de la prapatroj, kie la batatoj estis grava nutraĵo. Legendoj en Nov-Zelando diras, ke la batatoj estis portataj trans la maron per akvoveturiloj, kiuj ne estis kanotoj sed konsistis el "trunkoj kunligitaj per ŝnuroj".

Kiel konate Ameriko estas la sola loko en la cetera mondo kie la terpomoj kreskis antaŭ la tempo de la eŭropanoj. Kaj la

96

Supre: Neordinara litkunulo. Ni estis la unuaj homoj, kiuj vidis vivan serpentoskombron (lat. gempylus). Iun nokton ĝi saltis sur la floson kaj venis en la dormsakon de Torstein.
Sube: Venki la tunfiŝojn estis streĉa sporto. Estas tiom da fiŝoj en la maro, ke ili sufiĉus por tuta aro da flosoj.

Top left: The shift planner onboard the *Kon-Tiki* raft. Handcrafted by Thor Heyerdahl, it also shows who is in charge of cooking (*kokk*) that day.

Top right: Small, crude stone statue bartered from someone on Fatu Hiva.

Middle left: The official *Kon-Tiki* raft's radio, LI2B, QSL Contact Card.

Middle right: An illustration from one of the later *Kon-Tiki: Across the Pacific by Raft* editions.

Bottom left: Small stone statue without eyes bartered from someone on Fatu Hiva. The fine features of this statue reminded Thor Heyerdahl of the ancient stone carvers he believed also existed on Rapa Nui.

Bottom right: Ashtray from the restaurant "Kon-Tiki" at Norwegian Trade Fairs in Oslo, with a depiction of Kon-Tiki by Erik Hesselberg, artist, and navigator on the Kon-Tiki expedition, 1947.

Opposite: A letter from Thor Heyerdahl to John F. Kennedy, dated 20 August 1963, just a month before President Kennedy was assassinated in Dallas, Texas. Heyerdahl wrote and commended him for trying to "deminish world tension," which "has aroused admiration among thousands of us who confront the problems from outside the ring of politics."

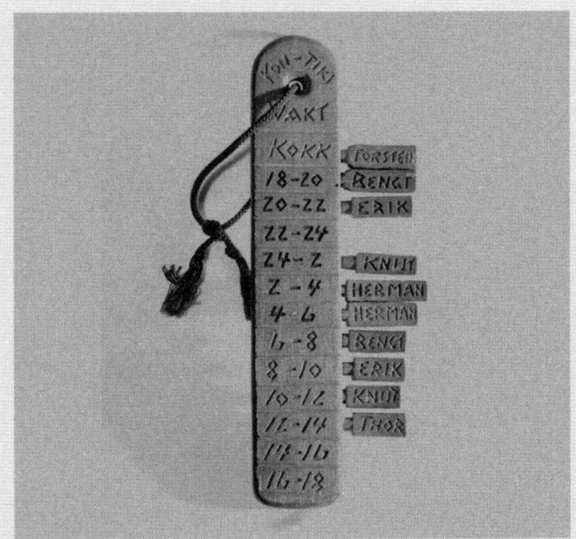

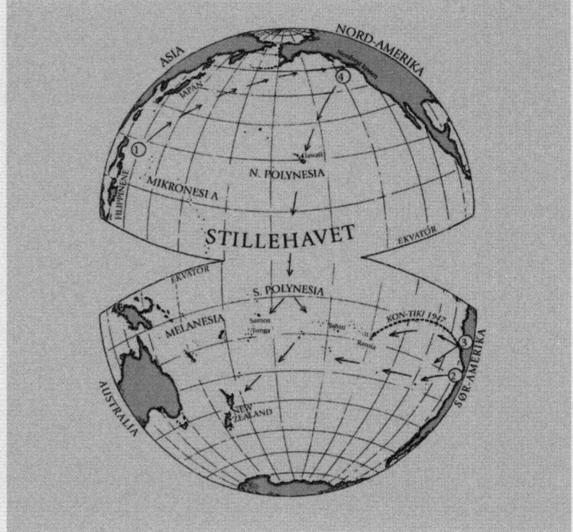

August 20th 1963
TH/ill/

President John F. Kennedy
The Waite House
Washington, D.C.
U.S.A.

Mr. President:

Your ability to overcome obstacles at home and abroad in the effort to arrest the bomb tests and deminish world tension has aroused admiration among thousands of us who confront the problems from outside the ring of politics.

One of your next tasks should be to deflate the growing tension in China by talking your countrymen and allies into admitting that infuriated giant into the United Nations. The U.N. should remove the clause restricting membership to peace-loving or better qualified nations, and thereby deprive communist China of any honor associated with membership. The U.N., and not the battleground, must become the place to meet your enemy. Friends can meet anywhere.

Please accept a copy of my book "The Kon-Tiki Expedition" as a very modest token of my great confidence in you as the right American in the right place.

Cordially yours,

THE WHITE HOUSE
WASHINGTON

November 20, 1963

PERSONAL

Dear Mr. Heyerdahl:

I am indeed sorry for the inadvertent delay in thanking you for your courtesy in sending the beautifully bound copy of your book, "Kon-Tiki," to the President. He is most appreciative of your thoughtfulness and deeply grateful for the warm sentiments expressed in your inscription.

With the President's very best wishes,

Sincerely yours,

Evelyn Lincoln

Evelyn Lincoln
Personal Secretary
to the President

Mr. Thor Heyerdahl
Casella 15
Laigueglia, Italy

Opposite: A letter from The White House, on behalf of President Kennedy, thanking Thor Heyerdahl for sending the president a copy of his *Kon-Tiki* book, written just days before President Kennedy was shot in Dallas.

Below: The diary from the Kon-Tiki expedition, from 28 April to 7 August 1947.

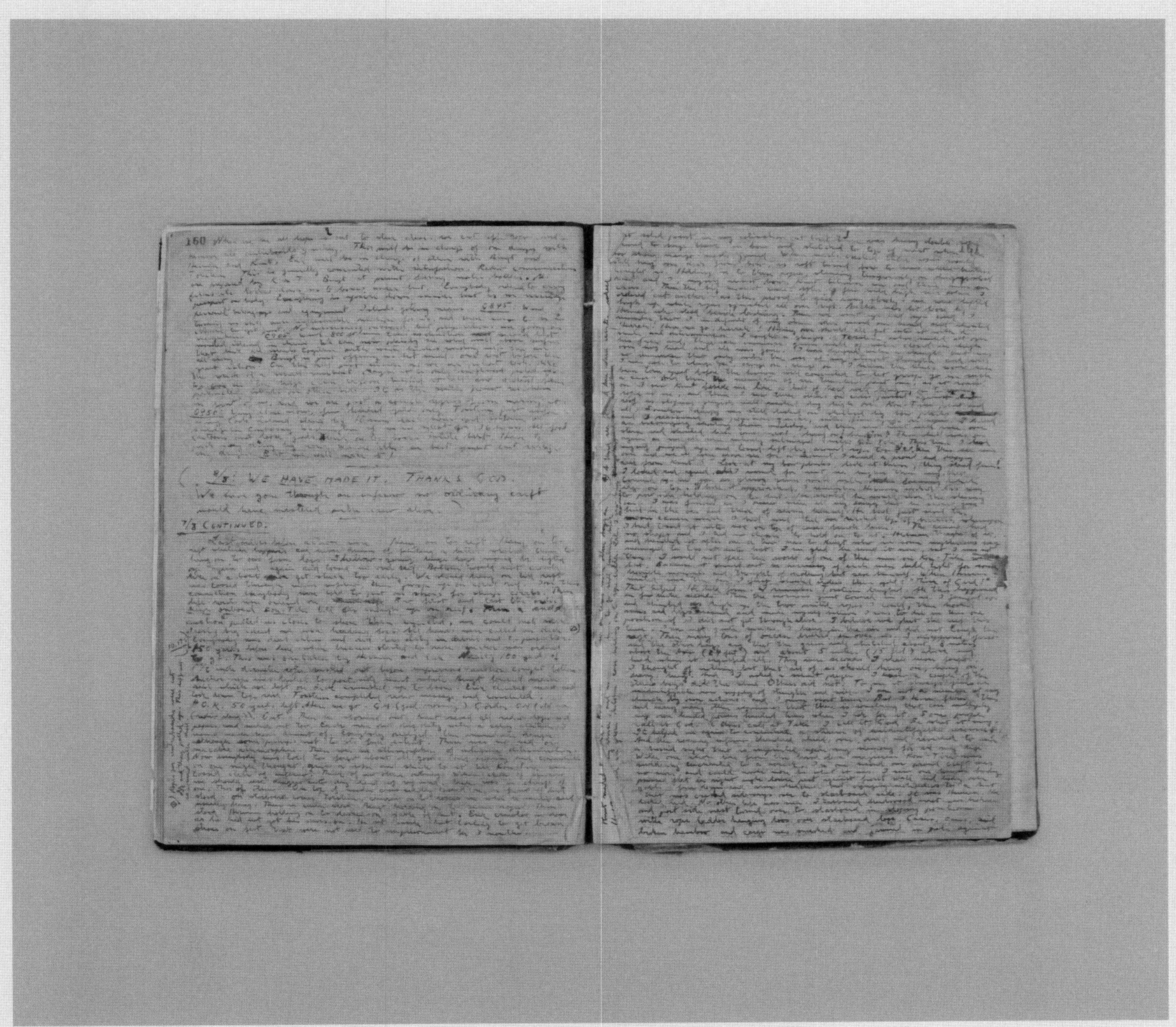

WE HAVE MADE IT. THANKS GOD.

1953

Galápagos Expedition

Notwithstanding his theory-substantiating Kon-Tiki expedition, and the prodigious scholarship encompassed within *American Indians in the Pacific,* Heyerdahl recognized the necessity for additional evidence for his unorthodox hypothesis and, therefore, sought further convincing archaeological evidence throughout the Pacific Ocean's islands and archipelagos. Galvanized by receiving a photograph from the French archaeologist Alfred Métraux of a stone statue on the island, on 10 January 1953, he set forth from Guayaquil, Ecuador, aboard the *Don Lucko,* toward the unimaginably remote Galápagos Islands, the archipelago of numerous volcanic islands instrumental to British naturalist Charles Darwin's natural theory of evolution, lying some 563 miles (906 km) west of continental Ecuador—and within the very midst of the ever-oscillating Humboldt Current that conveyed *Kon-Tiki* westward to Polynesia six years before.

Heyerdahl's intention was to conduct comprehensive excavations, the first to be executed upon the archipelago, accompanied by the archaeologists Erik K. Reed and Arne Skjølsvold. Clements Markham, a prominent Inca historian, first suggested in 1907 that Peruvian indigenous peoples conceivably voyaged to the Galápagos archipelago upon balsa rafts. Markham's hypothesis was drawn from ancient Peruvian accounts of Tupac Yupanqui, leader of the Inca, and his westward voyage from Ecuador to the mythical islands of Avachumbi and Ninachumbi, from which he returned with artifacts, treasure and prisoners; several scholars speculated he had in fact visited two of the Galápagos Islands.

In 1947, botanists Hutchison, Silow, and Stephens isolated and identified *Gossypium barbadense,* a cotton species found upon the Galápagos Islands that was originally raised and domesticated by the indigenous populations from along the coast of Northern Peru. That "remarkable ethno-botanical evidence,"[1] accompanied by the stone head in the photograph from Métraux (although subsequently revealed to have been executed by a German settler, Heinz Wittmer) and the vast seafaring capacity of balsa-wood vessels that he experienced firsthand upon *Kon-Tiki's* voyage, all suggested to Heyerdahl that indigenous peoples of South America may have frequently visited the Galápagos archipelago long before Christopher Columbus's 1492 voyage to the Americas. For *G. barbadense's* transplantation to the Galápagos archipelago could not have occurred "by birds or ocean currents, but only by human craft and care, and in an early pre-Columbian period."[2]

Heyerdahl's expedition also visited the islands of San Cristóbal, Santa Cruz, Floreana, Santa Fé, Santiago, Isabela, and several others, recovering some 2,000 fragmented water jars, cooking vessels and ornamental vases as well as flints from four ancient occupation sites. The expedition deduced that water jar fragments "concurred with a type well known on the South American mainland, frequently used also as funeral urns in Peru and Ecuador."[3] Recovered cooking vessel fragments also correlated, he believed, with those found among the indigenous Andean peoples of South America, while the ornamental vase fragments correlated with those manufactured upon the northern Peruvian coastline. Three ceramic Chimu frogs were also recovered, as was a terra-cotta whistle and a perforated stone disk. The latter, along with the many stone flints, suggested Stone Age importation, because the Galápagos archipelago remains exclusively of volcanic stone origin, where neither flint nor chalkstone naturally occur.

Acknowledging that "drawing far-reaching conclusions with regards to the past of the Galápagos islands [necessitated] much more evidence,"[4] Heyerdahl nevertheless believed that indigenous South American peoples had transported various vessels, stone implements, and cotton seeds to the archipelago long before Columbus's voyages and that the Incan account of Tupac Yupanqui encompassed descriptions of two long-unidentified islands found westward from the northern Peruvian coastline. He further speculated that South American indigenous peoples had frequently visited the Galápagos archipelago, but never established permanent settlements across the islands—the volcanic, arid landscape was unsupportive of cultivation and provided potable water only during the archipelago's wet season.

Heyerdahl then redirected his attentions toward balsa-wood vessels, journeying to Playas, Ecuador, to conduct experiments on an Incan navigational instrument: the *guara*, a type of centerboard. They proved that the rafts using a *guara* could alter course and sail against the wind. For Heyerdahl, that seafaring capacity confirmed his theory that pre-Columbian peoples could not only sail across the Pacific Ocean but they could also return to South America. Such an innovation was evidence of the ancient South American voyagers' ability to purposefully navigate as well as travel great distances.

Having illustrated that such vessels were wholly capable of navigating the Humboldt and Panama currents, both of which confluence about the Galápagos archipelago, Heyerdahl believed that voyaging back and forth across the vast ocean distances separating Ecuador and Peru from the Galápagos archipelago was "fully within the capacity of the aboriginal cultures on the northwest coast of South America"[5]—a hypothesis possessing innumerable parallels with Heyerdahl's macrocosmic theory of westward Pacific Ocean migration.

Top right: Small tortoise in Ecuador or the Galápagos Islands.

Bottom left: Farm, in Ecuador or the Galápagos Islands.

Bottom right: Local man with small tortoise, in Ecuador or the Galápagos Islands.

Opposite (top left): Archaeologist Arne Skjølsvold at the helm.

Opposite (top right): Arne Skjølsvold, standing with binoculars, onboard a local boat in the Galápagos Islands or Ecuador.

Opposite (bottom left): Thor Heyerdahl, Karl Angermeyer, and Erik Reed discovering something.

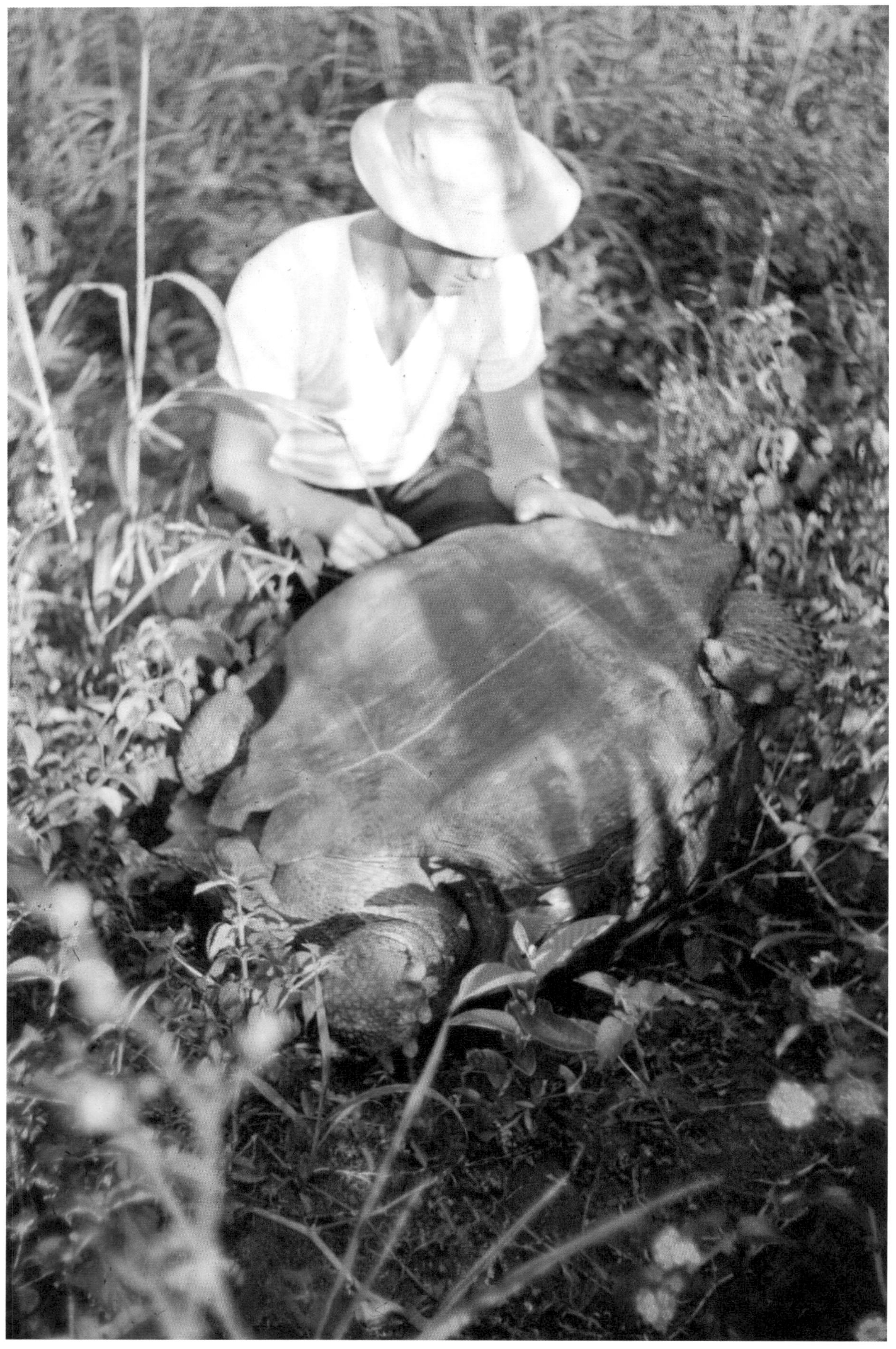

Opposite: A crew member meeting one of the giant tortoises of the Galápagos Islands.

Left: Lizard on the Galápagos Islands.

Right: Erik Reed and Thor Heyerdahl in the famous pirate cave on Floreana, Galápagos Islands.

1955~56,
1986~88

Easter Island Expeditions

"Bent on you is the silent gaze of a hundred and fifty eyeless faces... It was so when the sculptors went, and so it will always be."

"East of the sun and west of the moon," Heyerdahl declared with Norwegian fairy-tale evocation, stands Easter Island—Rapa Nui to her Polynesian inhabitants—that enigmatic, isolated, isle known within island mythology as *Te Pito o te Henua,* or "Navel of the World." "Mankind once had one of its most curious ideas. No one knows who had it, and no one knows why"[1] Heyerdahl wrote of the sculpting the island's numerous mysterious stone statues. These are monolithic human figures, known as *moai,* hewn from igneous tuff (solidified volcanic ash), with many possessing *pukao,* enormous blocks of red scoria (a variety of lava), symbolizing powerful topknots balanced upon their colossal heads. While European explorers believed "the world ended at Gibraltar," other accomplished navigators, Heyerdahl speculated, "plowed the unknown seas … off the desolate west coast of South America" and discovered Rapa Nui. Landing, these intrepid argonauts "whetted their stone adzes, and set about one of the most remarkable engineering projects of ancient times." Carving "gigantic stone figures in man's likeness, as tall as houses and as heavy as boxcars," the island inhabitants then "dragged them in great number across country and… [erected them] on huge stone terraces all over the island."

How had they achieved these Herculean endeavors? Such enormous figures were illustrative of unimaginable ingenuity, collaborative industry, and steadfast faith. However, one fateful day, the adze's blows upon the rock abruptly ceased. There was "a sudden silence, for tools were left lying and many of the figures were only half finished. The mysterious sculptors disappeared into the dark mists of antiquity." Heyerdahl wondered, "What had happened on Easter Island?"[2] How had the original inhabitants voyaged there? And what was the truth behind the arcane colossi's original construction? An expedition to the near-inaccessible island, at the time reachable only by Chilean warship (completing her annual voyage), would perhaps answer many of the questions about Rapa Nui that had perplexed scholars and visitors for centuries, and —Heyerdahl hoped—would serve to support his Polynesian migration theory. His three research ambitions for the expedition were to be: discovering early habitation and signs of the first settlement, creating a chronology (in particular, of the temple platforms), and solving the mystery of the stone statues.

Heyerdahl had long dreamed of visiting Rapa Nui, ever since December 1926, when at the age of 12 he had first read about the mysteries of the island as part of the English St. George expedition, an account of which was published in the 55th edition of the weekly magazine *Allers Familie-Journal.* This was ignited again in 1947, when *Kon-Tiki* had sailed north of the isolated island and he had ruminated on how voyagers in the distant past had navigated into the very midst of the Pacific Ocean. Eventually, in 1955, Heyerdahl, endowed with significant resources from the meteoritic sales of his *Kon-Tiki* travelogue and film, as well as the recent Galápagos documentary film made with Norwegian zoologist Per Høst, resolved to organize an archaeological expedition to Rapa Nui and several other yet-to-be-excavated nearby Pacific islands.

Requiring a vessel for the journey, with passage to the island an infrequent affair, Heyerdahl leased a Norwegian canning factory's trawler. "One feels like a conductor busy eating spaghetti while trying to drive his orchestra through a rhapsody by Liszt,"[3] Heyerdahl wrote while rapidly organizing the archaeological expedition. The members of the party included Heyerdahl's second wife, Yvonne Dedekam-Simonsen, his young daughter Annette Heyerdahl, Thor Jr., and five archaeologists: Norwegian Arne Skjølsvold; Americans Edwin N. Ferdon, Dr. Carlyle S. Smith, and Dr. William T. Mulloy; and Chilean Gonzalo Figueroa. They were also accompanied by a physician, Dr. Gjessing; a photographer, Erling Schjerven; and a ship's crew of 13. Heyerdahl's archaeological expedition transported spare parts, specialized equipment, and provisions for one year on an expedition patronized by H.R.H. Crown Prince Olav of Norway. He noted, "a crew had been signed on in spite of wives' and sweethearts' alarm over a year's absence in the romantic South Seas."[4] In September 1955, "The ship's bell sounded for the last time," Heyerdahl wrote, adding "Hands waved and handkerchiefs fluttered like treetops in a gale, while the captain made the siren utter a few heart-rending howls."[5]

The trawler M.S. *Chr. Bjelland,* which had been extensively remodeled for the voyage, was painted in contrasting white and yellow, with white symbolizing the chiefs and gods in Polynesian culture and yellow symbolizing the statues. Her funnel was emblazoned with a scarlet illustration of the Polynesian sun god, Kon-Tiki, the very same that appeared across the sail of Heyerdahl's balsa-wood raft, *Kon-Tiki,* (red being a sacred color in Polynesian culture), while her high bow was decorated with "a curious blue emblem … two of the sacred bird-men of Easter Island, half-bird and half-human (drawn) from one of the rare tablets of undeciphered hieroglyphics."[6] Thus, emblematizing the mythology of the intended destination, the ship sounded her melancholic horn and sailed forth from Oslo, "for Easter Island, the loneliest inhabited place in the world."[7]

Heyerdahl's 1955 expedition succeeded several others made to Rapa Nui in the preceding two centuries. Dutch explorer Admiral Jacob Roggeveen's 1721 expedition, sponsored by the Dutch West India Company, was the first to arrive, originally seeking *Terra Australis,* a long-speculated southern continent, and the opening of the western trade route to the Spice Islands—the Moluccas archipelago. Instead, Roggeveen's expedition encountered the Polynesian island of Rapa Nui on Easter Day, 1722. Observing a large population of islanders and several enormous statues, Roggeveen's captivated Dutch seafarers, the first Europeans ever to alight upon that enigmatic isle, bestowed the island with the well-known ecclesiastical eponym: Easter Island. Roggeveen's crew explored Rapa Nui for several days before finally sailing westward, while Roggeveen himself wrote of the encounter, "these stone figures caused us to be filled with wonder, for we could not understand how it was possible that people who are destitute of heavy or thick timber, and also of stout cordage, out of which to construct gear, had been able to erect them."[8] He erroneously concluded such statues were sculpted from clay.

Spanish Captain Don Felipe González's 1770 expedition to Rapa Nui, despatched there by the Viceroy of Peru, annexed the island to the Spanish crown and bestowed the name "San Carlos Island." Not long afterward, British explorer Captain James Cook visited Rapa Nui as part of his second voyage, reaching the island in 1774. He speculated that the island may have experienced a catastrophe subsequent to Roggeveen and González's expeditions, because only approximately 100 island inhabitants remained. Cook was naturally fascinated by the island's enigmatic statues, but he could not completely fathom how they were constructed without the aid of mortar or cement. Among Cook's expeditionary party was Omai, a young Raiatean (from the largest of the Polynesian Leeward Islands) acquainted with the Polynesian language spoken upon Rapa Nui, who determined that the statues were burial monuments erected for deified islanders.

Captain Jean-François de Galaup de La Pérouse of the French navy arrived next, visiting Rapa Nui on 9 April 1786 as part of his 1785 circumnavigatory expedition. He observed that the islands' population had significantly expanded and surmised that the islanders had concealed themselves in subterranean chambers and caverns when the Dutch, Spanish, and British explorers alighted. La Pérouse's departing expedition marked the beginning of Rapa Nui's long 19th-century history of intermittent visits by an American schooner, Chilean and Russian expeditions, Peruvian slave galleys, French Catholic missionaries, and two explorations, American and German. By the end of the 19th century, Rapa Nui was annexed by Chile.

The dawn of the 20th century witnessed the island's first archaeological surveys. British archaeologist Katherine Routledge's 1913–14 expedition, made with a ten-man party and her husband, William Scorseby Routledge, surveyed and excavated artifacts across the island. A subsequent 1934 Franco-Belgian expedition, directed by Belgian archaeologist Henri Lavachery and Alfred Métraux (the same ethnologist who had provided Heyerdahl with the photograph that catalyzed his Galápagos expedition), surveyed Rapa Nui's ethnography, collecting oral histories and authoring observations of rock carvings and stonework. However, no archaeological excavations were undertaken at the time of Lavachery's and Métraux's expedition, and, when Heyerdahl finally disembarked at Rapa Nui, the original construction of the stone monoliths had obstinately defied explanation by innumerable explorers, missionaries, archaeologists, and anthropologists for centuries.

⟿

"There, in the darkness, lay Easter Island … a deserted, petrified world," wrote Heyerdahl after 15 days of ocean voyaging from Panama (where he had joined the party) to Rapa Nui. He gazed awestruck "far away in the interior, [where there were] statutes standing scattered up the slope of an extinct volcano, like black caraway seeds against the red evening sky."[9] Watched over by the islands' motionless juggernauts, Heyerdahl's Greenland trawler "anchored … off the shore of an extinct world, where once had lived beings of a kind other than those on our own earth." With dusk's shadows lengthening over that surreal lunarscape, the red sun "descended slowly into the black sea and drew the night down over us."[10]

Heyerdahl's expedition selected picturesque Anakena Bay, on Rapa Nui's northeastern coastline, for the expedition's main campsite. The Bay remained readily accessible for expedition equipment, far from the village, where robberies and other troublesome incidents frequently occurred, and was situated in the region of the Miru tribe, where the legendary Hotu Matua, "the alpha and omega in the conceptions of Easter Island, a sort of hybrid between the Adam of religion and the Columbus of history,"[11] originally made landfall. Heyerdahl's converted Greenland trawler anchored at the bay and a shepherd directed the party to the site of Hotu Matua's residence, which was alongside a colossal fallen statue and an established camp. Introduced to the long-standing mayor of Rapa Nui, Pedro Atan, Heyerdahl now encountered perhaps the most powerful individual upon the island. In amidst the Polynesian inhabitants stood "a solitary white-robed form, his gown fluttering in the wind." Characterizing Father Sebastian Englert, from a Bavarian missionary, Heyerdahl wrote that he, "stood before me, broad and straight-backed ... he was like an apostle or prophet in his white gown ... his bare head and flowing beard against an incredibly blue sky. 'Welcome to my island', were his first words. 'Yes, I always say my island ... for I reckon it as mine.'"[12] Father Englert had authored *La tierra de Hotu Matu'a* (The Land of Hotu Matua), an academic account of Rapa Nui's history, archaeology, anthropology, and language (having become fluent in the local dialect), and Heyerdahl knew well of him, and the extraordinary, near-complete dominance he exercised over the island. Aided by the island's Chilean military governor, Arnaldo Curti, Father Englert would later prove instrumental to the success of Heyerdahl's excavations.

Expedition archaeologists undertook reconnaissance expeditions to the east and west while the equipment was assembled at Anakena Bay, the expedition's operations were arranged, and island labor was secured to assist with excavations. Some of the first of these were undertaken within Hotu Matua's pentagonal kitchen oven, which revealed an old stone bowl, spearheads, human-bone fishhooks, volcanic glass implements, and polished stones, as well as within a second pentagonal kitchen oven, beneath which lay fishhooks, shells, bone splinters, charcoal, and human teeth. They also eventually unearthed a blue Venetian pearl, an artifact, the expedition hypothesized, that originated from Roggeveen's 1722 visit—for the expedition's logbook recorded the gift of such an object to an island inhabitant. Heyerdahl, convinced that the island's archaeological artifacts had largely been appropriated for institutional collections and private collectors by fleeting expeditions possessing very superficial knowledge of Rapa Nui's history and culture, saw that the eradicated archaeological record lent an erroneous impression that the statues as Rapa Nui's only material artifacts, offering supercilious expressions "to the Lilliputians who come, stare, and go again"[13] as the centuries pass by. Rapu Nui remained, to his mind, enveloped by mystery. Indeed, he believed even the island's inhabitants' knowledge of the island's history to be lacking; however, such a dismissive attitude remained inaccurate, with the passing down and recording of history being a central element of Polynesian culture occurring across the islands.

Astoundingly, several of Rapa Nui's inhabitants were knowledgeable of Heyerdahl's

Kon-Tiki expedition, including the raft's passage far northward of the island and eventual passage westward. Inspired by Heyerdahl's journey, and convinced of their ancestor's voyaging capacities, several intrepid islanders undertook fateful expeditions upon inadequate wooden vessels, one of which washed ashore at Reao, an atoll within the Tuamotu Group, with the famished and fatigued sailors thankfully rescued and transported onward to Tahiti. With other island inhabitants also attempting comparable voyages, the practice was forbidden by the governor and enforced by vigilant watchmen, on account of the extraordinary dangers they entailed. Heyerdahl was emphatically encouraged to discourage this practice, to which he acquiesced. While many of these journeys were not successful, the eventual founding of the Polynesian Voyaging Society in 1973 led to a revival of ancient seafaring methods, illustrating both the voyaging capacity of such vessels as well as the sailors' ability to accurately navigate against the winds and currents.

While the excavations progressed, Heyerdahl was drawn away by two of the expedition's housekeepers, Eroria and Mariana, who were "the keenest cave hunters on the island," and they went on a search for additional caverns. "They crisscrossed the hills with a pocketful of candles, searching for old dwelling caves, where they dug ... to discover their ancestors stone and bone tools,"[14] he wrote. Heyerdahl and Schjerven, the expedition's photographer, accompanied the two elderly island women in spelunking a variety of darkened caves, extremely narrow warrens, and catacombs bored deep into the volcanic rock. "In these subterranean cave dwellings the old-time population of Easter Island had lived," Heyerdahl noted. People would retreat to the island's interior when threatened and when European vessels appeared upon the horizon. Within the darkened caves, Heyerdahl encountered human bone implements, obsidian spearpoints, and a cranium. Further excavations within the caves conducted by Carlyle Smith also revealed kitchen middens of fish bones, shells, fowl, an occasional turtle, rodents, and human bones, an indication of cannibal practices.

Evidence of such primitive existences was incompatible to Heyerdahl with what he encountered above ground. "How could a people of hunted cave dwellers have bred such unique engineers and ingenious artists as the creators of those gigantic monuments?"[15] he contemplated. Heyerdahl's inability to reconcile such apparently conflicting phenomena led him to wonder whether these ancient peoples had the capacity to create such a monumental achievement as the *moai*. Or, was it that Heyerdahl judged them as primitive, requiring him to assign fair-skinned ancestors to explain Easter Island's monolith-creation phenomenon? Regardless, the veneration of fair complexions was supported by island myth. During the cave excavations with Eroria, Mariana, and other islanders, Heyerdahl also visited Ana o Keke, the holy bleaching site of the *neru* virgins, specially selected young maidens confined to deep caves to keep their skin as pale as possible, then revealed within sacred festivals before adulating island audiences.

"Rano Raraku remains one of the greatest and most curious monuments of mankind" Heyerdahl wrote of Rapa Nui's verdant, water-inundated volcano, a surreal lunarscape that stood for him as "a monument to the great lost unknown behind us, a warning of the transience of man and civilisation."[16] He described how "the whole mountain massif has been reshaped ... greedily cut up as if it were pastry" and thousands of tons of impregnable stone extracted from the volcano's long-dormant crater. Within "the mountain's gaping wound ... lie more than a hundred and fifty gigantic stone men," in various phases of completion, Heyerdahl noted, amazed by the magnitude of such industry, with complete stone figures arrranged "like a supernatural army" side by side. "In Rano Raraku you feel the mystery of Easter Island at close quarters. The very air is laden with it. Bent on you is the silent gaze of a hundred and fifty eyeless faces. Nothing moves except the drifting clouds above you. It was so when the sculptors went, and so it will always be."[17]

Heyerdahl's expedition conducted extensive excavations and characteristically practical experiments in an attempt to resolve the mystery of how the statues were transported. Expedition members were enthralled by the legions of colossal sculptures, and their excavations revealed that many of the colossal heads were, in fact, attached to equally colossal torsos, stomachs, arms, and hands submerged within the island's soil. An exhilarating discovery, however Heyerdahl's excavations had then "solved none of the problems of Easter Island."[18] Instead, "The giants' mouths ... sealed seven times over" stand "proud, arrogant, and tight-lipped, as though defiantly conscious that no chisel, no power will ever open their mouths and make them speak."

"Even the engineers shook their heads resignedly."[22] Heyerdahl wrote of the island's colossal endeavors. "We felt like a crowd of schoolboys standing helpless before a practical conundrum. The invisible moon dwellers ... seemed to be glorying over us, saying: 'Guess how this engineering work was done! Guess how we moved these gigantic figures down the steep walls of the volcano and carried them over the hills to any place in the island we liked!'" Conveying the extraordinary magnitude of Rapa Nui's remarkable *moai*, and the equally extraordinary magnitude of labor necessary for the statues' construction, Heyerdahl likened the 55-ton (50-tonne) sculptures—the largest 72 feet (22 m) tall—to two 11-ton (10-tonne) boxcars, each containing 12 draft horses and five large elephants, which were then transported for miles around the island.

When examining the unfinished *moai* in the quarry, laying on their sides or standing upright, Heyerdahl observed thousands of stone picks scattered around them. Sculptors had hewn the bare rock to form the face and front part of the statue, then cut narrow channels along the figure's sides to create enormous ears and arms with long fingers wrapped around the torso—only the back, in the shape of a narrow keel, remained attached to the rock face. Once facial details were carved and the statue was polished, the juggernaut was then liberated from the quarry by cutting away the keel. All the statues received a flattened base without the semblance of legs, so that the *moai* stood only as a head and elongated torso. Could such extraordinary industry be considered impossible without modern machinery? Had "the oldest inhabitants of Easter Island mastered the impossible?"[19]

Heyerdahl remained convinced that the *moai's* construction "was not the work of a canoeload of Polynesian wood carvers who set to work on the bare rock faces when they landed merely because they could find no trees to whittle." Instead, he believed, "The red-haired giants with the classical features were made by seafarers who came from a land with generations of experience in maneuvering monoliths." Rano Raraku's summit remained for Heyerdahl, "the focal point of Easter Island's foremost riddle; this was the statues' maternal home." Standing upon "a sturdy embryo," at the summit's base, within and outside the crater, "the newborn stood erect, blind and hairless, waiting in vain to be hauled away on their long transport."[20]

Unable to fathom the engineering process by which the colossi were transported, Heyerdahl enquired of a shepherd, Leonardo, how it had occurred. "They went of themselves," Leonardo replied, bemused by Heyerdahl's incomprehension. That fantastical explanation was repeated by Heyerdahl's housekeeper Mariana, who relayed an enduring myth of an old witch who had long ago breathed life into these stationary automatons, then commanded them about the island. Katherine Routledge received the exact same explanation during her 1914–1915 expedition, and Heyerdahl discovered that such an explanation remained acceptable to all of the island inhabitants he questioned.

→»»

Abandoning Rano Raraku to Arne and his assistants' excavations, Heyerdahl next journeyed to Moto Nui—a nearby rock-strewn island of the tangata manu, or "birdman" cult—to examine several of the sacred caves there, within which were found ancient wooden tablets emblazoned with carved hieroglyphics called *rongorongo*, which were believed to visit death upon all those that came into contact with them. For centuries, Rapa Nui's most powerful men spent weeks in half-subterranean stone homes at the Rano Kao volcano (on Rapa Nui's southwestern headland), awaiting the annual migration of the sooty tern (*Onychoprion fuscatus*, or *manutara* in Rapanui, meaning "lucky bird") to Motu Nui, after which they competed in a voyage to the island upon reed floats to recover the first egg lain there. "The man who became owner of that egg was exalted to a kind of divinity: he had his head shaved and painted red, he was led in procession to a sacred hut among the statues at the foot of Rano Raraku," where he would remain confined for the year, without contact with common island inhabitants and attended to by special servants, having been "designated the sacred bird-man of the year."[21]

Orongo, a ceremonial village and the ancient site of the birdman cult, commanded a panoramic view of Moto Nui, and was situated along a precipitous ledge banked by a deep volcanic crater, some 1,000 feet (300 m) below which lay the cacophonous Pacific Ocean. Edwin Ferdon, an American ethnologist, excavated among the ruins of the abandoned birdman cult site, marked by a large rock face graven with numerous images of male figures with long, crescent-shaped bird beaks. Heyerdahl, having read accounts of these birdman ceremonies previously, unsurprisingly made the link between these and similar activities in South America. On Moto Nui, Heyerdahl also explored several partly overgrown caves within which the expedition discovered human bones and crania. However, frustrated by a perceived lack of cooperation by locals, little more was found. While these excavations were in some ways unenlightening, given that much of what they saw had been previously recorded, the threads of Heyerdahl's theory were, to him, continually strengthened.

→»»

Returning to Rapa Nui, excavations led by Mulloy and a party of 20 island laborers were now underway at the extraordinary ceremonial complex of Ahu Vinapu, one of the largest *ahu* (stone platforms with walls, ramps, and usually supporting *moai*). Everyone who encountered the stonemasons' remarkable work there, Heyerdahl observed, was "struck by its [the complex's] remarkable resemblance to the grand mural constructions of the Inca empire. There is nothing like it on the tens of thousands of other islands in the vast Pacific."[22] Ahu Vinapu stands alone in a "mirrored reflection of the classical masterpieces of the Incas or their predecessors ... all the more striking because it [the complex] appears on the particular Polynesian island nearest to the Incas' own coast." Had "the master masons from Peru ... been at work out here too?" Heyerdahl speculated, "could ... scions of their [the Incas'] guild ... [have] landed and begun to chisel gigantic blocks for the Easter Island walls." The evidence, he believed, overwhelmingly suggested that this was, in fact, the case.

Mulloy concluded that the central wall at Ahu Vinapu, which possessed classical stone masonry, "belonged to the very oldest building period of Easter Island" and was constructed by "masters of the complicated Inca type of technique" using enormous blocks of basalt. Substantiating Heyerdahl's hypothesis that a pre-Incan people originally settled Rapa Nui, Mulloy's excavation assembled a chronology from Vinapu's ruins, observing that where the *ahu* had been rebuilt in subsequent eras, a marked difference in construction techniques appeared, delineating a second epoch in which the island's inhabitants simultaneously dismantled or altered existing stone structures and erected Rapa Nui's innumerable *moai*. Excavations at Ahu Vinapu also revealed a third epoch of human activity in which all chiseling ceased and formless stone blocks were cast haphazardly together against the *ahus*, producing funeral mounds and burial vaults when war enveloped the island with the arrival of the present Polynesian inhabitant's ancestors.

As excavations progressed at Ahu Vinapu, Heyerdahl was also struck by the extraordinary parallels between an unearthed four-sided red-stone column (a find so important that it prompted Father Sebastian to write to Heyerdahl stating "Victory is yours"), and those he encountered upon the shores of Peru's Lake Titicaca in 1954. And, duly, the expedition unearthed several red-stone-carved figures unseen before upon Rapa Nui, yet they were familiar to Heyerdahl from Tiahuanaco, an ancient, pre-Incan cult site. Island belief held that Tiahuanaco's sculptors eventually migrated westward into the Pacific before the Inca's arrival, suggesting to Heyerdahl that Rapa Nui's artifacts, sculptures, and construction possessed South American provenance.

Accepted scholarship, however, suggested that Rapa Nui's remarkable stone architecture and sculptures had developed organically upon the island, independently of a pre-Incan civilization. Several scholars believed that the Polynesians, masterful wood-carvers, had simply begun carving stone, because Rapa Nui possessed few trees. Regardless, Heyerdahl remained skeptical of such isolationist hypothesizing, convinced that only contact between Polynesia and South American could account for Ahu Vinapu's remarkable construction. What's more, Heyerdahl's party were able to prove, through pollen analysis, the island once possessed a prehistoric forest, ensuring the hypothesis for why island inhabitants began carving rock remained untenable. Subsequent carbon-dating undertaken by the expedition also revealed that "a people of highly specialized culture, with the typical South American type of masonry technique, had been at work on Easter Island. These earliest discoverers of the island had arrived more than a thousand years before the ancestors of the present Polynesian population."[23]

Heyerdahl and the archaeologists of the expedition agreed on three epochs that characterized the island's chronology. First, an antecedent sun-worshipping South American population had settled Rapa Nui from the east, erecting meticulously built structures with steep walls, platforms, and trenches around Rapa Nui. In the second phase, these industrious long-eared people coexisted alongside a newly arrived Polynesian short-eared civilization, altering these early structures and constructing the island's colossal statues. The short ears subsequently perpetrated cannibalism on the long ears and waged warfare on them—an interpretation taken from local oral history—in a third phase delineated by the presence of *mataa,* obsidian spearheads used as a cutting implement and as weapons, which become prolific in the archaeological record and are unique to Rapa Nui. From that period until the early historic period, this state of intertribal warfare persisted occasionally.[i] "The population of [Easter Island] today is the freshest shoot sprung from the victorious warrior tribe of the third epoch,"[24] Heyerdahl declared. With perhaps some exaggeration, he wrote that there "was no peaceful affair when their Polynesian ancestors arrived from the palm islands to westward. Of the battles which followed their arrival, of the statutes which fell, of the time when adzes cut their way into men of flesh and blood instead of men of stone, we were soon to hear stories from the living population of the island."

⟶⟶

By November 1955, excavations were underway at Ahu Vinapu, Orongo, and Rano Raraku, Rapa Nui's largest volcano. Heyerdahl had traversed most of the island, gathering extensive evidence concerning the construction of the *moai* and regarding the inhabitants who had perhaps constructed them. Now, however, he wanted to pass an absorbing evening within the old stone quarry at Rano Raraku. "Not because I was suspicious and believed that the spirits of the long-ears would come and betray their secrets," he declared, "but because I would like to assimilate fully the peculiar atmosphere of the place. I clambered over huge stone bodies ... until I was in the midst of a swarm of figures ... where one giant had been removed from his birthplace. The rays of the evening sun filled the foaming crests [of the ocean] with gleaming silver, and silvery dust hung in the air at the volcano's foot. It was a sight for the gods. And among a multitude of giant gods I sat, a solitary little human being. Time had again ceased to exist. Night and the stars had always been there, and man who played with fire."[25]

Awakening with dawn upon the quarry's impregnable rock, having dreamed of ancient Rapa Nui, Heyerdahl—always the enthusiast for conducting practicable investigations, with *Kon-Tiki's* voyage being emblematic of such—resolved to augment the expedition's excavations with another remarkable experiment. "Why not start an experiment?" he wondered. "The stone picks still lay where the sculptors had flung them down, and the last long-ear still had living descendants in the village. Perhaps work could actually be started in the old quarry again."[26]

Several days later, Heyerdahl consulted with Pedro Atan, the island's mayor and eminent descendant of the long ears. While many Western academics had long speculated about the methods employed to carve, raise, and transport the enormous *moai,* none, apparently, had ever thought to simply ask the islanders themselves. Heyerdahl, ever critical of "armchair archaeologists," intended to reenact the process for creating the *moai*, with the aid of a number of local islanders.

Not long afterward, the expedition witnessed an ancient, nocturnal ceremony performed before the construction of the *moai* began, within which several figures garlanded with featherlike crowns of leaves and wearing paper masks to resemble birdmen, danced, sang the old stonecutter's song for the god Atua to assure good fortune, and struck the ground with elaborately carved war clubs, dancing paddles, and stone picks. "I felt far away from the South Sea islands," Heyerdahl wrote of the enigmatic ceremony. "Strangely enough there was something to the music which reminded me of visits with the Pueblo Indians in New Mexico."[27]

Assembling at Rano Raraku's old quarry the next day, Mayor Atan, his second-in-command Lazaru Hotus, and a team of workers sang the stonecutter's ancient song once again, then they began striking at the quarry's near-impenetrable face in rhythmical union. By the third day, the contours of Heyerdahl's new *moai* were now discernible across the quarry wall, the sculptors systematically whetting their stone adzes upon others, and casting water from their calabashes against the quarry face. Heyerdahl's party estimated from the stonecutter's work that the creation of a medium-sized *moai* would take upward of one year to complete. However, the *moai* must then be removed from the quarry, transported to a site, and erected. How had the island's ancestors accomplished such a herculean task, Heyerdahl questioned.

Mayor Atan Atan would soon reveal the ancient methodology of erecting a *moai*. After performing another nocturnal ceremony with 12 leaf and bough-clad island men, descendants of the fabled long ears, dancing to incessant drumming and performing the song of Kon-Tiki commanding the resurrection of a moai, they all assembled at Anakena, a beach on the island, before a fallen *moai*, some 10 feet (3 m) wide and weighing between 28 and 33 tons (25 and 30 tonnes). Inserting three enormous wooden poles beneath the colossal *moai's* head, Mayor Atan then began slipping gradually larger stones under the statue's enormous face. *"Etahi, erua, etoru!* One, two, three! One, two, three!" Mayor Atan commanded. "Once more! One, two, three! One, two, three!" Eventually, after several hours, the *moai's* head was raised 3 feet (1 m). Leveraging the *moai* upward, back and forth, gradually larger stones were inserted beneath the colossus, until after nine days the cumbersome *moai* lay horizontally across an expansive platform of some 12 feet (3.6 m) of gathered stones. On the 11th day, additional stones were piled beneath the juggernaut's head and chest, gradually inclining the *moai*, now secured with ropes lashed about the gargantuan forehead and staked into the ground. On the 18th day, Mayor Atan's laborers, employing ropes and wooden poles, leveraged the *moai* into an upright position, with thousands of gathered stones cascading about the giant's base. For the first time in centuries, an enormous *moai* arose again on Rapa Nui.

Mayor Atan had been able to answer, in practice, the enduring question of just how such colossal statues were once erected throughout the island. However, another enigma persisted: How were the immense *moai* transported about the island? While the most popular theory expounded by the islanders who Heyerdahl consulted was that they simply "walked" across the islands, he, of course, did not accept such (a fact he was to regret many years later). However, Mayor Atan now revealed that island inhabitants had, in fact, employed massive Y-shaped sleds made from forked tree trunks with crosspieces, known as *miro manga erua*, and drawn them with thick ropes made from the durable bark of the *hau hau* tree. Demonstrating how such *miro manga erua* were used, Mayor Atan assembled some 180 island inhabitants, who successfully drew a 13-ton (12-tonne) *moai* across the plain behind Heyerdahl's encampment at Anakena Bay. "We had seen how water and stone picks could gnaw the statues out of the solid rock," Heyerdahl wrote, "if only one had sufficient time; we had seen how ropes and runners could move the giants from place to place, if only there were enough hands to pull; we had seen how the colossi could be lifted … and raised on end if only one applied the right technique. An industrious and intelligent people had come to this tiny island [Rapa Nui] with its unlimited peace," he reflected. "Absence of warfare, ample time, and traditions of an old technique were all that was needed to raise the Babel towers of Easter Island."[28] The fascinated members of Heyerdahl's expedition had now seen Rapa Nui's long impenetrable mystery dissolve before the islanders' labors, entranced by ancient Polynesian civilization's intelligence, ingenuity, and industry.

⤜

While the *moai* had been the focus of much of Heyerdahl's expedition, an unexpected discovery was made when undertaking excavations at Oronogo. Several wall carvings, entirely different from those already discovered across Rapa Nui, were found. Most enigmatic was "a typical American Indian weeping-eye motif, and several … sculptures of crescent-shaped reed boats with masts. One of the reed boats had lateral lashings and a large square sail."[29] However, the old Rapa Nui inhabitants were not known to have built reed boats large enough to carry a sail, and Heyerdahl described how they "were suddenly confronted with illustrations of reed boats among old ceiling paintings … on the crater of Easter Island's largest volcano. We not only found pictures of the boats, but we also found a surviving supply of the boatmen's reeds."

That reed, known as totora, was employed by Rapa Nui's inhabitants for the construction of small vessels they called *pora*, which remained "something of a botanical curiosity," having been identified by botanists as an American freshwater reed. Remarkably, as Heyerdahl well knew, that same reed was also found upon the shores of Peru's Lake Titicaca and employed by Peruvian Indians for the construction of similar reed vessels. Heyerdahl himself had sailed upon the reed boats on Lake Titicaca. The Spanish conquerors of Peru, in fact, had observed large reed boats employed upon the open Pacific Ocean, off the coast of Peru, and pre-Incan ceramics also recorded such craft. How exactly had such extraordinary transplantation, cultural and botanical, occurred?

Heyerdahl, fascinated by these parallels, asked four of the island's community, the highly knowledgeable Pakarati brothers—Pedro, Santiago, Domingo, and Timoteo—to construct a *pora*. He then spent several days undertaking test boring in the reed swamp within the Rano Kao volcano, where the South American freshwater reeds were originally cultivated, in search of pollen samples that would assist in determining the ancient vegetable life of Rapa Nui. Arne Skjølsvold, who was excavating at Rano Raraku, then discovered an extraordinary illustration of an enormous reed vessel etched across a *moai's* abdomen. According to island mythology, the vessel was Hotu Matua's, the one he had originally voyaged to Rapa Nui upon. Heyerdahl speculated the island's inhabitants were once master sailors, evidently having successfully navigated across the Pacific Ocean to isolated Rapa Nui.

Heyerdahl's commissioned *pora*, constructed from sun-dried totora reeds within Rano Raraku volcano, were now ready. These were identical replicas, Heyerdahl believed, to the one-man vessels constructed by pre-Incan peoples along the Peruvian coastline. Heyerdahl, Father Sebastian, and Mayor Atan watched, mesmerized, as the four Pakarati brothers launched their two and one-man *pora* vessels into the Pacific Ocean—a craft recalled by ancestors but absent from Rapa Nui for generations.

That December, Heyerdahl's expedition also discovered, during the southern hemisphere's summer solstice, the first ceremonial solar observatory then known in Polynesia. The vast complex consisted of a series of stones aligned in rows, each carved with large circular eyes reminiscent of typical sun symbols, arranged across a paved area before an ancient stone structure, accompanied by a series of holes bored into the rock, within which wooden rods were once placed. Heyerdahl's thoughts invariably turned eastward once more. "The Incas and their predecessors in Peru were sun worshipers," he declared, revealing, "these new observations recalled to our minds the old cultures of South America." Resolving the mystery of Rapa Nui, he believed, required examination of the sun, "man's [divine] ancestor," and celestial worship. Drawing sailors westward across all the world's oceans, "the Incas believed … the sun-priest Kon-Tiki Viracocha abandoned his kingdom in Peru on a westward voyage into the Pacific in the wake of his father the sun."[31]

⟶⟶

Heyerdahl's expedition to Rapa Nui had, he believed, been a resounding success. While conducting the first scientific excavations on the island, Heyerdahl and his party had uncovered invaluable archaeological evidence regarding the *moai* and Rapa Nui 's enigmatic history, which would determine the island's narrative for several decades. Indeed, he now considered the mystery of the *moai's* carving and transportation altogether resolved.

Heyerdahl remained convinced by the geographical significance of Rapa Nui, the enigmatic island lying much closer to South America than Asia or "any other inhabitable speck of land in the entire Pacific,"[32] and the evidence of habitation by the oldest culture in Polynesia overwhelmingly suggested to him that the original settlers had arrived from the New World. Carbon dating conducted by the expedition and led by Carlyle Smith indicated that by AD 380, "organized labor was at work on Easter Island" and of all the island settlements found throughout the Pacific Ocean, this island alone possessed ancient Peru's highly specialized masonry techniques.[ii] The island's colossal *moai* also evidenced remarkable similarities to pre-Incan statues, with further carbon dating indicating many of the island's *moai's* construction, in fact, occurred within the same epoch as those constructed in South America.

What's more, Easter Island's horticulture centered about the kumara, sweet potato, and Peruvian totora reed, the principal raw material for house, raft, and textile construction. Later serological testing in the 1960s of island inhabitants revealed that Polynesians possess similar hereditary conformity with indigenous North and South American populations, separating that lineage from the Indonesians, Malays, Melanesians, Micronesians, and other Asiatic peoples of the Western Pacific. All incontestable evidence, Heyerdahl believed, that Rapa Nui, and much of Polynesia, was originally settled from peoples conveyed westward by the Humboldt Current.

Drawing the ship's anchor on 6 April 1956, Heyerdahl's expedition, after almost six months onshore, despondently departed Rapa Nui. Bidding farewell to each of the fascinating island's inhabitants, the party set sail, bound for the nearby islands of Pitcairn, Rapa Iti, and Nuku Hiva. "When orders from the bridge brought the anchor chain rattling up from the depths, and the bell to the engine room set wheels and pistons humming and beating down in the ship's bowels, there were few cheerful hearts either on board or ashore."[33] Heyerdahl gazed meditatively at the recently erected *moai* as they drew away from the island at last, remarking that the colossal stone figure "stood in solitude, once more betrayed, staring out over a sun-filled valley where no one lived any longer."

⇸

"Pitcairn had risen out of the sea, dead ahead," Heyerdahl wrote, as the expedition voyaged westward from Rapa Nui. "We had reached the island of the *Bounty* mutineers. The sky behind it was aflame with a low, red sun, as though the desperate fugitives were still burning their ship behind them."[34] Heyerdahl's party was welcomed by the descendants of the *Bounty* mutineers themselves, "robust, barelegged, picturesque characters … [accompanied by] Parkin Christian, great-great-grandson of Fletcher Christian," the infamous leader of the 1789 mutiny upon Lieutenant William Bligh's ill-fated merchant vessel. Heyerdahl himself was billeted within agreeable Parkin Christian's own home. Several indolent days passed on Pitcairn Island, while the expedition conducted unsucessful test excavations and visited various *Bounty* mutiny landmarks, including the sunken wreckage of the ship, reached by Heyerdahl's young boatswain, Johan Kloster, who became the first non-Pitkerner to do so. On Pitcairn, Heyerdahl found insufficient archaeological artifacts from which to draw any significant conclusions, because "the mutineers' descendants, as God-fearing Christians, had leveled the temple platforms to the ground, smashed the small red statues, and thrown them into the sea to rid their island of heathen images."[35]

Voyaging westward once again, the expedition sailed first to Mangareva, then onward to Rapa Iti, where Heyerdahl's ship landed on 28 April 1956, with the island lying "among the cloud banks to the southwest, like a dreamland sailing on the sea." Here, the expedition explored the ruins of the island's mountaintop fortifications, or *pare*, including the largest and oldest, Morongo Uta, a fort complex Heyerdahl described as a "fairy-tale castle, lulled in the slumber of centuries like the Sleeping Beauty. As in a spell, its towers and walls overgrown with brushwood and foliage … Although [the castle] stood free and heaven-soaring beneath the blue sky, there was something earthbound—almost subterranean—about this ancient edifice, which seemed to rise from underground."[36] There were 12 of these "castle-like formations," which could be seen on the summits of verdant hilltops all about the island.

Rapa Iti was first visited by a European expedition in 1791, led by Captain George Vancouver, a British Royal Navy officer, during his 1791–1795 expedition that explored and charted North America's northwestern Pacific Coast regions. The island was later sighted in 1813, by a sea otter fur trader, Stephen Reynolds; in 1815, by the *Endeavour* ship voyaging from New Zealand to the Marquesas; and in 1817, by the British missionary William Ellis, after which missionaries wandered ashore, the island's first nonindigenous visitors, in 1825–1826. The French diplomat Jacques-Antoine Moerenhout also explored Rapa Iti, while J.F.G. Stokes undertook fieldwork there in the 1920s. No intensive archaeological excavations were undertaken upon the enigmatic Pacific island, however. Enveloped by the ever-westward oscillating Humboldt Current, Heyerdahl believed Polynesian vessels would have naturally been conveyed here from Rapa Nui. Anxious to conduct excavations but now lacking essential provisions, the expedition sailed back to Tahiti, then returned to Rapa Iti. Enlisting a party of island laborers, with women eventually replacing men, Heyerdahl began excavating Morongo Uta. "Hibiscus and pandanus and giant tree ferns were powerless to withstand the assault; heavy tree trunks crashed down from the walls and went thundering into the depths, followed by leaves and ferns and brush."[37] The ancient fort complex and well-fortified village was defended by ramparts and an impassable moat. And had been constructed upon some 80 terraces of durable basalt stones lain masterfully together without mortar upon the summit of one of Rapa Iti's many mountains, overlooking the gentle valleys below. Heyerdahl's party unearthed several square stone ovens, wells, adzes, mortars, and taro storage pits. For Heyerdahl, the oval hut dwellings made from bent boughs, bound together and plastered with reeds and dried grass, remained "suspiciously reminiscent of Easter Island." The expedition continued to explore the other fortified village sites found across the palisaded island. Carved rock chambers, stone reliefs, a repository resembling a sarcophagus, and burial caves hewn into the rock face and sealed with masterfully cut stone slabs were also discovered. Regardless, the Cave of the Kings in Anarua Valley remained unrevealed, the royal cavern's whereabouts long forgotten by the island's inhabitants. Gazing forth from the island's terraces over the Pacific Ocean, Heyerdahl speculated that Rapa Iti's inhabitants "were afraid of a powerful outside enemy, an enemy who was known to them, and whose war canoes might appear above the horizon without warning."[38] He described how the "man-wrought peaks of Rapa Iti rise out of the sea like some elaborate monument to nameless navigators of a forgotten age—navigators who had many hundreds of miles behind them when they landed ... But many hundreds of miles were not enough to remove their fear that other seafarers might follow in their wake."[39]

Leaving Rapa Iti, Heyerdahl's party continued on to conduct excavations on the islands of Raivavae, Nuku Hiva and Hiva Oa in the Marquesas archipelago. Here, Heyerdahl explored the Taipi Valley, immortalized by Herman Melville in his 1846 novel, *Typee*. Heyerdahl's expedition, the first within the islands, uncovered several stone figures. Carbon dating from charcoal recovered at I'ipona me'ae, Hiva Oa, revealed that temple construction began about 1300, some 900 years after Rapa Nui's settlement—and that the statues found were dated to an even later period. This aligned with Heyerdahl's theory, "Assuming, as I did, that people of another culture, from early South America, had found their way into the Pacific before the present islanders, then ... Easter Island would have been [settled] first instead of last."[40] The artifacts unearthed on these smaller islands appeared insignificant to Heyerdahl in comparison with the remarkable colossi of Rapa Nui, and he believed that island's "deep-rooted culture, towered above the rest, a cornerstone in the prehistory of the East Pacific. No other island could possibly have usurped the proud title: 'Navel of the World.'"[41] Additionally, the expedition gathered blood samples from the islanders, which, after serological examination, revealed "all the hereditary factors directly arguing Polynesian descent from the original population of the American continent," further substantiating his east–west migration route.

Rapa Nui, Heyerdahl remained convinced, was the site of the original settlement, from which subsequent Pacific archipelago exploration and habitation occurred, with the ancestors of the island's present-day inhabitants supplanting another population. His archaeological excavations revealed a definitive "substratum of two distinct cultural epochs that antedated the final period of unrest and decadence concurring with the late arrival of the present population." Analogous masterful masonry appeared both upon Rapa Rui and across Peru, and the colossal *moai* resembled the pre-Incan statues found at Tiahuanaco, Peru. Rapa Nui's inhabitants, he believed, then settled the Marquesas archipelago and nearby islands. The islands' mythology of seafaring ancestors voyaging from the east, genealogy and serology, botanical species, and elaborate sculptures all evidenced South American origin.[42]

Finally, after many months away, Heyerdahl's expedition sailed away from the verdant valleys, scarlet mountains, near-impenetable jungle, and elegant coconut palms of Polynesia, with each member sorrowfully casting their kaleidoscopic floral wreaths into the Pacific Ocean, proffering "a wistful farewell to those departing" and disappearing at last into opaque shadow beneath the descending sun, subsumed by the vast seas.

"Thirty years would pass before I returned to Easter Island for further investigation,"[43] Heyerdahl recalled, to that "dream island sailing above the clouds," where to him mystery remained omnipresent, and ever tangible —a mystery and living history infinitely more fascinating than the paradisiacal white sand beaches of Tahiti. Heyerdahl remained convinced that the voyaging ancestors of the sun god Kon-Tiki had eventually settled upon Rapa Nui, and he eagerly returned in 1986 to substantiate his unconventional hypothesis, drawn by "a remarkable discovery made by one of the many young archaeologists who ... had tried to wrench more information out of the old ruins."

The transformative discovery was made on Anakena beach by Rapanui archaeologist Sonia Haoa Cardinali, as part of an expedition directed by Sergio Rapu. Cardinali unearthed an inlaid eye made of coral that had once graced the visage of one of Rapa Nui's colossi. For Heyerdahl, here was irrefutable evidence of an intercultural connection he had long advanced between the ancient cultures of Mexico and Peru; within both civilizations, colossi were adorned with inlaid eyes made from black obsidian and white shell. These were the inlaid eyes that he had predicted many years before would be inevitably unearthed. Archaeologist Rapu, now Easter Island's governor, had, in fact, witnessed Heyerdahl's 1955–1956 expedition to the island and invited him to conduct another archaeological excavation there, with Heyerdahl recalling the invitation as "a dream come true."

Heyerdahl returned to Polynesia, drawn by an irresistible desire to witness the "staring *moai*,"[44] where he experienced a profound sense of global interconnectedness: Rapa Nui "was part of the planet that had housed the other reed-ship builders."[45]

Throughout Heyerdahl's 1986 expedition to Rapa Nui, he was accompanied by a young Czech engineer, Pavel Pavel. He had written to Heyerdahl before the expedition enquiring why, as detailed in his 1957 book, *Aku-Aku,* Heyerdahl had never believed the inhabitants of Rapa Rui, when they claimed their ancestors had induced the colossal stone *moai* to walk about the island without the aid of sleds. Pavel, believing these claims, had himself constructed a 22-ton (20-tonne) *moai* replica, inducing the statue to walk with the aid of several ropes and assistants. Heyerdahl, therefore, invited young Pavel to Rapa Nui to replicate his extraordinary engineering feat. "We all felt a chill down our backs when we saw the sight that must have been so familiar to the early ancestors of the [Easter Island] people,"[46] Heyerdahl wrote of Pavel's successful experiment, which was achieved by synchronizing 15 laborers, drawing back and forth together upon ropes lashed about the enormous *moai's* head and base. He described the stone colossus of an "estimated ten tons 'walking' … behind a group of Lilliputians, with a little man in front beating his left and right fists in the air each time the Goliath had to take a step." Within Heyerdahl's mind, he saw "the blind colossi being guided on their rough keels down across the empty … [hollows] in the crater wall, to be set up and have their dorsal keels chopped away before the long march began." He visualized "the terrifying sight of several of the carved giants wriggling along the roads in different directions, like robots from another planet, through a green landscape of palms and cultivated fields."[47] His longstanding ethnocentric dismissal of the Rapanuis' *moai* creation mythology methodologies as simply apocryphal was now illustrated as fallacy, with Heyerdahl acknowledging the necessity of further integrating indigenous belief systems into archaeological and ethnographic hypotheses.

⥲

"The mysteries [that] had confounded visitors and armchair scientists since the days of Roggeveen and Captain Cook existed no more,"[48] Heyerdahl victoriously declared. "The genesis of the blind giants dotting the slopes of the volcano was known, and how they walked to the *ahu* before they received their eyes. The way each of these incredible feats had been accomplished with help from neither machinery or outer space—all these former puzzles now had their answers." All of Rapa Nui's history had, however, already been relayed, Heyerdahl acknowledged, by the island's inhabitants, in oral histories, memories, and mythologies, the handing down of which had supported the expedition throughout. Heyerdahl's deeply fortunate position as both a European male and internationally celebrated archaeologist and explorer, and his capacity to subsume indigenous mythologies and narratives within Western anthropological discourse cannot be underemphasized, but his excavations on the island did serve to further research and discussion of migration theory and Pacific archaeology among the international scientific community. Returning to the island's inhabitants their own history, they could at least give it back to them "written in our own letters with a stamp of scientific approval."[49]

Vestiges of Kon-Tiki Viracocha's westward exodus from Pacific Coast South America and settlement upon Rapa Nui remained evidenced, Heyerdahl believed, within the island's totora reeds, statues, reed vessels, elaborate illustrations of mythological birdmen, and botanical specimens. Specifically, "Reed boats, bird-men and ear-lengthening were three phenomena typical of Easter Island and conspicuous by their absence in Polynesia." And all three of these, Heyerdahl observed, appeared upon a gilded silver earplug from the pre-Inca period, from the coast of northern Peru. Enigmatic Rapa Nui, he was now wholeheartedly convinced, was originally settled from the east.

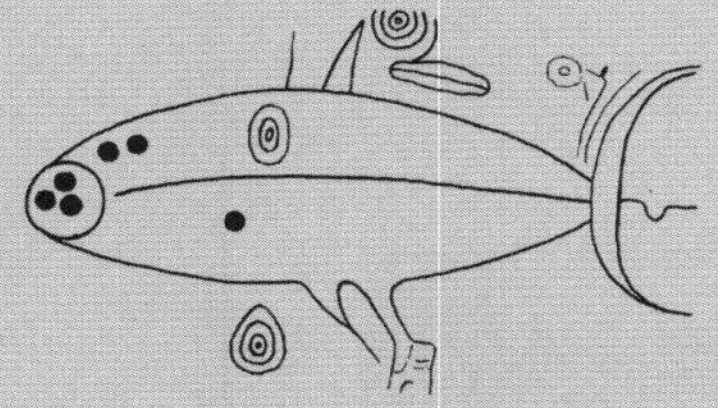

i There was a consensus on the three epochs until 1968, when Mulloy changed his view on the chronology of the Vinapu ceremonial site where he worked.

ii Research since this assertion has since ruled out the AD 380 date. Susan J. Crockford and Helene Martinsson-Wallin analysed the total C-14 record from settlement activity and concluded that the few outliers of which the AD 380 was the most extreme, had to be discounted. The main reason for this being that the interpretation of a fortification ditch by Carlyle Smith may be erroneous, in fact being attempts at wetland agriculture of taro, which would mean the site was reexcavated many times. The earliest settlement of the island is now supposed to be either *c.*AD 1200 or later (the late school) or AD 800-1000 (early school). Ref: "Early Settlement of Rapa Nui (Easter Island)" by Helene Martinsson-Wallin (KTM) and Susan J. Crockford, published in Asian Perspectives, 40:2:2001.

Top: Excavating the famous kneeling statue on the outside slopes of Rano Raraku. From left: unidentified, Silvestro Pakarati, Arne Skjølsvold, and Elias Rapu.

Bottom: Father Sebastian Englert and local workers restoring a stone statue close to the village of Hangaroa.

Opposite (top): Lazaro Hotus, the second in charge of the crew, and other local Rapanui in the process of erecting a *moai* on the Ahu Ahure Tuki, Anakena.

Opposite (bottom): Arne Skjølsvold and his work party are arriving in Rano Raraku quarry to begin archaeological excavations.

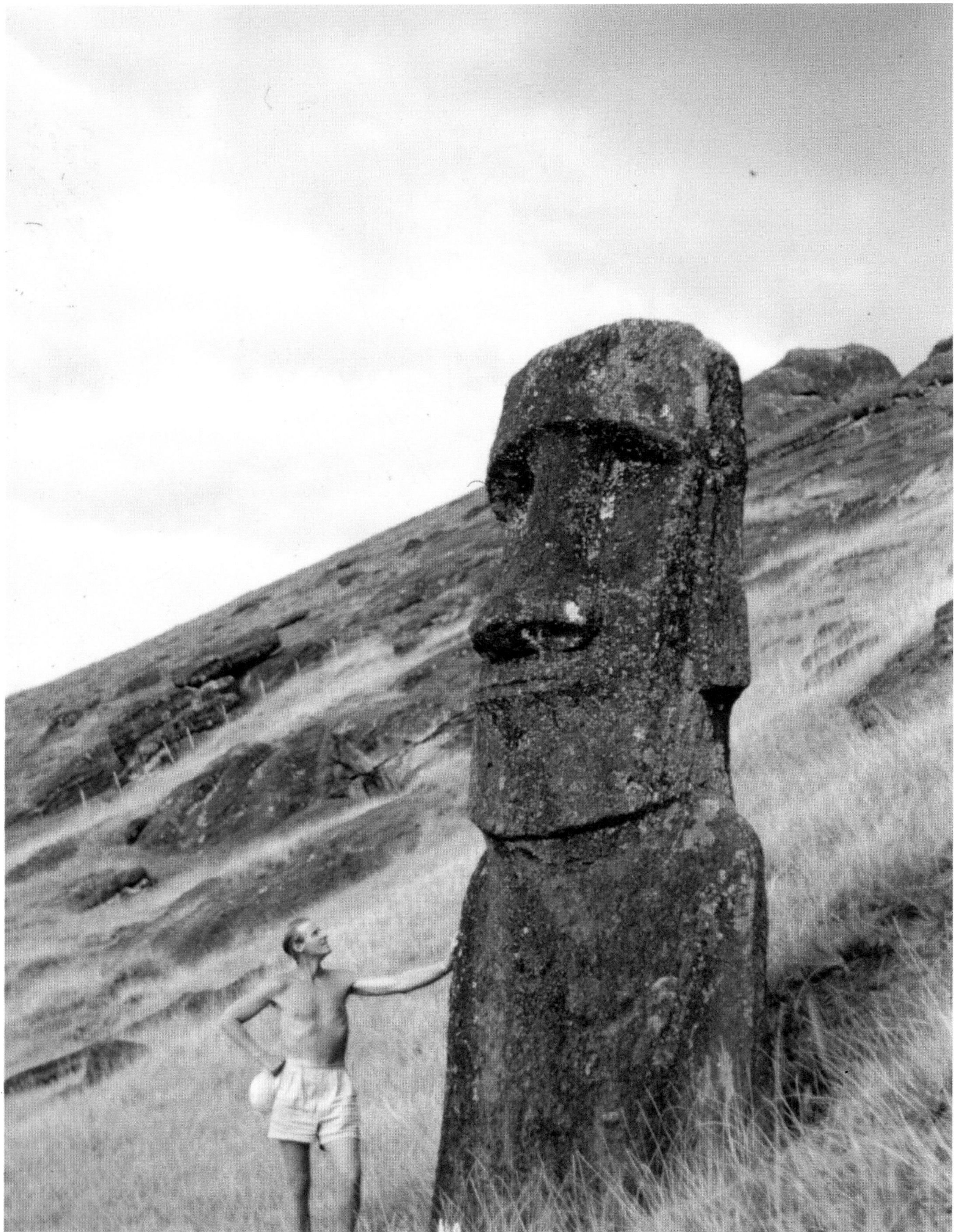

Opposite: Thor Heyerdahl beside a *moai* statue in Rano Raraku.

Top: Close-up of the statue after restoration.

Bottom: Local Rapanui workers in the process of erecting a statue close to the village of Hangaroa.

Opposite (top): Desolated *ahu* on Rapa Nui (unknown location).

Opposite (middle left): Two brothers, Timoteo and Domingo Pakarati, testing their reed boat, or *pora*, in the sea outside Anakena.

Opposite (middle right): Timoteo, Domingo, Santiago, and Pedro Pakarati paddling in their reed boat, or *pora*, in the sea outside Anakena.

Opposite (bottom): Local Rapanui workers in Rano Raraku.

Top: View of Hat Brim Hill and Anakena from the northwest.

Bottom: On the coast below Rano Kao volcano with the famous Orongo ceremonial site, waiting for a trip to Motu Nui.

Milagrosa Pakarati dancing in traditional costume, at Anakena.

Opposite: Edwin N. Ferdon sitting sketching petroglyphs at Orongo ceremonial site. (The ship's doctor Emil Gjessing in the background.)

Left: Thor Heyerdahl Jr., Thor Heyerdahl, Yvonne Heyerdahl, and their daughter Annette on the deck of M.S. *Chr. Bjelland* prior to departure from Oslo to Rapa Nui for the 1955–56 Easter Island expedition.

Right: Ahu Nau Nau, Anakena, Rapa Nui restored by local archaeologist Sergiou Rapu in 1978.

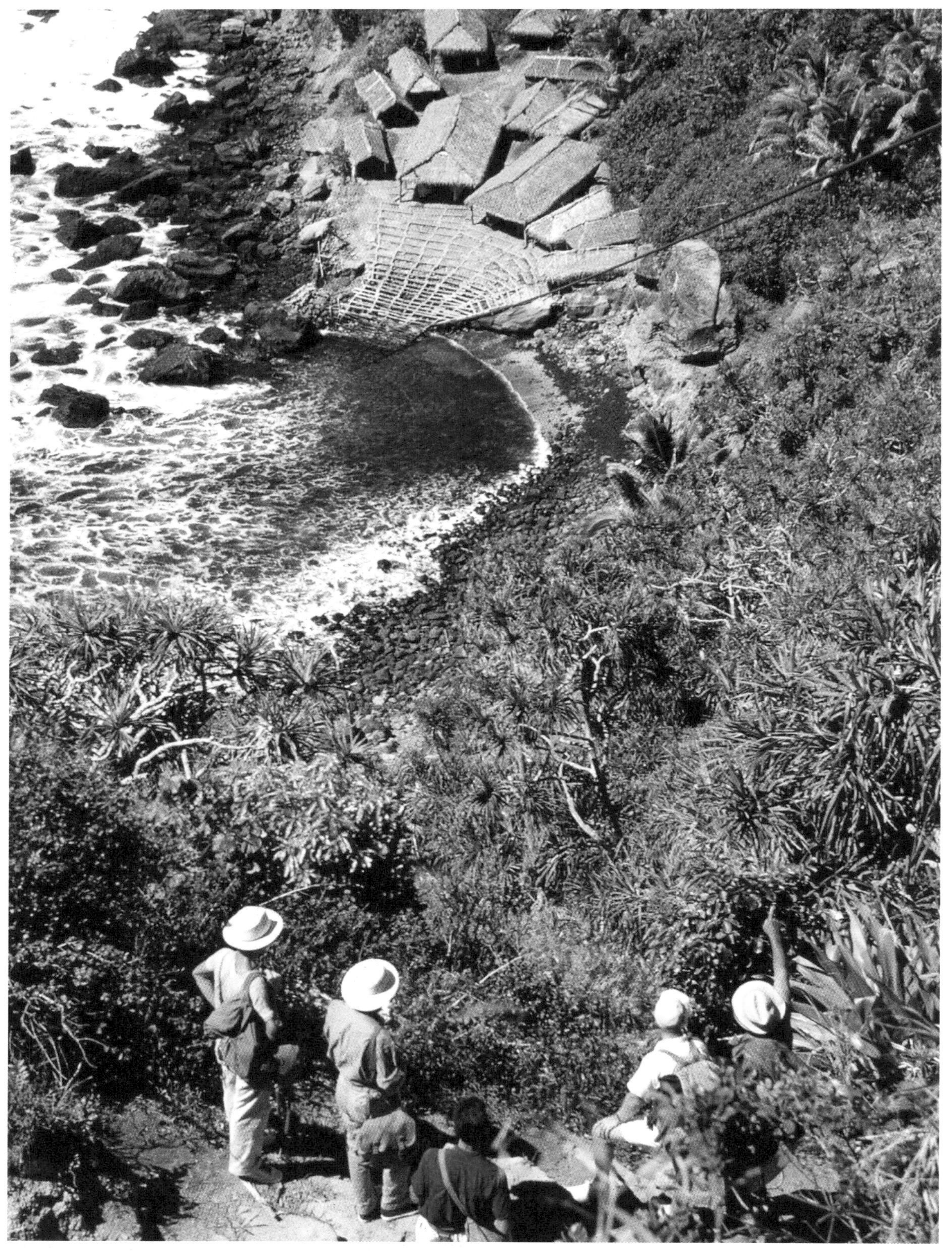

Opposite: The only place for landing boats on Pitcairn Island.

Bottom: On the way down from Morongo Uta, Rapa Iti.

Daily life on Rapa Iti
in 1956.

Opposite: Canoes meeting M.S. *Chr. Bjelland,* Rapa Iti.

Top: Thor Heyerdahl Jr. (in front), Edwin N. Ferdon, Eduardo Sanchez, and Captain Arne Hartmark, with two locals dragging something across the lagoon, Rapa Iti.

Top: Tiki Makii Tau'a Pepe, a unique statue in Polynesia, at the famous ceremonial site of I'Ipona me'ae in Puamau Valley, Hiva Oa, Marquesas Islands.

Middle: Local architecture on Hiva Oa, Marquesas Islands, during the Easter Island expedition in 1955-56.

Bottom: The main statue, Tiki Takaii, at the famous ceremonial site of I'Ipona me'ae in Puamau Valley, Hiva Oa, Marquesas Islands. Sitting on the left is archaeologist Gonzalo Figueroa, a member of Thor Heyerdahl's 1955-56 Easter Island expedition, and on the right is the Norwegian expat Henry Lie.

Opposite: The fort on Morongo Uta, Rapa Iti, after clearing has taken place.

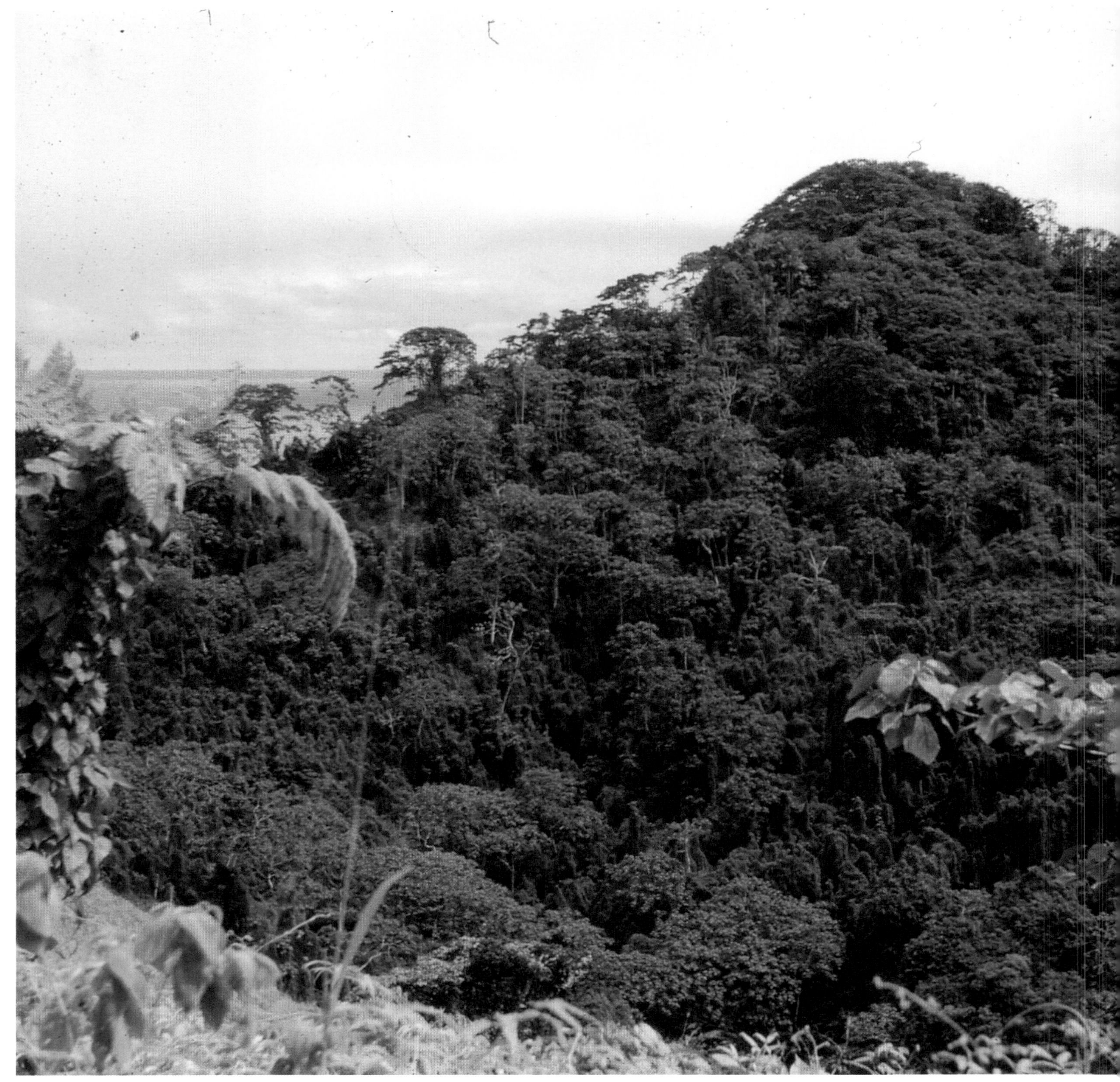

Vegetation cover on Coccos Island, 1956.

Opposite: Thor Heyerdahl with a local on Morongo Uta, Rapa Iti.

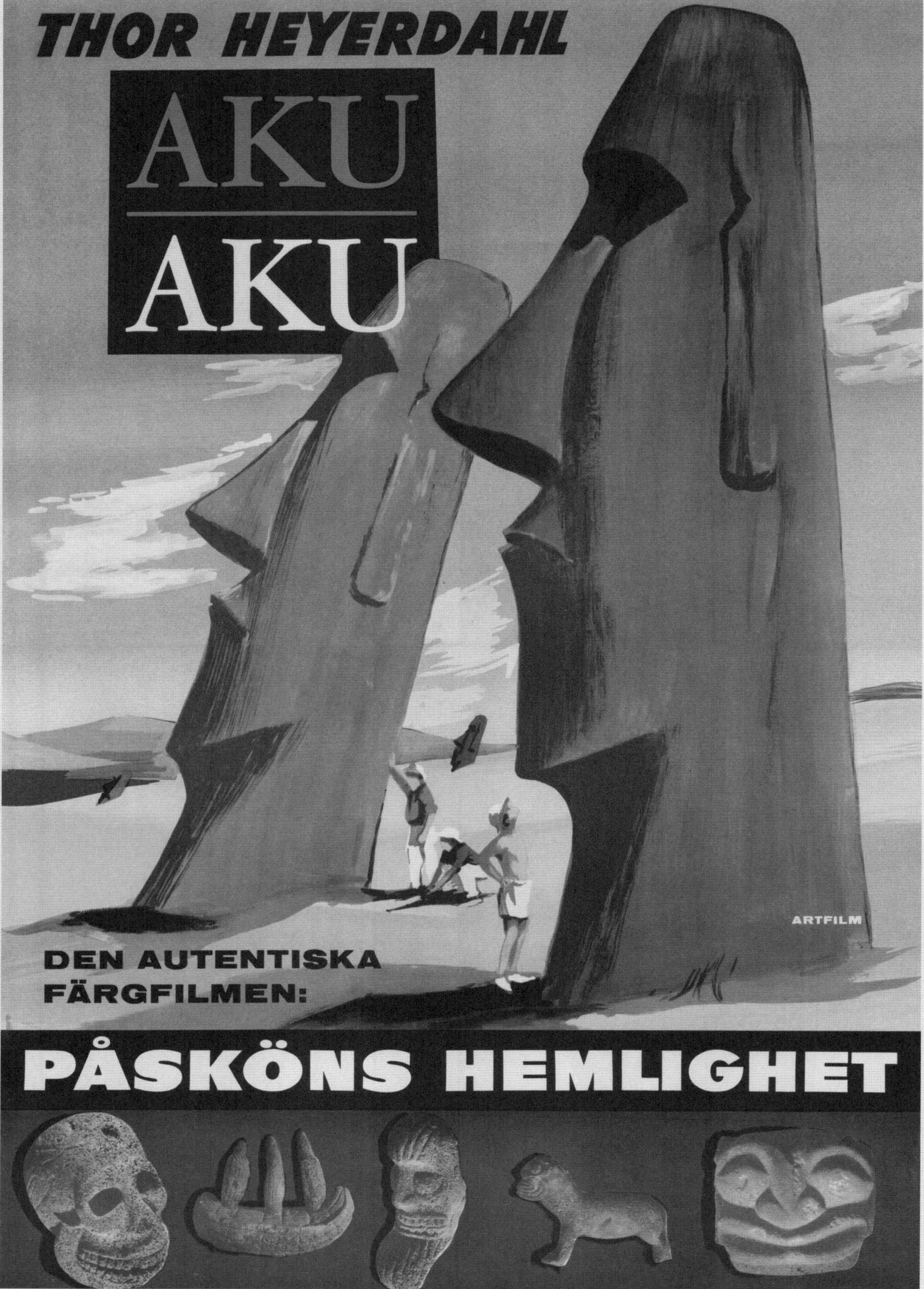

Swedish movie poster for *Aku Aku. The Mystery of Easter Island* released in 1960.

Opposite:
A selection of cave stones collected by the expedition on Rapa Nui.

1962

1979

1677

11157

11012

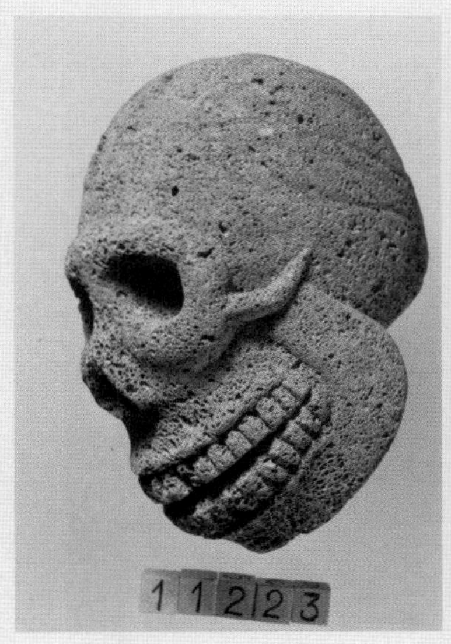
11223

11133

11189

11156

Top left: Basalt stone axe from Rapa Nui, 3⅛ × 6 in. (8 × 15.2 cm). These crude stone axes, called *toki*, were used in carving the *moai*. To resharpen them, one axe was simply used as a hammer on the other to remove small pieces.

Top right: From our collection: Basalt stone axe from Rapa Nui, 3 x 6 in. (8 x 15.2 cm), made by a crude percussion technique. Everyone knows the giant stone statues from Rapa Nui, called *moai*, made from a yellow-green tuff inside the extinct Rano Raraku volcano. Less well known are the crude stone axes, called toki, which were used in carving the giants. To resharpen them, one ax was simply used as a hammer on the other to remove small pieces. Surprisingly, these axes fit pretty well in your hand.

Middle: Stone bead with birdmen, ½ in. (1.5 cm) high, found on Puna Island, Ecuador, in 1965. These particular birdmen are identical to birdmen carved in stone on the high slopes of the ceremonial center of Orongo on Rapa Nui.

Bottom left: One-piece fish hook from Rapa Nui, $4\,^{3}/_{8}$ in. (11 cm) wide and $5\,^{1}/_{8}$ in. (13 cm) high, in fine-grained black basalt. Made by grinding and polishing. Rapa Nui is known for its fine, almost completely round one-piece, stone fish hooks. This fish hook, which was a personal gift to Thor Heyerdahl, is exceptionally large but not unique. Such hooks were probably used in a ceremonial context, perhaps for human sacrifices, which in Polynesia often were termed two-legged fish.

Bottom right: Stone head from Rapa Nui (Easter Island), in light gray or white unspecified rock, 131/2 in. (34 cm) high and 11 in. (28 cm) wide. The stone head has carved eyes, nose, and mouth. On the front of the cheeks there are three rings under the eyes. The Polynesian pantheon had four gods who each ruled a "department" or aspect of life. Hiro/Rongo was the god of agriculture and when the god wept it rained. This statue comes from Rapa Nui (Easter Island).

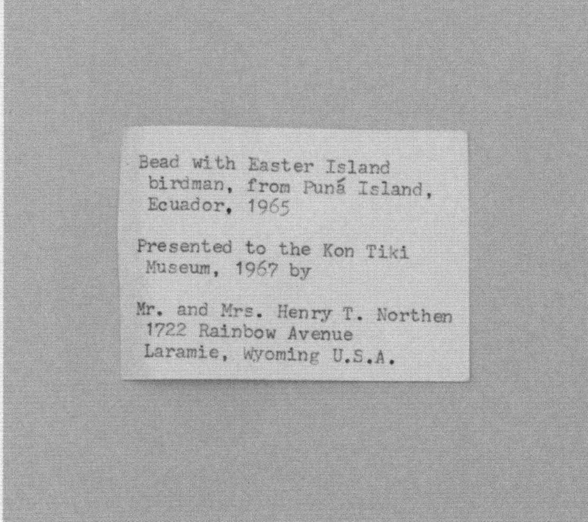

Bead with Easter Island
birdman, from Puná Island,
Ecuador, 1965
Presented to the Kon Tiki
Museum, 1967 by
Mr. and Mrs. Henry T. Northen
1722 Rainbow Avenue
Laramie, Wyoming U.S.A.

Top: A *tapa* beater made from whale bone, Pitcairn Island, about 16⅝ in. (42.3 cm) long and 1⅞ in. (4.7 cm) wide at the head. In Polynesia, garments were made of bark cloth, or *tapa*, by hammering layers of paper mulberry bark together with a flat club with grooves. This item is square, and each of the sides have a higher density of groves; the *tapa* was used to beat with successively finer groves at perpendicular angles. This process made the bark stick together more strongly and would also create a pattern on the cloth. This is one of only a handful of *tapa* beaters made in whale bone from Pitcairn Island. Thor Heyerdahl acquired it on his expedition in 1956.

Middle: Replica of a *rongorongo* board in bone from Rapa Nui. On the small, isolated island of Rapa Nui in the far eastern Pacific, the population developed its own written language called *rongorongo*. No one has been able to decipher this script, but it is probably a syllabic language, where each syllable is represented by a figure. The figures are engraved on wooden boards, where every other line is upside down, starting from the opposite side of the previous text. The reading starts in the upper, left corner. When you reach the end of the line, you turn the board 180 degrees and read the next one, in a continuous line of text. There are only 25 tablets in the world.

Bottom: *Rongorongo* booklet with 16 pages from Rapa Nui, 11 x 153/8 inches (28 x 39 cm), dating to about 1915. On the tiny, isolated Polynesian island of Rapa Nui, culture innovation was greater than most places. They invented their own written script, called *rongorongo*, probably a syllabic sign language, written on wooden tablets. No one today can read this script. Around 1915, a native, knowledgeable in myths and legends, sat down with an old Chilean school ledger and wrote down a translation of each sign and a few local legends in the Rapanui language. This manuscript was a gift to Thor Heyerdahl from Juan Haoa.

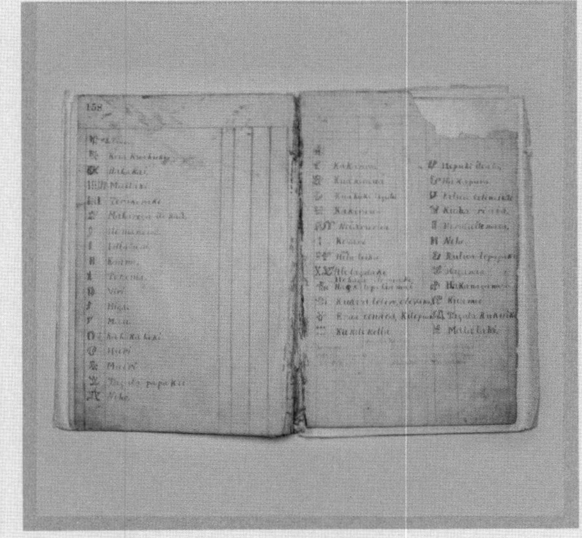

1969, 1970

Ra & Ra II Expeditions

“I wanted to find out if a reed boat could make the journey to America.”

"Two hundred thousand reeds flutter in the wind. A whole meadow billows like a green cornfield along the shore. We cut it down. We tie it into bundles, like great corn sheaves. The bundles float. We go on board. A Russian, an African, a Mexican, an Egyptian, an American, an Italian, and myself, a Norwegian, with a monkey and a lot of clucking hens. We are off to America."[1] Remarkably, Heyerdahl was now in Egypt, an eternal landscape of incandescent sunshine, cloudless desert-blue heavens, maelstroms of ever-oscillating sand, and enormous palisades of golden papyrus reeds.

Heyerdahl had encountered evidence of ancient reed vessels, "tusk-shaped one-man boats, *pora*,"[2] during his 1956 Rapa Nui expedition, and also at Andean Lake Titicaca. When he first acquired knowledge of their employment throughout the Incan Empire, from the Pacific coast of Peru northward to Mexico and California, at the time he had considered such watercraft largely novel. "One usually thinks of reed and straws as exceptionally fragile, delicate things," he declared. "One clings to them, figuratively, when all else has failed. One does not put to sea on flower stalks of one's own free will."[3]

Heyerdahl had discarded reed vessels from his thoughts, content with balsa-wood rafts, until 1965, when visiting Egypt's Valley of the Kings. He was astounded to find several remarkable wall paintings depicting reed vessels which bore an extraordinary resemblance, in his mind, to those illustrated upon ancient northern Peruvian ceramic jars. Pharaonic tomb paintings also included ancestor-worshipping depictions of the divine sun god, Ra, sailing upon crescent-shaped, upswept vessels, accompanied by entourages of bird-headed figures. Recalling the illustrations and stone monoliths he encountered some ten years before on Rapa Nui, Heyerdahl immediately began to formulate hypotheses around these "strange parallels"—mythological and astronomical continuities and comparable pyramidic structures, which evidenced simultaneous arrival at almost identical conclusions even across vastly distant lands.

Heyerdahl's hypothesis was further encouraged by American archaeologist John Howland Rowe's January 1966 article, "Diffusionism in Archaeology." Rowe was an intractable cultural isolationist but, nevertheless, he had identified some 60 remarkable cultural parallels between ancient Egyptian and Peruvian civilizations—with reed vessels constituting one of these astounding similarities, which, Rowe believed, developed independently of one another due to the seemingly unnavigable oceans between them. Indeed, in 1925 eminent American anthropologist Dr. Franz Boas had declared, "on the Atlantic side the broad expanse of water made immigration impossible,"[4] a pronouncement long held as gospel by the international anthropological community.

While believing that transatlantic mariners must have transplanted wooden shipbuilding knowledge to South America, Heyerdahl also recognized that archaeological evidence of such wooden vessels was paradoxically absent on that continent, nevertheless remained unconvinced that transatlantic voyages upon reed vessels across the Atlantic Ocean were unachievable. "Plank-built ships were known on only one side of the Atlantic [the eastern coast]," he wrote, "but reed vessels were known on both."[5] Observing that such reed vessels were once employed throughout numerous Mediterranean islands, as well as coastal Morocco and in Mexico, Heyerdahl noted that the distance between these nations were "not as startingly absurd as the distance between the farthest points, Egypt and Peru,"[6] but he also reasoned that these vessels could have conceivably voyaged across the Atlantic Ocean. Ancient Egyptian sailors had once navigated the placid waters of the Nile River upon similarly constructed papyrus vessels before developing magnificent boats from dovetailed wooden planks. He wondered therefore whether such antecedent reed vessels were capable of voyages far beyond the Nile Delta.

Heyerdahl was fascinated by the speculation that the ancient Egyptians had transplanted their culture to distant lands and continents, including South America; however, he possessed no conclusive evidence for such a theory—unlike in the case of his Pacific migration theory, which had been substantiated, to some extent, by *Kon-Tiki*'s successful Polynesian voyage. Heyerdahl was eager to discover whether "the ancient Egyptians had originally been able boatbuilders and seafarers" and whether "a reed boat could withstand a sea voyage of 250 miles [155 km], the distance from Egypt to Lebanon,"[7] from where the Phoenicians had, scholars believed, sailed to the Nile Valley to gather papyrus reeds for vessel construction. What's more, Heyerdahl wanted to know whether "a reed boat would be able to sail even farther, even from one continent to another," which would offer evidence regarding just who may have conceivably been the first seafarers to reach the American continent.

Fascinated by the population of continental America, Heyerdahl had always accepted the conventional migration hypothesis that nomadic hunter-gatherers had once crossed the Bering Strait—which is just 51 miles (32 km) wide at the narrowest and separates the Pacific and Arctic oceans, as well as the continents of Asia and North America—and that they gradually migrated southward, populating North, Central, and South America. However, Columbus's and subsequent Spanish and Portuguese explorers' landfall at Mexico and Peru elicited no surprise from indigenous peoples. Instead, Spanish explorers "were not received as 'discoverers' but as voyagers repeating an ocean crossing held to have been achieved long before by culture bearers who had come to their forefathers at the dawn of traditional history."[8] Indeed, Heyerdahl believed that at least two—if not three or four—waves of migrations to the Americas had taken place before Columbus landed.

Fascinated Spanish explorers, erroneously believing they had circumnavigated the world, reaching the extraordinary civilizations of distant India, now encountered advanced civilizations, such as the Aztecs, with literate populations producing paper books, advancing scholarship in the fields of astronomy, geography, history, and medicine, and with accurate calendar systems and surgical advancements. What's more, they lived within structured societies of developed metropolises with aqueducts, waste management systems, schools, observatories, elaborate palaces, pyramidical temples and monolithic tomb monuments, vast marketplaces, and sturdy adobe houses constructed from sun-baked clay bricks arranged along planned city streets. Inhabitants produced remarkable textiles upon sophisticated looms, ceramic artifacts equal to those manufactured in the Old World and elaborate jewelry superior in execution, while artificially irrigated and terraced fields ensured superabundant cultivated fruits, vegetables, medicinal plants, and cotton plants.

"Who discovered whom?" Heyerdahl wondered. "Those who were standing on the shore watching the ships arrive from beyond the eastern horizon, or those who were standing on the decks spotting people ashore as land emerged from the western haze?"[9] Within several devastating decades, Heyerdahl lamented, the extraordinary, dynamic American civilizations Columbus encountered were largely annihilated by the conquistadors' avarice, missionary zealousness, and colonial disease. "What had really happened in Mexico and Peru before Columbus and followers had turned up America?" he speculated. "Was the ignorant Stone Age man from the Arctic tundra alone responsible for planting the seeds of all that the Spaniards found?" Or had their descendants "received voyagers who landed in the Gulf of Mexico in the morning of time, when civilization also spread from Africa and Asia Minor up to the coasts of barbaric Europe?"[10]

Archaeological excavations conducted in South America had failed to evidence local development of the extraordinary civilizations that had appeared there, and Heyerdahl speculated that importation of such cultures may have occurred from elsewhere. Where and when, however, remained unanswered questions. Late-19th century New Zealand ethnologist Percy Smith had first speculated that contact might have occurred between Egypt, South America, and Polynesia. Was ancient Pharaonic Egypt the original source of Central and South American cultural importations: sun gods, reed vessels, bird-headed men, masterful architecture, creation mythologies, and linguistic parallels could all be found, improbably, between Rapa Nui, Peru, and Egypt. "Perhaps it was there [Rapa Nui], geographically speaking, that the history of reed boats had finally come to an end."[11]

Envisaging another practicable experiment, Heyerdahl resolved now to construct his own papyrus vessel as an accurate scale reproduction of ancient Egyptian vessels depicted in sketches, photographs, and tomb wall paintings. "I wanted to find out if a reed boat could make the journey to America."[12] To that end, Heyerdahl resolved to commission a group of indigenous Buduma carpenters from Chad, who still constructed similar vessels, to revive "a boatbuilder's art which the Pharoah Cheops and his generation were already beginning to abandon at the time when they ordered the building of those mighty forms, those pyramids."[13] "A paper boat" scholars from Cairo's Papyrus Institute pejoratively declared. "What reason had I to think such a craft could be used outside the Nile Delta?"[14] Heyerdahl wondered.

→»»

Journeying to Fort Lamy on 26 April 1968, the capital of the recently independent Chad Republic, Heyerdahl sought to visit the enormous, 10,000 square-mile (3,860-km^2) Lake Chad. Such an expedition was an exceedingly arduous undertaking, because the country at that time lacked an extensive internal transportation infrastructure, while the lake's ever-metamorphosing dimensions and geographical location remained imprecise, impeding ready access. The reed vessels, which were constructed upon the papyrus-suffused shores of Lake Chad from floating reed islands resembling "thick bouquet[s] of bristly golden papyrus flowers,"[15] possessed remarkable resemblances to the reed vessels Heyerdahl encountered across South America, Rapa Nui, and the Gulf of Mexico. Anthropologists hypothesized that Chad's population had partial origins in the Upper Nile Valley, suggesting that the reed-vessel craftsmanship preserved within the vast continent's isolated interior was once employed throughout ancient Egypt and that their ancestors, journeying southwestward, had long ago transplanted traditional *kaday* construction practices to Central Africa.

Heyerdahl undertook the onerous day's journey along the Sahara's southern frontier, where "sand lay like snow on bare mountainsides … over low, rolling crests and hollows in the landscape, where only sparse desert scrub broke the sun-drenched infinity of sand,"[16] to Lake Chad, where the celestially beautiful lake was "shining like cold steel … behind a belt of sappy spring-green papyrus reeds,"[17] a miraculous, near-illusional oasis. Along with two expedition photographers, Michel and Gianfranco, Heyerdahl now encountered Lake Chad's papyrus vessels, "mirrored in the lake and the reflection, sailing upside down, reminded me of those other reed boats which now actually were sailing upside down … on the other side of the globe, on Lake Titicaca."[18]

After an audience with Sultan M'Bodou M'Bami, Heyerdahl was introduced to two Buduma fishermen, Omar M'Bulu and Mussa Bulumi, who would be able to provide him with a practical education in the millennia-old construction of reed vessels, or *kaday.* M'bulu and Bulumi, aided by two other Buduma tribesmen, scythed large masses of 6-foot (1.8-m) tall green papyrus reeds from the lakeshore, then began weaving individual reeds together by splitting them lengthwise into four parts, inserting additional reeds into these four junctures, entwining the porous fibers, and binding them inextricably together with handwoven ropes made from durable white palm fibers. Eventually, they created an increasingly larger bound, tapering papyrus bundle, which was then bent in the center, trampled upon, and curved to resemble "a huge elephant tusk."[19] With this bundle now forming an upswept prow, two additional reed bundles were bound to the center bundle and the superfluous reed lengths cut with machetes to create the vessel's "thick, flat, sawn-off stern." M'bulu and Bulumi's *kaday,* some 12 feet (3.6 m) in length and constructed over the course of one laborious day, was now ready for sailing upon Lake Chad.

Heyerdahl, preparing to embark upon an inaugural *kaday* voyage, now serendipitously encountered a carpenter, Abdullah Djibrine, who offered to act as a translator, as he was able to speak both Arabic and French. Heyerdahl immediately accepted, noting "How else was I to learn anything from Omar and Mussa when the three of us were out on the lake in the little vegetable boat?"[20] Heyerdahl passed an entire day aboard the rapidly constructed *kaday,* marveling at the vessel's buoyancy, loading capacity, and durability. After Djibrine accompanied him across the placid waters of Lake Chad, he would later become instrumental to another of Heyerdahl's papyrus vessel voyages—across the vast Atlantic Ocean. Several days passed before Central Africa finally evaporated away beneath Heyerdahl's airplane, as the expedition returned northeastward to Egypt, with "jungle and desert … blinding sun and our own giant aircraft casting the racing shadow of the twentieth century over the Sahara."[21]

⟿

"To build a reed boat you must have reeds. I needed papyrus reeds," Heyerdahl declared, "Where would I find them?"[22] Reed-vessel construction, he surmised, necessitated wading into the vast papyrus fenlands along the Nile's shores, like Pharaoh's aides would have, to gather fresh reeds. However, voyaging back and forth along the Nile upon camel and horseback, automobile, train, weather-beaten fishing vessels, and freighters, he saw that the once-plentiful papyrus reeds no longer grew in abundance on the antediluvian riverbanks. "No papyrus grows in Egypt now," Georges Sourial, an Egyptian chemical engineer and champion free diver (who would later also accompany Heyerdahl across the Atlantic Ocean), assured him. Papyrus had disappeared from Egypt sometime in the late 19th century, simultaneously erasing the masterful construction knowledge of the old Nile River navigators. Heyerdahl required enormous quantities of papyrus for the construction of any large-scale vessel. However, although papyrus may not have survived in Egypt, elsewhere along the Nile, abundant sheaves of verdant papyrus reeds still appeared.

Heyerdahl journeyed northward to the Blue Nile's ancient source, Lake Tana in the Ethiopian Highlands, the potential location of those mythopoeic Mountains of the Moon and home to a monastery of hermetic, island-dwelling Coptic Christian monks. Flying over the upper reaches of the ocher-colored Nile, Heyerdahl watched the river's turbulent masses of water inscribing "mighty hieroglyphs … gouging … down through the very mountain rocks, gnawing with the inexorable teeth of time … of Ethiopia's mountain landscape,"[23] where papyrus reeds still thrived. Here, Heyerdahl again encountered reed vessels similar to those he encountered at Lake Chad, Lake Titicaca, and Rapa Nui. He resolved to transport papyrus reeds from Lake Tana and boatbuilders from Chad (where he believed more durable reed vessels were constructed) to Egypt, where ancient wall illustrations would inform the reconstruction of a seafaring vessel, which he would then audaciously sail across the Atlantic Ocean.

⟿

"Archaeologists say that papyrus boats can never have sailed beyond the mouth of the Nile because papyrus dissolves in sea water and breaks up in the waves,"[24] one unconvinced Egyptian minister declared to Heyerdahl, who had returned to Cairo. The minister shared both the president of the Egyptian Papyrus Institute and the Cairo Museum director's immense skepticism. "That is exactly what we want to test in practice," Heyerdahl replied. He himself had witnessed the papyrus reed vessels in operation and was also convinced by the seaworthiness of Peru's totora reed vessels, making him, therefore, somewhat assured of the papyrus reed's natural buoyancy and durability. Heyerdahl, however, did deliberate. Scientists, scholars, Coptic Christian monks, and the Laki people of Iran all believed that papyrus vessels retained a maximum of 14 days' buoyancy in calm, fresh water. Would papyrus reeds fatally absorb seawater at greater rates than that of the South American totora reed when at sea?

Regardless, compelled by an enthusiastic letter from Abdullah Djibrine that expressed his readiness to construct an enormous *kaday* with Omar and Mussa, who "knew more about the floating capacity of papyrus than all the scholars in the world,"[25] Heyerdahl resolved to implement his somewhat quixotic plan. That evening, he telegrammed a resourceful Italian merchant in Addis Ababa, Ethiopia, who ordered his laborers to harvest 5,000 cubic feet (140 m^3) of papyrus reeds from the western shores of Lake Tana. These were sheaved, sun-dried, and transported 450 miles (725 km) across the Ethiopian mountains, northward to the Red Sea, along the Suez Canal, then across Egypt to Cairo, where construction would commence. When completed, Heyerdahl's papyrus vessel would be transported to the Moroccan coastline, from where the expedition would voyage forth toward the intended destination of Barbados. However, the perilous hurricane season in Barbados typically begins in June, necessitating voyaging from Africa in May. With Christmas Day rapidly approaching, Heyerdahl had only five months to organize the entire expedition. And with only one telegram sent just now to distant Ethiopia, time was of the utmost essence.

→⟫⟫

Immediately recognizing the importance of assembling suitable expedition members, Heyerdahl first thought of once more enlisting the five original members of the 1947 Kon-Tiki expedition. However, not content with merely undertaking the Herculean task his Atlantic voyage was to be, Heyerdahl decided to gather seven men from seven nations for the expedition, each representative of different ethnicities, geographies, and ideologies. His reasoning for selecting such varied individuals was that he wanted to conduct another experiment within the experiment itself. Heyerdahl was well cognisant of globalization's tumultuous force and technological advancements, which forged a closer world in many respects, but also made modern life, he believed, increasingly more detached and cleaved apart by sectarian violence. Declaring that the papyrus reed's voyage would constitute a journey into "the crowded, overpopulated world of tomorrow," he imagined that "a papyrus boat, sailing along in the grip of the elements could be a micro-world, a practical attempt to prove that men could work together in peace regardless of country, religion, color, or political background … fighting for a common cause."[26] Heyerdahl's multinational expedition would simultaneously emblematize his personal social and political perspectives (which emphasized a one-world outlook[i]) and replicate how he believed such voyages were made in prehistory, with navigators from multiple backgrounds and cultures.

Subsequently, he engaged American Navy commander Norman Baker, his translator and friend Abdullah Djibrine from Chad, the free diver Georges Sourial from Morocco, Italian alpinist Carlo Mauri, Mexican anthropologist Santiago Genovés,[ii] and Russian physician Yuri Alexandrovich Senkevich to constitute his papyrus vessel's expedition members. Baker would serve as navigator and radio operator, Djibrine as papyrus expert, Sourial as diver to check the condition of the vessel, Mauri as photographer, Senkevich as ship's doctor, and Genovés as provisions director. Heyerdahl would examine, to some degree, ancient methods of food conservation and preparation as part of the experiment. Rather omininously perhaps, Djibrine, Genovés, Senkevich, and Sourial were all largely unacquainted with sailing and seamanship.

→⟫⟫

After several weeks of logistical arrangements and infuriating bureaucratic wrangling, construction—directed by Djibrine and aided by

Omar and Mussa along with several Egyptian laborers—began on Heyerdahl's archetypal papyrus *kaday* in front of the Great Pyramids of Giza. The vessel, knowledge of which was harvested from the labors of ancient predecessors, was constructed amidst desert maelstroms and a scarcity of water beneath the incessant Saharan sunshine. Heyerdahl's vessel construction immediately aroused national fascination, appearing in Egyptian newspapers and television and drawing vast assemblages of inquisitive tourists, as well as journalists and photographers drawn to Egypt by the Arab-Israeli Six-Day War.

The vessel was eventually completed on 28 April 1969, which was also the 22nd anniversary of Heyerdahl's famed Kon-Tiki expedition. Heyerdahl described the vessel as a large "golden hen brooding on round logs in the sand in front of the pyramids."[27] It was transported first by an enormous wooden sled, hauled across the sand dunes in biblical fashion by 500 Egyptian male gymnasts, to a large freight transporter, then overland from Cairo to Alexandria at the Nile's palm-enveloped mouth. The improbable craft was then carried along the war-ravaged Suez Canal to Tangier, Morocco, and finally to the ancient African harbor of Safi.

On 17 May 1969, the Pasha of Safi, the Egyptian ambassador, swathes of photographers, journalists, and expectant spectators were present when the 50-foot (15-m) long, 16-foot (5-m) wide, 26-foot (8-m)-tall single-mast vessel, which had a sail and would be navigated with two-parallel oarlike rudders, was christened *Ra*—named, as *Kon-Tiki,* for ancient Egypt's omnipotent sun god. Upon *Ra*'s deck was a basket cabin of flexible wickerwork, measuring 12 feet (3.6 m) long and 8 1/2 feet (2.6 m) wide, with a height that would accommodate a standing man with his head bent, within which all seven expedition members would be housed. An open storage alcove, an extension of the diminutive cabin's walls and ceiling, would contain the vessel's numerous baskets of provisions. On 25 May, after the expedition's seven members had acquainted themselves with one another and the reed vessel's buoyancy had been augmented by saltwater absorption, traditionally crafted amphorae of sheep's cheese, olive oil, baked bread, flour and butter, fresh eggs and vegetables, dried fish, almonds, dates and honey, and mutton sausages were stored onboard and *Ra* sailed forth from Safi, southwestward down the western African coastline, into the North Atlantic Ocean, bound for Barbados, 8,790 miles (6,100 km) away.

"We were alone with the sea," Heyerdahl wrote. "Seven men, a monkey [Safi] gamboling gleefully ... and a wooden cage full of cackling fowl and a single duck [Simbad]. It was suddenly so strange and quiet, with only the sea swelling and frothing round our peaceful Noah's Ark,"[28] an elysian analogy that neglected the unfortunate fact that most of the accompanying animals were to be devoured onboard. With day now waning and land completely disappeared from *Ra*'s sailors' sight, Heyerdahl's fatigued expedition, Senkevich excepted, withdrew into the wickerwork cabin to collapse into exhausted sleep.

—»»»

Sinuous papyrus *Ra,* Heyerdahl whimsically zoomorphized, was like a live sea serpent, "a great, puffing sea monster, swimming with long undulations and snarling, snorting and bellowing," the large sailcloth "a huge distended dorsal fin,"[29] accompanying the rhythmic undulations of *Ra*'s muscular papyrus sheaves. Within the vessel, a cacophony of banging, crashing, creaking, and wailing sounded as each wave caused the papyrus bundles to bend, buckle, and strain within their rope constraints. It "sounded as if a hundred thousand Sunday editions of the *New York Times* were being torn to shreds."[30]

Visited by large schools of dolphins and, infrequently, by majestic whales, *Ra* sailed southwestward toward the treacherous, savage rock and low sandbank-riddled passage lying between southern Morocco's Cape Juby, the westward-oscillating Canary Current, and the Canary Islands. The expedition, having successfully sailed from Safi to Cape Juby, had sailed "farther than from the Nile estuary to Byblos in the Phoenician kingdom … as far as from Egypt to Turkey,"[31] illustrating, Heyerdahl believed, ancient Egyptians' ready capacity to sail the coastline of Asia Minor.

After 11 days of sailing, "that timeless perception of eternity that I had experienced on *Kon-Tiki*"[32] returned to Heyerdahl. Enveloped by the constellations above and phosphorescence below, he and *Ra*'s sailors voyaged across "a billowing mirror," over seawater of such transparency they "could see right through it to myriads of stars on the other side of the universe." *Ra*'s ancient Egyptian-designed trapezoid mainsail "turn[ed] the calendar back thousands of years … silhouettes of sails like these are not seen against the sky of today … We were living at a time when the earth was still large and flat and full of unknown seas and continents, when time was the common prerogative."[33]

"What a phenomenal boat-building material!"[34] Heyerdahl declared of the papyrus reeds on 31 May, having been submerged in seawater for two weeks and neither rotting nor disintegrating. *Ra*'s interwoven reeds remained "stronger and more pliant than ever. Not a single reed had been lost." The expedition rejoiced by slaughtering three fowl for a celebratory banquet, which they ate accompanied with glasses of an orange liqueur distilled by Senkevich as *Ra* prepared to sail past the ominous Cape Juby. Assailed by a storm of several days, including 18–20-foot (5.5–6-m)-high seas, Heyerdahl's vessel sailed hazardously close to Cape Juby's shores before triumphantly continuing southwestward into the Atlantic Ocean, where they lost sight of land. "Good-bye Africa. Good-bye, Old World,"[35] Heyerdahl triumphantly declared. "Despite broken rudder-oars and yard, despite the maltreatment of inexperienced, non-Egyptian landlubbers, and despite storms and waves, *Ra* was as buoyant as ever … We sailed on in high seas which had little in common with the serene waters of the Nile."[36]

Continuing southwestward toward the perilous coastlines of Mauritania and Senegal, within one of the heavily populated transatlantic shipping lanes, Heyerdahl and his sailors encountered indelible evidence of the ocean's degradation. Djibrine, setting out to perform his ritualistic cleansing before prostrating himself eastward toward Mecca, discovered the ocean suffused with endless coagulated oil masses, refuse, and ceaseless flotsam and jetsam from passing freight liners. The Atlantic Ocean had become befouled, an opaque gray-green reminiscent in Heyerdahl's mind of a port city's squalid waters, unusable even for the sailors' superficial ablutions. He had encountered nothing of such devastating ocean degradation while onboard *Kon-Tiki* for 101 days in 1947. Now, in June 1969, they found that humankind was polluting their "most vital well-spring, our planet's indispensable filtration plant, the ocean. The danger to ourselves and future generations was revealed to us in all its horror."[37]

Ra's expedition members, intimately acquainted with the ocean by now, recognized that for shipowners, industrialists, and authorities, such degradation was abstract. Was humankind, Heyerdahl wondered, laboring beneath an anachronistic delusion that the sea was infinite? He now understood, while sailing past whole continents, "the sea is not so limitless after all; the water that rounds the Africa coast in May passes along the American coast some weeks later with all the floating muck that will neither sink nor be eaten by the inhabitants of the sea." Heyerdahl, gazing despairingly from *Ra*'s papyrus foredeck at humankind's devastating pollution of the Atlantic Ocean, realized the profound interconnectedness of the world's oceans and its inhabitants and the necessity for immediate international environmental advocacy. International awareness of, and allied intervention against, oceanic pollution, he gradually believed, remained the only solution to ameliorating humankinds' devastation of our natural world. "We must make an outcry about this to everyone who would listen," he resolutely declared. "What was the good of East and West fighting over social reforms on land, as long as every nation allowed our common artery, the ocean, to become a common sewer for oil slush and chemical waste?"[38]

→»»»

By late June, *Ra* was about 500 nautical miles (925 km) west of the West African coastline, sailing directly for the mountainous Cape Verde Islands. Having completed 25 successful days at sea and more than 1,000 nautical miles (1850 km), Heyerdahl's papyrus vessel's afterdeck had become gradually inundated, caused in large part by the expedition's neglect in attaching an essential bowstring between the afterdeck and stern prow. Nevertheless, Heyerdahl was more concerned by the gradual development of "'expedition fever'—a psychological condition that makes even the most peaceful person irritable, angry, furious, absolutely desperate, because his perceptive capacity gradually shrinks until he sees only his companions' faults."[39] Recognizing the expedition members' varying cultures, geographies, ideologies, and theologies, he remained vigilant, from the voyage's outset, noting "our paper boat was loaded with psychological gasoline and the heat generated by friction in the little basket capsule could only be extinguished by the ubiquitous waves."

Heyerdahl focused on how the expedition's seven crewmembers would ultimately survive increasingly intensified interactions with one another. "We were stuck together like seven-headed … twins," he declared, "with seven mouths all speaking different languages. We were not only black and white, from communist and capitalist countries, we also represented the extremes of educational level and living standards … One crewmember could not read or write; another was a university professor. One was an active pacifist; another a naval officer … Abdullah was a fanatical Mohammedan … Norman was a Jew. Georges was Egyptian."[40] Vigilance against substantial conflagration would be of paramount importance to any expedition leader, he believed, aware that escalating interpersonal tensions could invariably effect mutinous catastrophe. Notwithstanding a few incandescent verbal bouts, mercifully, level temperaments prevailed among the seven argonauts, and expedition fever was miraculously evaded because "each man tried to understand why the others behaved as they did," and Heyerdahl credited Genovés' "philosophy and research on peace versus aggression" as being beneficial to all expedition members.

Heyerdahl's argonauts attempted to repair the gradually subsiding afterdeck with several ingenious interventions, including the unanimous decision to destroy *Ra*'s only green rubber life raft, repurposing parts of the raft to aid buoyancy. However, the sailors' desperate measure only temporarily palliated the floundering vessel's ailments: the stern section was gradually being inundated, slowing their westward pace like a lobster tail and the vessel's diminutive cabin was frequently deluged by ocean waves cascading over the collapsing papyrus bulwarks. "I felt as if Neptune himself had taken hold of the oar blade out there in the darkness of the sea," Heyerdahl wrote on 19 June,"Vast forces wrenched the oar… and the whole vessel heeled, while white furies thundered out of the darkness … The sail thrashed. The water seethed. Ropes and timber screamed louder than shouted orders."[41] Nevertheless, *Ra,* now deeply wounded, voyaged valiantly forth farther into the solitude of the Atlantic Ocean, as Heyerdahl's thoughts became increasingly trepidatious.

→>>>

As *Ra* triumphantly crossed the 40th longitude west, entering the Atlantic Ocean's Continental American half and the sun gradually descended into the sea, Heyerdahl remarked that the incandescent sun god himself was calling "our own swan-necked *Ra* westward, ever westward." An eternal enticement for ancestral sunworshippers, the sun's "resplendent lancets which no royal crown could match radiated like a diadem from the sea's edge into the western sky."[42] Elated by *Ra's* progress, Heyerdahl's crew, despite their vast individual differences, continued their peaceful coexistence upon the narrow, overcrowded vessel. *Ra* herself performed remarkably, with each sailor astounded by the "incredible strength and loading capacity of the papyrus."[43] Defying the dismissal by theorists, anthropologists, and papyrus scholars of the bundled reeds' strength within seawater, *Ra,* Heyerdahl observed, was a sophisticated Egyptian vessel "made of first-class materials," much more functionally complex than the balsa-wood raft, *Kon-Tiki.*

Heyerdahl's practicable experiment defied academic experimentation and ready rejection. "Papyrus could be tested in a bathtub," He declared of the dissonance arising between detached scholarship and practicable experiment. "Scientists work in libraries, museums, laboratories—not on the Atlantic, playing savages."[44] Set adrift on the vast ocean, the expedition obtained answers that notably contrasted those advanced within conventional textbooks. Papyrus researchers had anticipated a maximum of 14 days of reed buoyancy before inevitable decay. By 5 July, *Ra* had sailed 2,150 nautical miles (4,000 km), supporting seven sailors, innumerable provisions, scientific equipment, and, of course, Safi the monkey and Simbad the duck. The experiment irrefutably illustrated that reed vessels were entirely capable of expansive ocean voyaging.

Having examined illustrations of reed watercraft gathered from the stone ruins at Nineveh, in modern-day Iraq, and the burial chambers of the Nile Valley, Heyerdahl speculated that papyrus vessels were employed throughout the ancient civilized world, from Mesopotamia to the Atlantic coast of Morocco. He further theorized that reed vessels, depicted within ancient Peruvian tombs, indicated the vessels' construction and employment throughout South America. The ancient civilizations of Asia Minor, North Africa, Polynesia, and South America, he believed, were all entwined by common vessel construction. Were Old World and New World vessels truly as separated as scholar's long insisted, Heyerdahl wondered? Was the Atlantic Ocean truly separated by two distinct hemispheres of vastly varying cultural influence? And was *Ra* herself, in fact, a modern-day successor to ancient reed-vessel passages across the Atlantic Ocean?

Archaeological evidence indicated that ancient Phoenician fleets systematically circumnavigated Africa, colonizing and establishing complex trade relationships throughout the outlying islands and African continent. Had these accomplished sunworshippers voyaged even farther afield, away from the treacherous African coastline, across the Atlantic Ocean, to South America and the New World? Not only had they proven these journeys possible, numerous archaeological, mythological, linguistic, physiological, and technological parallels existed between the ancient civilizations of South America, Mesopotamia, Egypt, Babylon, Assyria, and Phoenicia. What's more, the ocean's currents ensured that even without navigational systems, a vessel sailing from Africa would inevitably arrive in the Gulf of Mexico, via nature's own nautical thoroughfare.

Heyerdahl rejected the prevailing isolationist theories of separate cultural evolution occurring upon continents separated by the Atlantic Ocean—an evolution manipulated within the New World by European exploration, colonization, and exploitation. "I remembered the isolationists' claim that there was an insuperable distance between the inner Mediterranean and Peru,"[45] Heyerdahl observed. "Had I also allowed myself to be fooled by this dogmatic claim?" Had he unintentionally overlooked the possibility that cultures found upon either side of the Atlantic Ocean possessed a common cultural heritage? And was he now dogmatically insisting that transatlantic cultural transmissions from the Old World authored such cultural parallels. "We seven men from seven nations were here on board a reed boat to prove how alike human beings are, whatever their homeland," he declared. "And yet one often finds it difficult to understand that the same likeness pursues us through time as well, from the days when the ancient Egyptians were writing love songs … or the Phoenicians were laying the foundation of our own writing or struggling with sails and rigging to explore the riches of West Africa."

However, Heyerdahl's leisured diffusionist contemplations aboard *Ra* were interrupted by the arrival of July's mid-Atlantic hurricane season, an arrival that the beleaguered papyrus vessel's compatriots met "with devastating calm." On 8 July 1969, a catastrophic storm began gathering beyond the horizon.

⇻

"Never had I seen the Atlantic so clear and so deep as through that cleft in our own little papyrus world,"[46] Heyerdahl declared on 9 July, with *Ra* now cleaved apart lengthwise by the ocean's waves, thundering over the gradually submerging reed vessel. Although they successfully sutured the two papyrus halves together with an enormous iron sewing needle and rope, *Ra* continued to be assailed by relentless seawater cascading over the vessel's collapsing bulwarks, savaging the disintegrating cabin, subsuming the heeling bridge, enveloping the listing mast, suffocating the tearing sail, and debilitating Heyerdahl's unimaginably fatigued sailors. By 18 July, with *Ra* no longer navigable yet still floating toward her destination—"a giant lifebuoy"—Heyerdahl sorrowfully summoned the expedition's members.

Onboard the papyrus vessel *Ra* for two months, and having sailed more than 3,000 miles (5,500 km) across the North Atlantic

Ocean, the expedition had more than confirmed the long-dismissed seaworthiness of papyrus vessels. Heyerdahl himself was satisfied by all that *Ra*'s voyage had illustrated; a papyrus vessel "handled by a group of uninitiated landlubbers … zigzagging the open ocean for eight weeks,"[47] was, indeed, theoretically capable of voyaging from the Africa in the Old World to the New World, because *Ra* was just a week away from the West Indian islands of Barbados.

Despite the enthusiasm of the expedition's members to still continue their voyage westward and mindful of the immunence of innumerable tropical hurricanes now gathering momentum, any one of which was almost certain to destroy the rapidly disintegrating *Ra,* on 8 July, Heyerdahl reluctantly ended the practicable experiment at last. "Sand from the Sahara was raining over the jungles of Central America. And ahead and behind us, clots of oil were drifting from the coast of Africa toward the beaches of Central America. It was to become *Ra*'s fate to travel alone with the elements on their passage to the tropical land ahead,"[48] he sorrowfully declared. That abdication of the voyage would be Heyerdahl's decision alone to make.

→>>>

"I had sworn to myself that I would never attempt such a thing again," Heyerdahl declared, referring to a voyage and *Ra*'s voyage and foundering. "And here I was. The same wickerwork cabin around me. The same low, wide opening out into the wind and the naked world, where savage waves, streaked black and white, reared up against the night sky. Ahead the same big Egyptian sail stood unchanged, set taut on the straddled mast … and astern the slender tail of the papyrus boat soared above us in an elegant curve."[49] "Why a second *Ra*?" Heyerdahl meditated, sailing again toward Cape Juby. "Why was I beginning a thick expedition journal from page one again? Could I answer?"[50]

Persuaded by *Ra*'s tenacious crewmembers, conscious of Atlantic Ocean migration theory skeptics, and compelled by unsatisfied inquiry, *Ra II* addressed for Heyerdahl an unrealized desire to discover whether "we could cross the ocean in a better built papyrus boat, now that we had practical experience."[51]

Before preparations for the next voyage began, Heyerdahl set out to conduct further research with some of his crew. Examining Sardinia's ancient Nuraghi towers with Carlo Mauri, Heyerdahl was astounded to discover the towers' architecture, "an extraordinary composition," was constructed on the same plan employed by the Mayans in a complex astronomical tower, "the famous 'caracol' of Chichen Itza on the Yucatan peninsula." Had, Heyerdahl speculated, "the unknown masters of the Mayan architects, the earlier Olmecs, also built ceremonial observation towers like the towers of Sardinia?"[52] Gazing toward the Mediterranean, "the home of man's earliest ventures at sea, the home of deep-sea navigation, with the Straits of Hercules as an ever-open gateway to the world beyond," he wondered once again whether a connection, facilitated by reed vessels—humankind's earliest mode of watercraft, which had been constructed all around the Mediterranean Sea, in Egypt, Mesopotamia, Corfu, Sardinia, and Morocco—existed between the ancient cultures of Asia Minor, Africa, and Central and South America.

"Lost civilizations. Lost ships," he wrote. "No wonder the prophet Isaiah could speak of messengers visiting the Holy Land on boats of reeds that sailed across the sea."[53] Reed vessels had drawn Heyerdahl to the archaeological site of Lixus, at the mouth of the Lucas River, on Morocco's Atlantic Ocean coastline. He was astounded by the masterful masonry technique displayed at the Eternal Sun City's ruins. Unknown and "almost inimitable … the technique appeared as a sort of signature carved in stone whenever reed boats had once been in use, from Easter Island back to Peru and Mexico … back to the great civilizations of Africa and the inner Mediterranean."[54] Contemplating the ruins, Heyerdahl found the Americas and the eastern Mediterranean drawing closer together in his mind, Lixus connecting these disparate cultures while at the same time halving the enormous distance separating the two civilizations. Mediterranean sailors had, he believed, sailed beyond Cape Juby and away from the African coastline, during the same era within which the "Olmecs appeared on the opposite shores of the Atlantic and set about clearing glades in the jungle. Just when Mediterranean stonemasons were pouring out through the Straits of Gibraltar, the unknown Olmecs began to introduce stonemasonry and civilization to the … [indigenous Central and South American inhabitants] that had roamed the wilderness for many thousands of years."

With Chad engulfed by civil war, rendering Mussa and Omar, *Ra*'s original boat builders unreachable, and Heyerdahl recognizing that the Central African vessel construction method was unsuitable for extensive ocean voyaging, he now sought alternate boatbuilders who were still crafting vessels using an ancient Mediterranean design. He enlisted four indigenous Aymara boatbuilders from Bolivia: Demetrio, Jose, Juan, and Paulino. Nestled high within the altitudinous Andes, upon tempestuous Lake Titicaca, the Aymara, Quecha, and Uru peoples still constructed watercraft identical to those built in ancient Egypt and Mesopotamia. Accompanied by an interpreter, Señor Zaballos, they were to construct the second papyrus vessel, *Ra II*, from Ethiopian papyrus in Morocco.

The prow and stern sections of the improved craft rose equally, with the entire hull—two enormous cylinders of papyrus reeds—enveloped within woven papyrus sheaths that were encircled by ropes and bound about a third central cylinder, producing a double-cylinder hull of enormous strength that was hoped to be impenetrable by ocean waters. When construction ended, *Ra II* stood 39 feet (12 m) long, 16 feet (4.8 m) wide, and 6 feet (1.8 m) thick, encompassing a 13-foot (4-m)-long, 9-foot (2.7-m)-wide basket cabin constructed upon 10 crossbeams for the eight sailors, a pair of steering bridge poles, and a heavy straddled mast. *Ra II*'s design and execution illustrated, Heyerdahl believed, the Aymara people's inheritance of boatbuilding knowledge from ancient Mediterranean sources. The remarkable vessel's ingenious construction was "quite inconsistent with the style and quality of the Aymara Indians' other earthly possessions."[55]

Manned by the original *Ra* crew, minus Abdullah Djibrine and Georges Sourial, who were substituted by photographer Kei Ohara of Japan and ecologist Madani Ait Ouhanni of Morocco, who would be in charge of collecting ocean degradation samples (oil and other pollutants), *Ra II* was as "rigid as a block of wood,"[56] lashed from stern to deck with a continuous spiraling rope, with her cargo concentrated upon the vessel's leeside. Nevertheless, the vessel encompassed numerous "unknown qualities." *Ra II*'s long narrow rope, disquietingly only half an inch (5 mm) thick, was "all that held us together" and might easily "snap in heavy seas." They would discover that, while *Ra* "lay on the water as comfortably as a mattress, *Ra II* rolled so that we could neither sit nor stand without holding on to something." Heyerdahl's expedition would also learn that *Ra II* was capable of extraordinary speed, sailing across the heads of waves, ensuring that sail manipulation proved at times immensely difficult. The uncontrolled mainsail, some 26 feet (8 m) high, tapering from 25 to 16 feet (7.6 to 4.8 m) wide, was "a gigantic flag, battering, flapping and slapping until we expected the whole vessel to disintegrate."[57]

On 17 May 1970, *Ra II* voyaged triumphantly forth into the Atlantic following celebrations at Safi harbor. "I name you *Ra II*," declared Aicha, Pasha Taieb Amra's wife, anointing the "bone-dry papyrus boat" with goat's milk. After just three days at sea, however, *Ra II* began to submerge. Heyerdahl's seven argonauts desperately cast every superfluous provision, equipment, article, and feature of the craft overboard. Thankfully, now sufficiently lightened, the vessel was able to carry on calmly southwestward of the treacherous Canary Islands. Here, after seven days into the journey, the lackadaisical sailors, bathing beneath the golden sunshine, once again encountered constellations of coagulated oil floating across and beneath the ocean's surface. The original *Ra*'s samples and records of similar devastating ocean pollution had aroused enormous interest from the United Nations' Norway delegation, and Secretary General U Thant had asked Heyerdahl to make daily observations on the next voyage. With the aid of Ouhanni, *Ra II* would be able to undertake more systematic observations of the Atlantic Ocean's wholesale degradation.[iii]

On 26 May, a northeasterly trade wind arose to starboard at last, inflating the papyrus vessel's sail and sending *Ra II* past treacherous Cape Juby and southwestward into the open Atlantic Ocean, devouring upward of 80 nautical miles (150 km) per day. Remarkably harmonious, interpersonal relationships characterized life aboard Heyerdahl's papyrus vessel, because all expedition members "shared the same trials and the same blessings … without anyone thinking about family trees, certificates of baptism, membership cards or passports." With the vessel encompassing a formidably narrow foredeck and just a small basket cabin, "we knew each other's swear words, snores, table manners and jokes."[58] There was "no room for secrets. At all times of day and in every situation, we were all there, at the closest possible range." Despite Cold War hostilities, American Baker and Russian Senkevich were now thoroughly acquainted. Although, "If the Almighty did not allow Himself to be worshipped under many names, we would have had a religious war on board," Heyerdahl observed. Representing "a babel of eight different languages," with English, French, and Italian spoken among *Ra II*'s sailors, each argonaut became intimately well-acquainted with one another's culture, nationality, and faith. Geopolitical and sectarian adversarial international relations were supplanted by sincere, individual altruism, empathy, and cohesion. "We argued, told funny stories and sang in chorus whenever we had leisure … We discussed politics, and never pulled our punches. For here the arguments for East and West were uncensored; no one was standing by with loaded pistols … we mulled over the Palestinian problem, the tribal feuds in Africa, the intervention of the Americans in Vietnam and of the Russians in Czechoslovakia."[59] They agreed. "We discussed religion and no one felt a holy wrath. Copt and Catholic, Protestant and Mohammedan, Buddhist, atheist, free-thinker and half-Christian Jew, there was no space for a greater mixture on our little ark." Identifying "the highest common factors of mankind," remained, Heyerdahl believed, easier than identifying differences between individuals. "Whether we tried to understand one another or not, we were packed close enough together on board our papyrus ark to see each other as slices cut from the same loaf." He had noted, "In their innermost hearts human beings are amazingly alike, regardless of geographical location."

A month of largely uneventful days sailing westward across the Atlantic Ocean had now elapsed. On 16 June, *Ra II* once again encountered "an absolute plethora of oil pollution,"[60] accompanied by large constellations of flotsam and jetsam, kaleidoscopic gasoline clouds, deceased marine invertebrates, and crustacea floating sorrowfully westward.

On 18 June, a moderate gale rose, and *Ra II* was assailed by the largest waves, upward of 30 feet (9 m), that Heyerdahl had ever encountered upon either *Ra* voyage. Navigating unrelenting palisades of water, beneath thickened storm clouds and ceaseless rain, *Ra II*'s admirable efforts were nevertheless curtailed by the disintegration of the vessel's formidable port rudder-oar shaft. Cast diagonally into the waves' crushing valleys, *Ra II* was assailed by successions of powerful, engulfing swells, all of which threatened to entirely inundate the papyrus vessel. The storm ignited tensions among the previously peaceful crew, with Mauri and Sourial infuriated by Genovés, "the quiet professor of anthropology" who "lay in the corner psychoanalyzing others while they worked." They were preserved by rapidly lowering the craft's mainsail, casting several anchors anxiously overboard, and installing sailcloth barriers to puncture the ocean waves breaking over the vessel's bulwarks. After several days, the sodden vessel was finally able to sail rapidly westward, across now temperate West Indies waters, toward Barbados, with the incensed sailors' tempers quelled, too.

On 12 July, American sailor Norman Baker excitedly sighted land upon the horizon, to the northwest. Later that afternoon, escorted by a flotilla of more than 50 vessels of every conceivable variety, *Ra II* victoriously sailed into the harbor at Bridgetown, the picturesque colonial capital of Barbados. Heyerdahl's argonauts had successfully voyaged 3,270 nautical miles (6,100 km), over 57 days, from Morocco across the Atlantic Ocean, to the West Indies, and the Antilles, the archipelago that demarcates the Caribbean Sea from the Atlantic Ocean. Casting a long, contemplative glance "at the vanquished ocean … seemingly boundless, as in Columbus' day, as in the golden age of mighty Lixus, as in the days of the roving Phoenicians and intrepid Olmecs,"[61] Heyerdahl contemplated the sustainability of Earth and ocean life. "Would man at the eleventh hour learn to dispose of his modern garbage, would he abandon his war against nature? Would future generations restore early man's respect and veneration for the sea and the earth, humbly worshipped by the Inca as … 'Mother-Sea' and 'Mother Earth'? If not, it will be of little use to struggle for peace among nations, and still less to wage war. Has humankind changed? Nature has not. And man is nature."[62]

Several months later, Heyerdahl sat meditatively at his expansive desk within his booklined bureau at home in Colla Micheri. "Africa to the right, America to the left; the North Pole up, the South Pole down"[63] he declared, gazing at his large-scale, illustrated map of the vast Atlantic Ocean. Rendered as a "flat, lifeless implement, dividing a rectangular world in two," the mapmakers, he deplored, had authored an abhorrent "misconception of the most dynamic, vigorous, never-resting, ever-rushing conveyor that Nature ever set in motion!" The Atlantic Ocean appeared "motionless like the Sahara, petrified like the Alps," illustrating nothing of the immense ocean's ceaseless vitality and astounding capacity to initiate great change for humanity. "If only the rumbling sea could speak!"[64] he implored, for the sea would tell of "unrecorded voyages of antiquity that would match any of those recorded in the medieval age." The people of Egypt and Mesopotamia "bred sailors as able as their architects, and on distant [Mediterranean] islands that formed stepping-stones to the north and to the west they caused seaborne civilizations to blossom … with different languages and different scripts."[65]

Speculating after *Ra II*'s extraordinary voyage upon the relative merits of diffusionist and isolationist models and offering a new paradigm for transatlantic migration in which Egyptian and Mesopotamian sailors catalyzed these seaborne civilizations, Heyerdahl acknowledged that, "I have no theory, but that a reed boat is seaworthy and the Atlantic is a conveyor."[66] Of the countless maritime expeditions undertaken throughout antiquity, he speculated that surely some of these vessels did not break "their rudders outside Gibralter, or were swept off course while trying to avoid shipwreck in the perilous currents of Cape Juby. Did the crew of *Ra* drift to America … because of unprecedented ability in staying on top of bundles of reeds?"

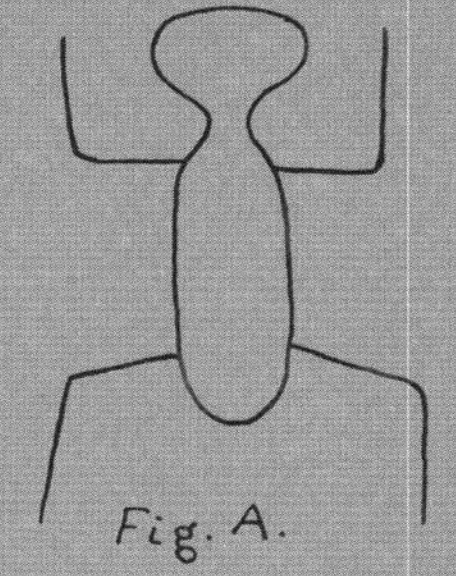

Fig. A.

i Heyerdahl was then Vice President of the World Association of World Federalists, a non-profit, non-partisan organization founded in 1947 committed to the realization of global peace and justice through the development of democratic institutions and the application of international law.

ii In 1973 Genovés attained international notoriety for a 101-day transatlantic expedition he organised upon the raft *Ocali*, dubbed the 'Sex Raft' by the world's press, within which he sought to explore sexual rapacity and extreme violence amongst eleven multinational expedition members.

iii Oil clumps were encountered on 43 of the voyage's 57 days. Heyerdahl presented reports regarding oceanic pollution on various occasions including at the UN's third Conference on the Law of the Sea. In 1972, the international community passed a ban on dumping of waste oil in open seas.

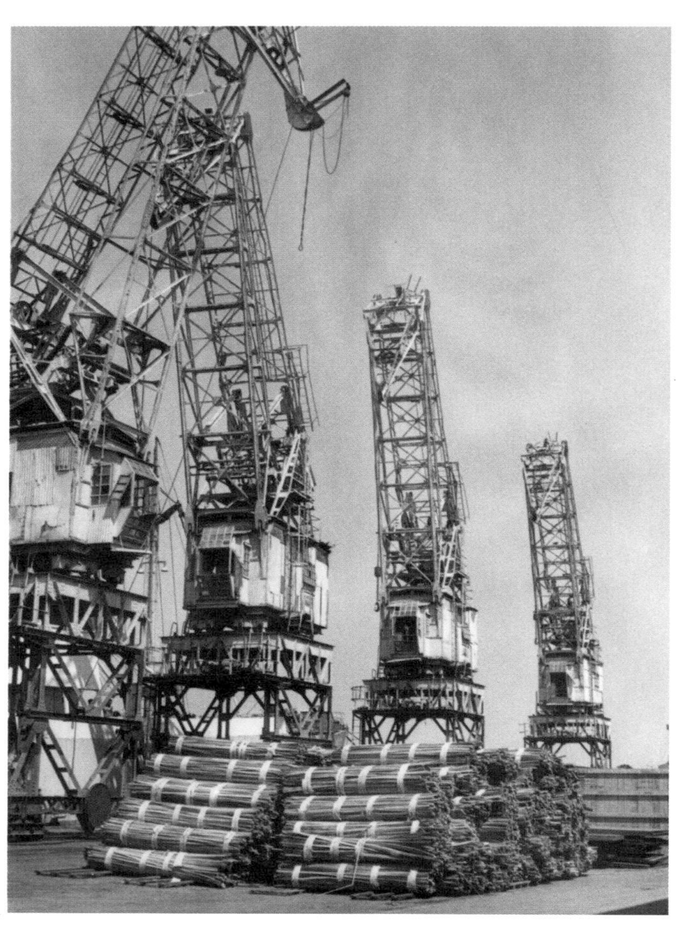

2.50
3.00
0,50
0,50

Opposite (top): The reed for Ra is arriving at the building site by the Pyramids of Giza.

Opposite (bottom left): Ra was built with 500 bundles of reed, weighing 13 tons (12 tonnes), harvested from Lake Tana, Ethiopia, and shipped by truck and boats to Egypt.

Opposite (bottom right): Bundles of reeds on their way to Egypt.

Top: Boatbuilders from Lake Titicaca, Bolivia—Demitrio Limachi, Paulino Esteban, and José Limachi—constructing the *Ra II* in Safi, Morocco.

Bottom: *Ra II* hoisted aboard M.S. *Sagaholm* for its voyage home to Oslo, 1970.

Opposite (top): Having a coffee break in 1969 with Adbullah Djibrine, an unidentified Egyptian worker, Mussa Bulumi, Omar M'Bulu, and another unidentified person.

Opposite (bottom): Inspecting the progress on Ra in 1969: from left, Abdullah Djibrine, Thor Heyerdahl, Omar M'Bulu, Mussa Bulumi, and Björn Ladström.

Top: *Ra* transported through the town of Safi, Morocco, in 1969.

Bottom: *Ra* in front of the Pyramids in Giza, ready to be transported, in 1969.

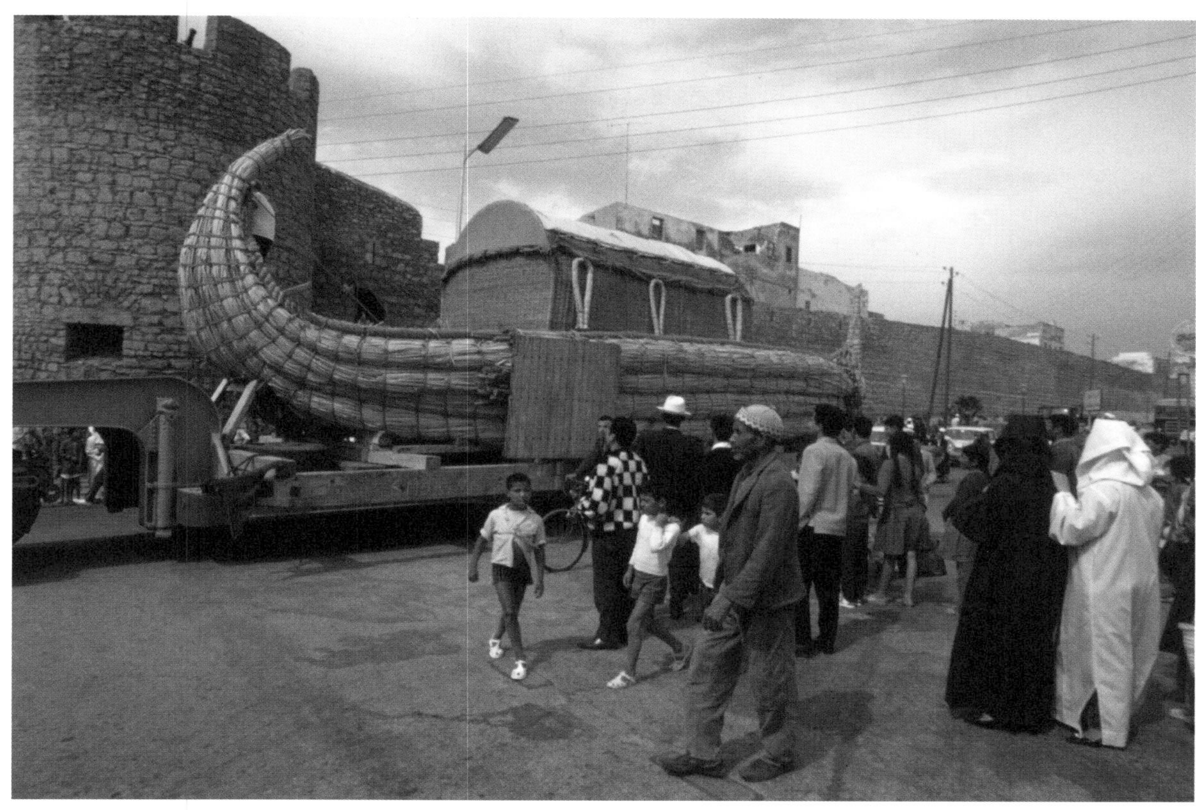

Abdullah Djibrine, boatbuilder and translator, talking to a local beauty.

Opposite: *Ra* is lifted onto the docks from the transport boat, in Safi, Morocco, in 1969.

Opposite (top):
In Morocco with the *Ra* team.

Opposite (bottom):
L-R: Carlo Mauri, Yuri Senkevich, Thor Heyerdahl and Georges Sourial.

Bottom: Running to protect the *Ra* building material of reed in 1969. From left: Bjørn Landström, Abdullah Djibrine, Thor Heyerdahl, Mussa Bulumi, and Omar M'Bulu.

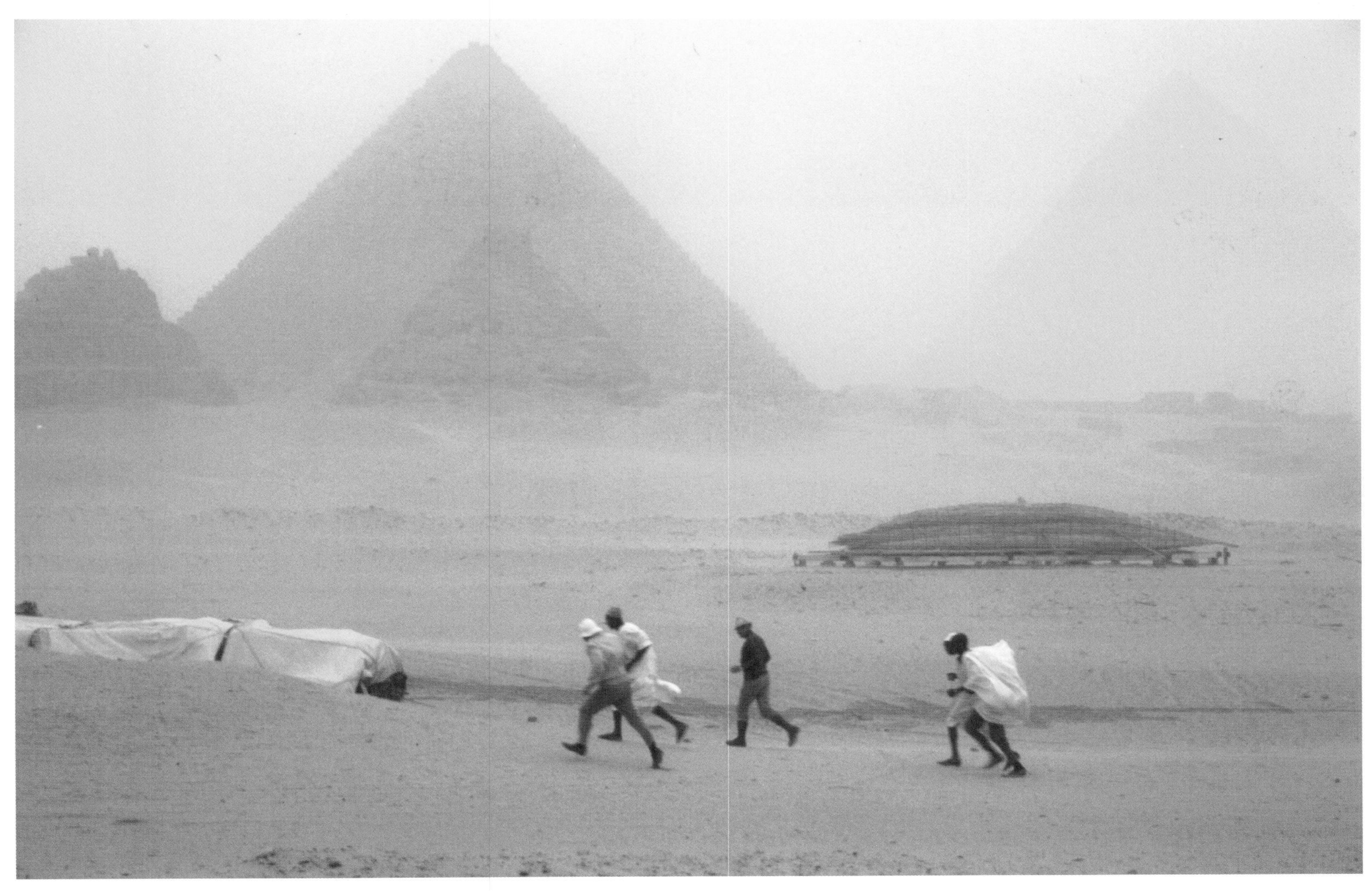

Norman Baker measuring the height of the sun for navigation.

Opposite (left): The deck of *Ra* sinking dangerously close to sea level.

Opposite (right): Santiago Genovés during the Ra II expedition in 1970.

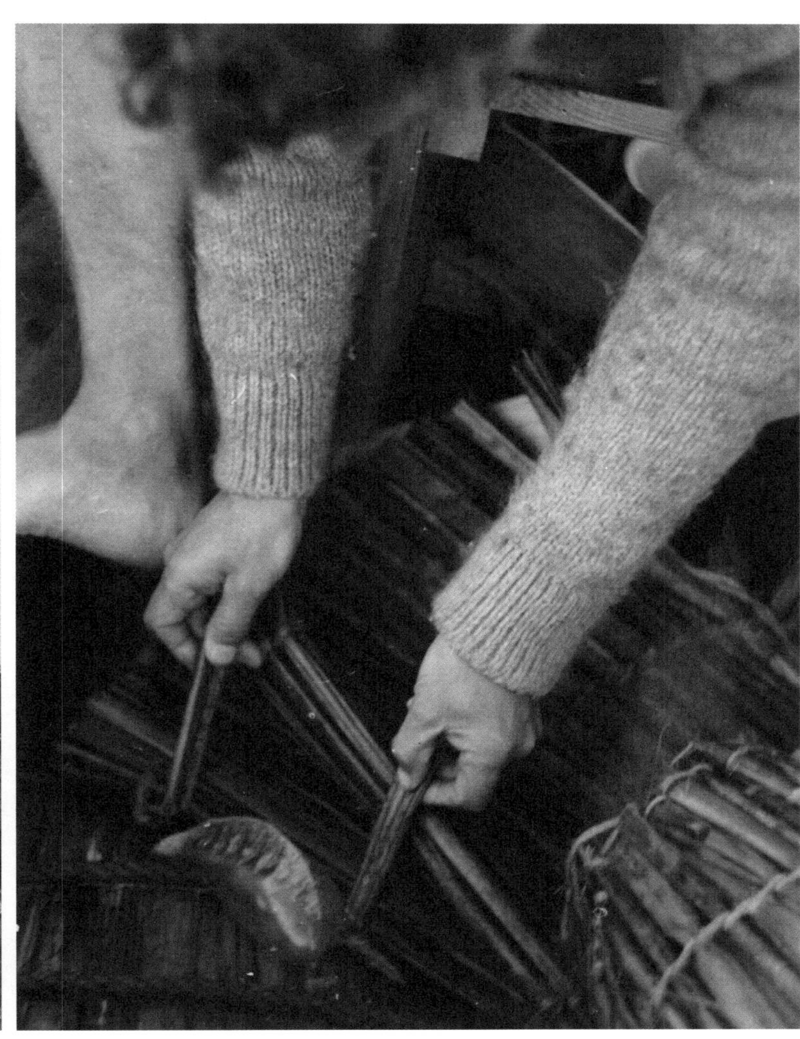

Georges Sourial, Norman Baker, and Carlo Mauri in the process of reparing one of the giant steering oars on *Ra II*.

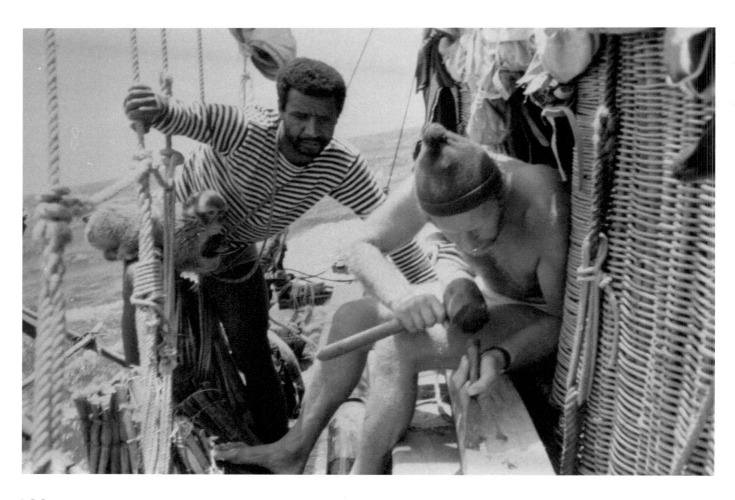

Top: The stern of *Ra II*.

Bottom: Thor Heyerdahl is doing some carpentry on *Ra II* while Safi the monkey and Madani Ait Ouhanni are observing.

Opposite: Georges Sourial, diver from Egypt, relaxing with Safi the monkey, during the *Ra* voyage.

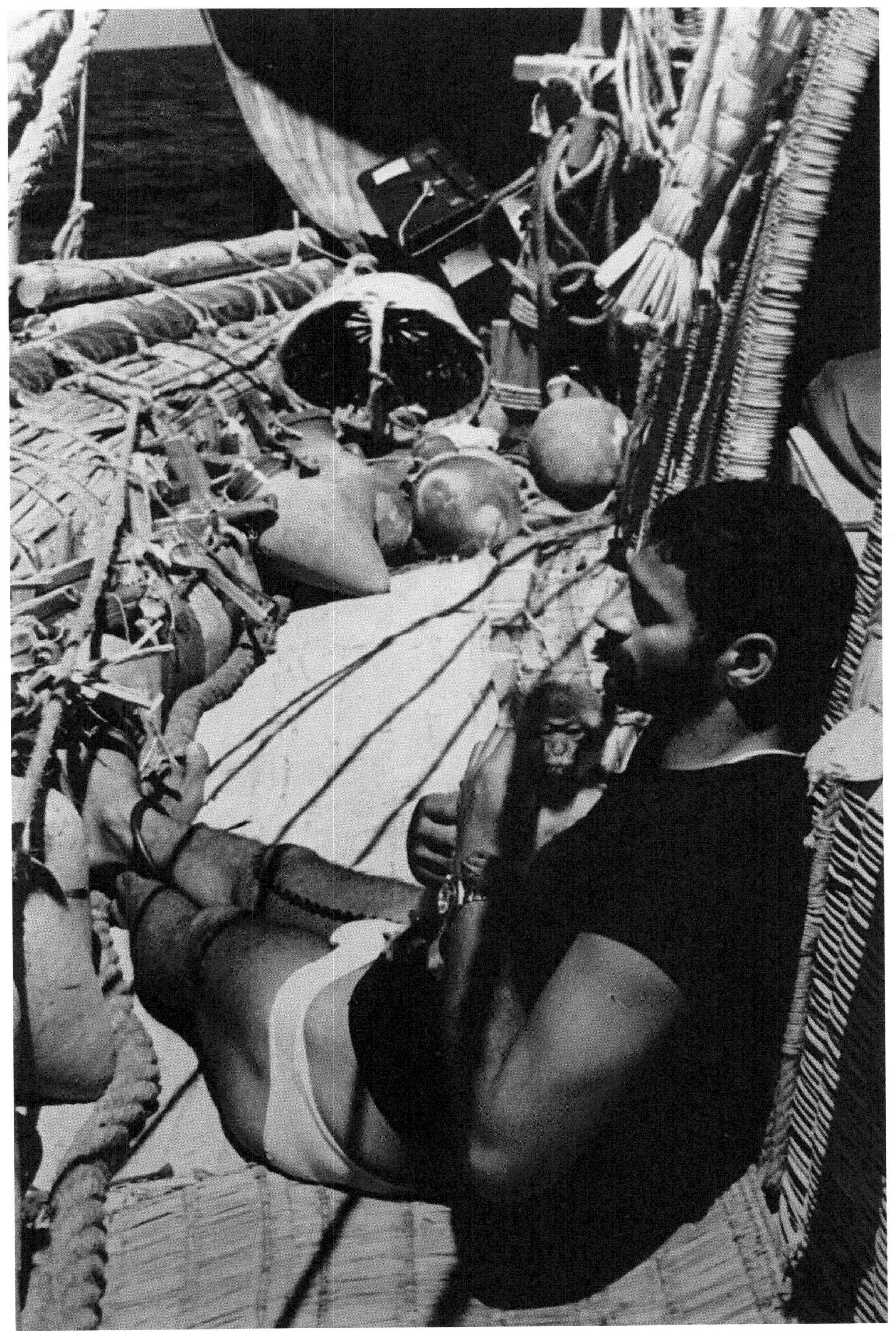

Thor Heyerdahl doing chores onboard *Ra II*.

Opposite (top): Norman Baker daring the waves while making repairs on *Ra II*.

Opposite (bottom left): Madani Ait Ouhanni holding one of the oil clumps found during the *Ra II* voyage in 1970.

Opposite (bottom right): Painting of a reed boat on wood, 16⅜ × 5¼ inches (41.5 × 13.2 cm), from Egypt, in the Kon-Tiki Museum collection.

1977~1978

Tigris Expedition

“Perhaps Thor Heyerdahl will consider a voyage from Babylon to Mohenjo-daro, for his next venture?”

"We now know that the merchant adventurers of Dilmun were sailing the Indian Ocean from the west coast of India to Mesopotamia—a distance greater than from Africa to Central America—at least as early as 2500 BC,"[1] declared British archaeologist Geoffrey Bibby in August 1971. "Representation of Indian Ocean ships of the third millennium BC are few and inaccurate, but we must now look at them with fresh eyes, and speculate whether they might have been of reeds (which grow in such abundance in lower Mesopotamia). Less than three months ago I was aboard a boat in the Arabian Gulf built on the lines of *Ra*, but of palm-leaf stems rather than reeds," Bibby revealed. "Perhaps Thor Heyerdahl will consider a voyage in such a craft from Babylon to Mohenjo-daro, for his next venture?"

Mesopotamia, Heyerdahl observed some six years later, was where "written history began … where mythology began." It is the source of the three most powerful religions in human history, "the spot chosen by God to give life to mankind." It is the site that "most of mankind believes was the cradle of *Homo sapiens*, paradise lost."[2] That archaic region is situated between the Tigris and Euphrates rivers, encompassing modern-day eastern Syria, southeastern Turkey, and Iraq. "The rivers from Noah's distant mountain [Mount Ararat] seem to ignore the scorched landscape of former Mesopotamia throughout its length to overflow in joy at encountering the timeless Marsh Arabs. They alone of Noah's descendants seem to have been blessed with eternal life, while all the great city-states and kingdoms around them have followed one another in collapse."[3] The ceaseless expansion of the desert has eradicated the region's colossal temple-pyramids, cities, irrigation systems, and shipping canals, rendering the once-fecund landscape, "as silent and lifeless as the North Pole," creating "the cemetery of an entire civilization, the oldest ancestor to our own."[4]

Heyerdahl was once again pursuing an enduring enigma—human history's known beginning. After the successful *Ra II* voyage, he examined the ancient civilizations around Mesopotamia, and was, in particular, fascinated by one quality of ancient vessel design: buoyancy. "Practical research into ancient types of watercraft leads one upon many untrodden trails,"[5] Heyerdahl wrote. And that indefatigable fascination with ancient vessels now drew him to the region once known as Sumer (Southern Iraq), "the home of the Marsh Arabs. There began my quest for human history beyond the zero hour." Heyerdahl journeyed to southern Iraq in 1976 to examine archaeological artifacts and obtain practical lessons from the regions' marsh-dwelling indigenous peoples, the Ma'dan. Here, he could return to antiquity, where yesteryear's argonauts were enticed beyond the horizon by "unknown and unforeseen worlds … worlds with plants and animals never imagined …

separated by barriers of wilderness and united by the open sea."[6]

The Sumerian's origins in Mesopotamia, Heyerdahl noted, "begins with civilized mariners coming in by sea. This is no real beginning. This is the continuation of something lost somewhere in the midst."[7] The seafaring Sumerians were believed to have originated from an eastern land known as Dilmun, frequently accessible by Sumerian vessels from Sumerian ports. Where Dilmun originally lay, and what the seafaring capacity and range of these Sumerian vessels were, remained unknown, "forgotten with the men who built them and sailed them, their range lost with their wakes." Had the earliest civilizations that emerged in Mesopotamia, the Indus Valley, and Egypt somehow been in contact with each other, facilitated by the nearby seas, Heyerdahl wondered.

Conventional scholarship held that the Sumerians possessed vessels with sails but assumed their seafaring capacity remained limited to the region's rivers and coastal waterways. And also held that Sumerian reed's rapid water absorbency precluded extensive voyages by the *elep urbati,* or reed vessels. However, such assertions were discarded by Heyerdahl following his successful *Kon-Tiki, Ra,* and *Ra II* voyages. Indeed, ancient Mesopotamian reliefs frequently depict illustrations of vast reed vessels captained by Assyrian and Babylonian legionnaires during Mesopotamia's civilization. "How could this modern verdict be reconciled with the ancient texts and illustrations?"[8] Characteristically, he decided to disentangle the theoretical controversy by a practical experiment. "I wanted to see how long a berdi [Iraqi freshwater reed] ship would float, and to attempt to retrace some of the obscure itineraries recorded … with references to Dilmun, Makan, Melunha and other disguised and long forgotten lands." Heyerdahl resolved to sail from Iraq, out onto to the Arabian Sea, upon a reed vessel constructed to archaic design.

Visiting with the Ma'dans, whose "culture had been proved viable and sound by persisting while the Assyrian, Persian, Greek, and Roman civilizations progressed, culminated, and collapsed,"[9] he discovered, from a sage village elder, Hagi, the traditional methodology for the construction of *jillabie* reed vessels. Berdi, freshwater reeds, were harvested exclusively in August. These were then gathered and bound impenetrably together with handmade ropes, lashed to additional bundles and plastered with natural bitumen, impermeable by water, to create an arcing, buoyant vessel, narrowing to a slender bow and stern. They were analogous, Heyerdahl observed, to the boatbuilding principles ascribed to Noah and his Ark of salvation in both Christian and Islamic creation theologies. Such practices, accompanied by contemporaneous descriptions, suggested to his mind, that ancient Assyrians, Mesopotamians, and Sumerians were all long acquainted with large, highly complex, reed-vessel construction and navigation.

The following year, Heyerdahl returned to the Ma'dan village to commence the gathering, transportation, and drying of vast quantities of verdant berdi in the southern Iraqi sun. The masterful reed-house builder Gatae was introduced to Heyerdahl by the village elder Sha Lan and was "not in the least surprised that I wanted to build a reed ship and sail away into the sea."[10] Under his direction, construction of Heyerdahl's enormous 60-foot (18-m) vessel began in August where the Tigris and Euphrates rivers conjoined. The vessel would "consist of two compact reed cylinders each ten feet [3 m] in diameter amidship, getting narrower as they curved up in bow and stern to the height of about twenty feet [6 m]."[11]

The original Aymara boatbuilders of Heyerdahl's *Ra II* were flown to southern Iraq along with Señor Zaballos, the curator of a museum in La Paz, having recently repaired *Ra II* in Norway. The boatbuilders would, Heyerdahl hoped, transform the enormous berdi bundles "to obtain a sickle-shaped ship that would neither capsize nor lose its shape in the ocean waves."[12] Expansive mats of handwoven berdi reeds, the full length of the vessel and uniform in reed orientation, were placed within a cradle-shaped jig and filled with compacted bundles of bound berdi, creating two large cylinders. Enveloping these two colossal berdi cylinders with further handwoven reed mats, the vessel gradually assumed a sickle form that October, as enormous sheafs of berdi "carried on the shoulders of thirty men, and, winding like sixty-foot [18-m] Chinese dragons between the date palms and stacks of reed, they were carried up on to the feeble scaffolding."[13]

Anticipating three traditional Dhow sailmakers' arrival from Bombay (Mumbai), all inexplicably delayed (and eventually revealed to be unqualified), Heyerdahl's expedition members, now began assembling the vessel. "Our ages ranged from twenty to sixty-three," he noted. "Our nationalities and characters were no less diversified."[14] Three of the sailors had accompanied Heyerdahl upon *Ra* and *Ra II*'s transatlantic voyages: American expedition navigator, Norman Baker, the U.S. Navy commander and construction contractor who was "agile as a monkey, strong as a tiger, stubborn as a rhinoceros"; fellow *Ra* crew member and expedition doctor, Yuri Senkevich, "our robust Russian bear … built like a wrestler, as peaceful as a bishop, doctor to Soviet astronauts," and Italian alpinist, Carlo Mauri, "one of Italy's most noted mountaineers," who was "Latin by temperament" and "could turn from a domesticated lamb into a roaring lion."[15] With them was Japanese underwater cameraman, Toru Suzuki, who had spent several years documenting the Great Barrier Reef's marine life and was now the proprietor of a Japanese restaurant in Australia; Mexican explorer and industrialist, German Carrasco, whose corpulent figure illustrated "no relationship between his body and his soul,"[16] an intrepid amateur filmmaker and archaeological collector frequently traversing the world; Danish college student Asbjørn Damhu and Norwegian college student Hans Peter Bøhn, who were inseparable, resourceful, technically inclined, and physically able, and "as much at home in turbulent water as in a bathtub"; Iraqi arts student, Rashad Nazir Salim, lithesome and athletic, who possessed a sharp mind and was "always eager to listen and learn"; German merchant marine captain, Detlef Soitzek, "an enthusiastic sportsman" who was, for Heyerdahl, "a good representative of post-Hitler Germany," a naturalist, idealist, calm, inclusive, and an unwavering pacifist; and, finally, American film cameraman Norris Brock, who was assigned by the National Geographic Society to document the voyage. These varied sailors constituted the vessel's multinational crew, now an established Heyerdahl practice.

Arduous construction continued throughout October, and in November, "Noah's Ark lay ready to float as new rain clouds gathered on the horizon."[17] Heyerdahl's golden reed vessel, the largest constructed in more than 3,000 years, was now emblazoned along the bow by hand marks stamped by the Arabian craftsman with the blood of six beautiful, latterly sacrificed, now-devoured sheep. After that, in a separate ceremony, the vessel was finally christened: *Tigris*. On 11 November 1977, with the last structural adjustments made and provisions for the long voyage ahead stored, the great reed craft was launched onto the eponymous Tigris River herself. "Let go the moorings!,"[18] Heyerdahl triumphantly announced. "Hoist the sail!" *Tigris* "obeyed beautifully,"[19] he noted, as the vessel sailed rapidly away down the Shatt-al-Arab, the mythical confluence of the Tigris and Euphrates rivers. After several fatiguing hours of rapidly acquired river-navigation practice, *Tigris*'s elated crewmembers anchored her upon the vast tidal river's west bank, acquainting themselves with one another while bathed by kerosene lamplight under the southern moon.

⇝

Several days later, having readjusted her rudder-oars and oar-steering shafts, *Tigris* began sailing farther southeastward down the rapidly flowing Shatt-al-Arab, entering a phase of languorous riverine days, framed by date palms, water buffalo, geese, ducks and *kassab* canes, picturesque villages, gleeful children, leisurely fishermen, and colorfully dressed women shepherding livestock or gathering water. Sailing toward the Persian Gulf, almost a week after their departure, *Tigris* passed the industrial towns of Abadan and Fao, the last upon the river's banks. Polluted cities of smokestacks, radio towers, and oil tanks appeared silhouetted against the dawn sky. The dismayed sailors encountered river degradation unfamiliar to the ancient Sumerians; an old riverside paper mill's thick, near-phosphorescent chemical waste washed forth into the Shatt-al-Arab river, appearing "like whipped cream with streaks of yellow butter"[20] across the river's surface, conjuring, in Heyerdahl's mind, Artic floes and ice flakes coagulating about *Tigris*'s golden bow. Baker would become convinced such chemical degradation had penetrated the reed vessel, damaging the freshwater reeds; many of the expedition members believed *Tigris* now lay significantly deeper in the river's water. "From a paradise of a kind our golden ship had suddenly found herself in a modern inferno," Heyerdahl wrote, with the city's air thick with the scent of oil—the harbor's water, between large vessles and dock installations, was "neither sea nor river water, but a thick soup of black crude oil and floating refuse ... Sumerians would have been horrified to see the environment modern man prefers."[21] Assailed by an industrialized landscape largely absent of life and beauty, Heyerdahl and the other expedition members yearned to voyage beyond the vast expanses of degraded gulf estuary to the gulf itself, "where brackish water would turn to salt and seagulls waited to escort us into the freedom of the open sea."[22]

⇝

Entering the Persian Gulf that December, *Tigris* was now traveling beyond the parameters that scholars had long defined as the capacity of Mesopotamian reed vessels: only the Sumerian's development of wooden vessels had, they believed, facilitated access to the open seas. "Zero hour," Heyerdahl observed, "for marine history and cultural contact by sea were both tied to the ... [evolution] from compact bundle craft to the hollow hull."[23] That evolution, scholars held, determined whether cultures and civilizations, separated by vast expanses of water, arose independently. By sailing beyond the Shatt-al-Arab and into the Persian Gulf, Heyerdahl sought to authoritatively illustrate how, in antiquity, reed vessels may have facilitated frequent contact between cultures previously supposed to have developed independently.

While on her journey toward the island of Bahrain and the Saudi Arabian coastline, *Tigris* became cast unexpectedly westward, closer to Kuwait and Failaka Island, an island of enormous Sumerian archaeological significance. Numerous Babylonian, Egyptian, and Sumerian artifacts had been previously unearthed upon the island, including five stamp seals depicting sickle-shaped and masted reed vessels similar to *Tigris,* as well as three seals incised with Egyptian petroglyphs of a sailing gazelle. These remarkable artifacts suggested that ancient Failaka once operated as a mid-gulf shipping center, engaged in the regular, long-range navigation and contact between Mesopotamia, Bahrain, the Indus Valley, and ancient Egypt.

Heyerdahl became impatient to set ashore and directly encounter the island's fascinating history. However, before the vessel could land, *Tigris* was waylaid by the gulf's oscillating tidal currents and was instead sent perilously close to the island's limestone coastline, where she began foundering in the mud-suffused shallows. At first aided by the amicable crew of a 18,700-ton (17,000-tonne) Russian freighter, *Slavsk* of Odessa, three Kuwaiti dhows eventually appeared in rapid succession, each demanding extortionate ransoms for the reed vessel's necessary extrication, "and waiting like jackals for our disaster."[24] Desperately conceding to their demands, *Tigris* was at last liberated from Failaka's treacherous shallows by the three dhows, aided by *Slavsk.* Damaged from her near catastrophe, *Tigris* entered the rapidly flowing Persian Gulf, where she sailed southward toward Bahrain for essential repair work.

Gazing heavenward at the sickle-shaped new moon as they drifted toward Bahrain, Heyerdahl was immediately transported back to "the days when the great reed-ship builders of Sumer, pre-Inca Peru, and lonely Easter Island shared the tradition that the new moon was a god ship, on which the sun god and the primeval ancestor-kings traveled across the night sky. The ancient Sumerians and Peruvians expressed this belief in both words and in art."[25]

The next morning, the expedition entered Bahrain's modern, industrialized harbor, where they were met by the eminent British archaeologist Geoffrey Bibby, who had originally challenged Heyerdahl to construct and sail a Mesopotamian reed vessel. Bibby's extensive excavations in Bahrain had in Heyerdahl's mind, "proved that seafaring had been a basic element in human society since the very beginning of civilization,"[26] demonstrating that Bahrain was, in fact, Dilmun, the trading center recorded in ancient Mesopotamian inscriptions. Examining the fascinating excavations with Bibby, Heyerdahl again contemplated the diverse phenomena that gave rise to intercontinental diffusions of culture. "At the peak of evolution most civilizations tend to possess ships and be involved in some kind of seafaring," he declared. "We should not be surprised then to find that most ancient civilizations seem to appear without local background and often to disappear again without a trace. We … expect every civilization to have grown like a tree," but, "civilizations spread like seeds with the wind and the current once the tree is grown and in bloom."[27] Rivers, seas, and oceans, acting as ancient thoroughfares, had all, he believed, ensured the transmission of civilizations and cultures across vast, seemingly unconquerable distances, for millennia. Repairing *Tigris*'s punctured hull with palm stems, and awaiting construction in Germany of another enormous dhow sail, Heyerdahl's expedition passed 21 vexed days in Bahrain before setting forth again on 26 December, back into the Persian Gulf, with Heyerdahl's 11 men "as free as man can be."[28]

As *Tigris* headed toward the Hormuz Strait —the narrow, hazardous entranceway to the Gulf of Oman and the Arabian Sea—she was nearly shipwrecked against the towering coastline of the Omani peninsula that rose vertically, 6,400 feet (1,950 m) above the gulf, a mountainous mirage to Heyerdahl's anxious expedition. Encountering the forbidding landscape and "assaulting seas," they experienced "tossing and leaping waves of a treacherous kind never encountered in the free ocean spaces,"[29] Heyerdahl again considered the "illusory" speculation by anthropologists that pre-European voyages were feasible only if sailing alongside mainland coastlines, and that ocean passages remained an impossibility before the advent of 15th-century Spanish caravels. Contrary to these assumptions, in Heyerdahl's mind, nowhere remained more treacherous for navigation than where waves and currents encounter seashores and shallows. Only the open seas and oceans, he believed, offered tranquil sanctuary to watercraft, reed vessels, or otherwise.

Tigris's successful evasion of the Omani peninsula's hazardous palisades galvanized Heyerdahl's expedition's cohesion, the 11 expedition members immediately discarding age, culture, ethnicity, and individualism in favor of common survival. "Anyone acting otherwise," he wrote, "becomes like a drummer trying to play a symphony without the conductor and the rest of the orchestra."[30] *Tigris* battled valiantly against the formidable northern wind before the vessel miraculously turned westward, catapulting the vessel at devastating speed directly into the central double-traffic lane of the Hormuz Strait, then the world's busiest shipping channel. "Boys, we've navigated!"[31] came Norman's jubilant exclamation several hours later as *Tigris,* sailing masterfully across the heavily utilized strait, voyaged into the peaceful Gulf of Oman and the Arabian Sea, the eventual gateway to the Indian Ocean.

Heyerdahl and his crew continued to journey southward along the Arabian Peninsula toward Oman, where a Sumerian ziggurat had recently been discovered, the first of such step-sided pyramids to be unearthed beyond Egypt and Mesopotamia, which was additional evidence to substantiate the intrepid Norwegian's diffusionist hypothesis of Middle Eastern migration. *Tigris* arrived at the harbor in Muscat, Oman's capital, on 4 January 1978.

Guided by renowned Italian archaeologist Paolo Costa, the expedition members examined the half-submerged structure, which was remarkably similar to those Heyerdahl had encountered among pre-Columbian ruins in Mexico. He noted the Sumerian ziggurat had been constructed "in the fashion characteristic of the temple-pyramids of the sun worshippers of Mesopotamia and pre-Columbia America."[32] For Heyerdahl, the plausible explanation was that "the unidentified [ceremonial] structure ... had been built by, or for the service of, the sun-worshipping merchant mariners from the great civilizations... [of Mesopotamia], who had come here in large numbers ... for mining and smelting copper."[33] After all, had not *Tigris,* itself an ancient Sumerian vessel, successfully voyaged from Bahrain to Oman?

In mid-January, *Tigris* resumed her journey into the heavily frequented Gulf of Oman before sailing, at Heyerdahl's impulsive command, northeastward toward coastal Pakistan, the site of the great Indus Valley civilization. Abundant archaeological evidence illustrated frequent contact between Mesopotamia and Meluhha (the accepted ancient Sumerian name for a trading partner in the Indus Valley). Heyerdahl's overwhelming desire to examine that supposition was the impetus behind *Tigris*'s eventual landing at Ras Ormara, Pakistan, by 30 January.

Visiting Karachi, Heyerdahl's expedition examined the archaeological ruins of the ancient metropolis Mohenjo-Daro, or "Mound of the Dead." Heyerdahl equated the complexity, intellect, and inventiveness of that sophisticated metropolis with contemporary society and speculated whether the creators of the city, one deliberately oriented toward the sun, "had either in record time surpassed all other human generations in inventiveness, or that, like later Aryans, they were immigrants bringing with them centuries of cultural inheritance."[34] Were Mohenjo-Daro's founders intrepid seafarers originally from Mesopotamia, he wondered, the city founded simultaneously alongside the Egyptian and Sumerian dynasties, prospering for millennia before being annihilated by Aryan invaders from the north?

At Mohenjo-Daro, an illustration on a steatite seal of a sickle-shaped, cross-lashed, double-masted, double-rudder oared reed vessel—a sea-going *ma-gur* that was remarkably similar in design and construction to that of *Tigris* and *Ra*—had Heyerdahl wondering whether the ancient Indus peoples may have also had access to papyrus reeds. Indeed, while examining Mohenjo-Daro's desert landscape, and the nearby Indus River's banks, Heyerdahl's expedition discovered abundant berdi reeds, the same material *Tigris* had been constructed from almost 2,000 miles (3,200 km) northwestward, at Shatt-al-Arab. Berdi, Heyerdahl deduced, was the material that the Indus Valley peoples used to construct reed vessels which were remarkably similar to those manufactured in Egypt and Mesopotamia. This, he believed, evidenced sustained engagement between the Indus Valley and Mesopotamia across the vast Persian Gulf.

Reflecting upon the Eurocentric and dogmatic isolationist theories of cultural evolution within the Middle East region, Heyerdahl remained bemused by "the desperate desire of so many historians and anthropologists to reserve the first possible crossings of the Atlantic to the Spaniards and the Vikings." There is an element of "religious fanaticism in the attempts by the western world to see America as a European creation, completely protected by sea until the local barbarians were found by civilized Christian pioneers. We should try to be more open-minded," he declared. "The art of navigation, literacy, even the symbol of the cross and the religion we carried to America, we had first obtained from Asia."[35]

Heyerdahl, however, remained completely cognizant of the technological limitations of the reed vessels, observing that his practicable experiments, although illustrating the extraordinary seaworthiness of such craft, also demonstrated their weaknesses. "I had always tried to make the point that though certain primitive craft were seaworthy, not even a reed ship could succeed in doing what the early Spanish caravels found impossible: force an old-fashioned sailing craft eastward along the equator to tropical America. The Pacific Ocean fills half the surface of our planet, and in this unsheltered hemisphere, ocean currents and trade winds are rigorously propelled by the rotation of the earth. In the entire tropical belt, sea and air, set in nonstop movement from Peru and Mexico to Indonesia and the China Sea, are too strong to permit aboriginal mariners to reach America across the Pacific,"[36] subarctic latitudes and voyages originating from the American continents notwithstanding. "For eastbound voyagers from the Indus Valley, China would be the end of the line. Any effort by us to sail our primitive reed craft from Asia through the mid-Pacific island area would have failed, just as it would have failed Chinese junks and as it did fail Spanish and Portuguese caravels."

Transfixed by such thoughts, Heyerdahl returned to Karachi with his sailors. The Tigris expedition had evolved now from an experiment to test the buoyancy of a berdi reed vessel, with no predetermined destination in mind. Instead, Heyerdahl's vessel had pursued the trade routes of Sumerian merchants. Navigating toward predetermined destinations, he observed, had become much more difficult than simply completing long-distance voyages. "We had so far voyaged between the legendary Dilmun, Makan, and Melunha of the Sumerian merchant mariners," he observed. "Across the Indian Ocean lay the Horn of Africa, Somalia, considered by all scientists to be the legendary Punt of the Egyptian voyagers. If we could reach that coast also, then ... we would have tied all three great civilizations of the Old World together with the very kind of ship all three had in common."[37]

Heyerdahl's *Ra* and *Ra II* had demonstrated the feasibility of transatlantic contact between Africa and the New World, while *Kon-Tiki* demonstrated transpacific contact between continental America and Polynesia. Perhaps *Tigris* would also illustrate transcontinental engagement across vast distances, together illustrating diffusionist migration throughout antiquity. In January 1978, *Tigris* set forth once again into the Gulf of Oman, bound southwestward this time, after much deliberation, for the Horn of Africa and Somalia.

⇸

"The philosophers of the most ancient civilizations believed mankind to be the descendants of mother sea and father sky," Heyerdahl wrote that February. "Modern science has come to a somewhat similar conclusion ... What else was there for the first living species to descend from?"[38] As dusk descended upon *Tigris* sailing in the Arabian Sea, heading toward the Gulf of Aden and Somalia, the immutable stars became deeply integrated into the sailors' lives on *Tigris*, just as they had within the lives of antiquity's sailors. These mariners experienced the sense that "only life in the wilderness can give, of time fading away, and past and present becoming one. Time was not divided in ages, only into day and night." Gazing heavenward, evening after evening, Heyerdahl experienced a sublime integration with the celestial bodies and constellations, all long familiar to the master astronomers of ancient Egypt and Mesopotamia, infallible aids to seafaring navigation. *Tigris* was soaring "with our black sail ... among the stars."[39]

Nearly five months of passage upon *Tigris* had offered Heyerdahl abundant opportunities to meditate upon how little information humanity possesses of our genesis and chronology. British evolutionist Charles Darwin's transformational theory of evolution, and the discovery of our civilizations' genesis in Egypt and Mesopotamia, had only answered humanity's origin narrative. Rejecting again the isolationist paradigm of diverse civilizations developing independently of one another, Heyerdahl emphasized the relative inaccessibility of inland geographies as well as the universal interconnectedness of Earth's rivers and oceans.

Acknowledging that "most of the human past is totally lost,"[40] He contemplated how, over the course of some two million years of human activity "between the oldest hominid [human] bones found under the silt in Africa and the evidence of seafaring inside and outside the Straits of Gibraltar only six or seven years ago," there was lacking knowledge of our past. At the same time, enormous geological forces had cyclically transformed Earth. "Ice has come and gone. Land has emerged and submerged. Forest humus, desert sand, river silt, and volcanic eruptions have hidden from

... view large portions of the former surface of the earth. The sea level has altered, [and] 70 percent of our planet is below water." Tectonic plate activity and geological metamorphoses have cyclically transformed Earth's seas and oceans. What imaginable human vestiges lay now undiscovered upon the ocean's floor? And what may they reveal of long effaced civilizations, such as the apocryphal Atlantis, or of the genesis of inland and coastal civilizations, upon either side of the Atlantic Ocean, evading, perhaps, catastrophic oceanic transformations? In our interrogations of the genesis of humanity, were we authoring a fragmentary, inaccurate narrative drawn from archaeological discoveries and cultural observations of an Earth vastly different from that inhabited by our long-deceased hominoid ancestors?

Heyerdahl's meditations were interrupted on 29 March 1978, on sighting the blue mountains of Africa. Having voyaged about 4,200 miles (6,800 km) and 142 days, and after much negotiation with the governments of Ethiopia, Yemen, and Eritrea, *Tigris* was granted permission to land at the neutral republic of Djibouti, upon the Gulf of Aden's western coastline, at the entrance to the Red Sea. Heyerdahl's elation, however, rapidly evaporated when confronted by the humanitarian crisis besieging the surrounding area. Despite "twenty centuries of progress since the time of Christ, the peace-loving moralist," he wrote, "wonderful people were taught to kill each other ... and were helped to do so by the most advanced methods man had invented at the end of five millennia of known history."[41]

Deeply sorrowed by the "unbelievable nightmare of modern war and the suffering of the refugees,"[42] Heyerdahl and the expedition's members resolved to end the voyage, and incinerate triumphant, still-buoyant *Tigris* at the Red Sea's entrance. It would be "a torch that would call men of reason to resume the cause of peace ... where civilization first took foothold," a "protest against the accelerating arms race and the fighting in Africa and Asia."

Addressing United Nations Secretary-General Kurt Waldheim, Heyerdahl declared *Tigris* would be incinerated within the Djibouti harbor as an appeal to "the innocent masses in all industrialized countries ... to wake up to the insane reality of our time" and to demand from decision-makers "that modern armaments must no longer be made available to the people whose former battle axes and swords our ancestors condemned." Humanity, Heyerdahl urged, must recognize "the desperate need of intelligent collaboration to save ourselves and our common civilization from what we are about to convert into a sinking ship."[43]

On 3 April 1978, as the sun descended behind the them, *Tigris* was ritualistically set alight, her reed structure doused with kerosene lantern oil and rapidly engulfed by rapacious flames. As *Tigris*'s majestic mast and sail was subsumed at last by the waters of the Gulf of Aden, Heyerdahl elegized from the harbor's shores before the 11 silent argonauts: "She was a fine ship."

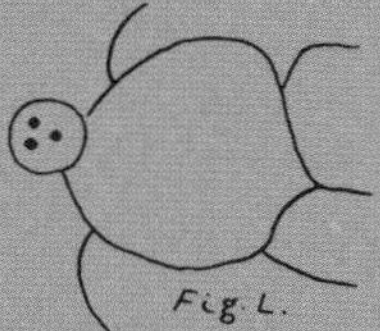

Opposite: In the reed house of village leader Hagi Suelem in Om-el-Skuekh, in the area of Arab al-Ahwār or Ma'dān, or Marsh Arabs.

Right: Working on the world's largest reed ship in the grounds of Hotel Garden-of-Eden by the side of the Tigris River.

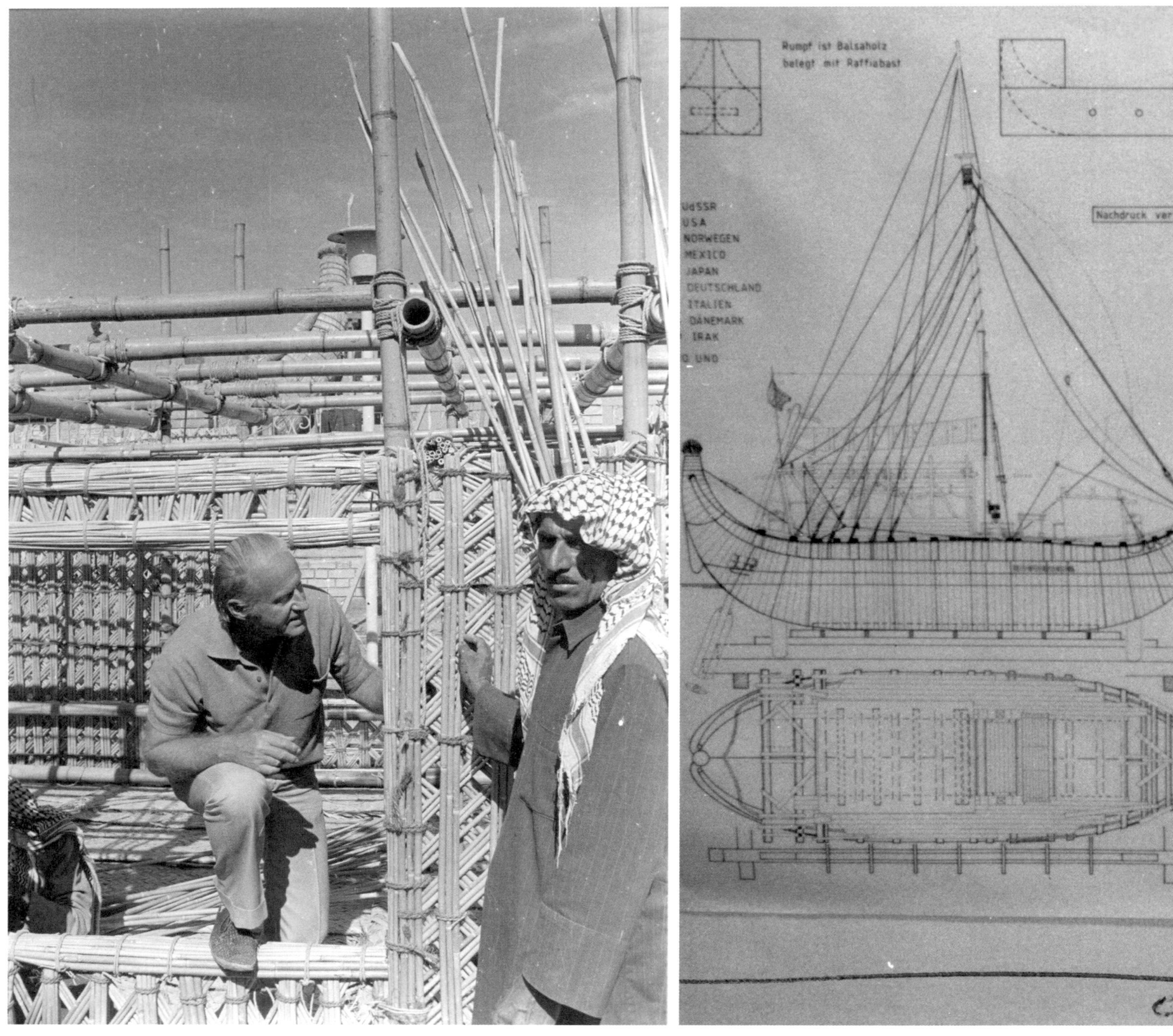

Left: Thor Heyerdahl, with one of the local Ma'dān or Marsh Arab workers, in the hut of the *Tigris* during construction.

Middle: Technical construction drawing of the *Tigris* reed boat.

Right: The crew of the *Tigris:* Asbjørn Damhus (Denmark) and Norris Brock (USA) on top; Rashad Salim and Germán Carrasco (Mexico), second from top; Hans Petter Bøhn (Norway), Toru Suzuki (Japan), and Detlef Soitzek (Germany) third from the top; Norman Baker (USA), Thor Heyerdahl (Norway), Yuri Senkevich (Russia), and Carlo Mauri (Italy).

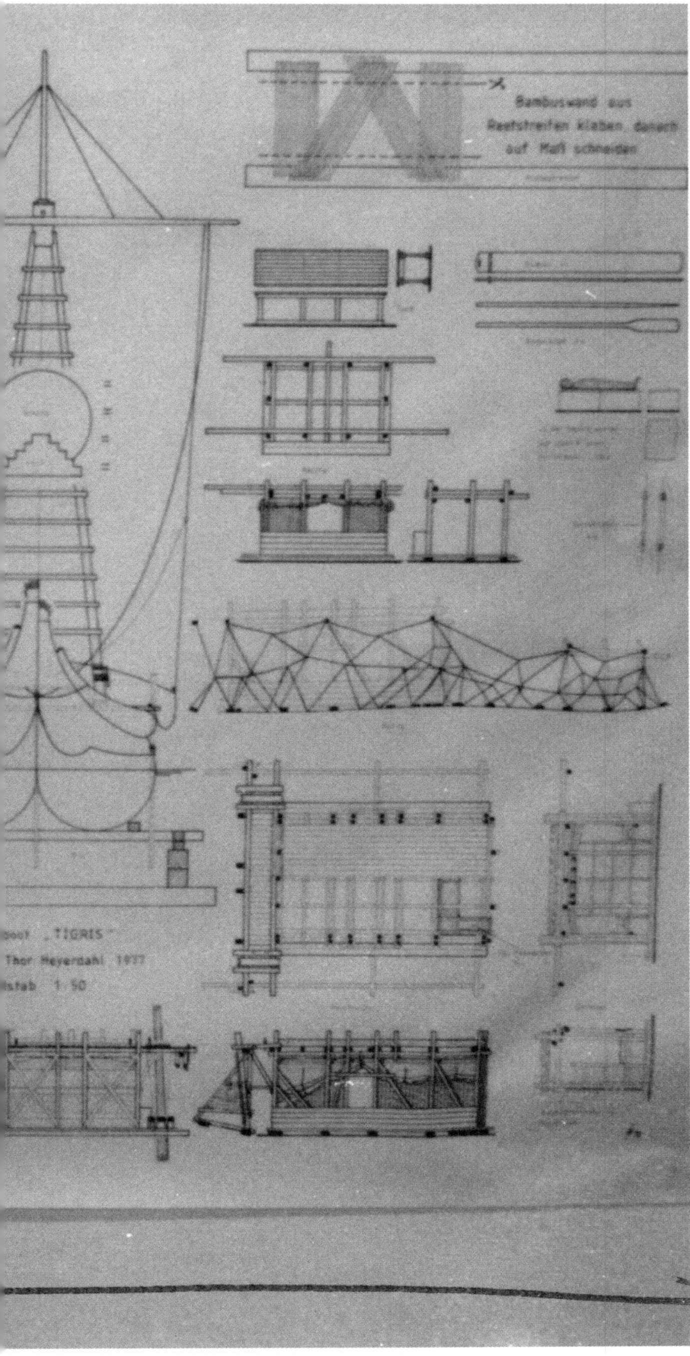
Bambuswand aus
Reetstreifen kleben, danach
auf Maß schneiden
„TIGRIS"
Thor Heyerdahl 1977
1:50

Readying the *Tigris* for ocean sailing with the spare sail.

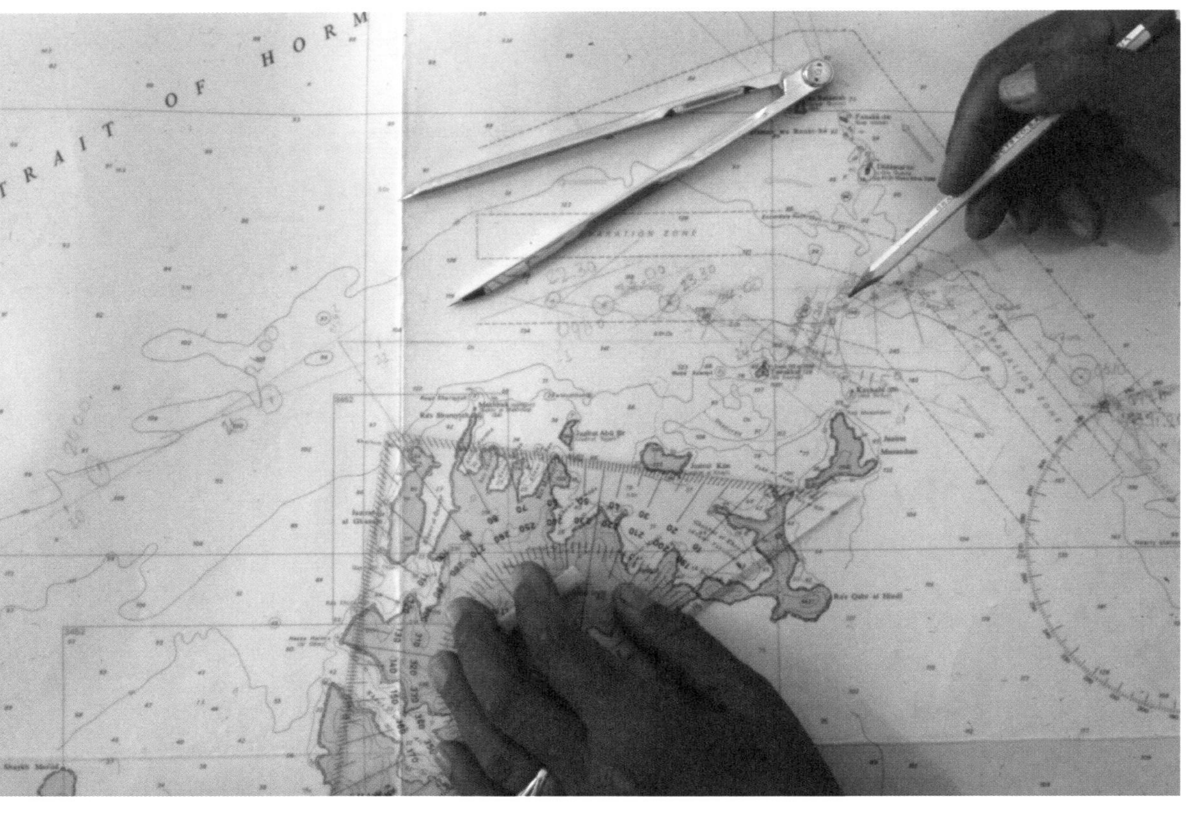

Top: Norman Baker charting their course through the Straight of Hormuz.

Bottom: Yuri A. Senkevich, the Tigris expedition doctor, writing in his notebook in 1977.

Opposite: Asbjørn Damhus, from Denmark, on the hunt.

Thor Heyerdahl burned the *Tigris* outside the Djibouti harbor as a protest against arms sales from the superpowers of the world to small countries in Africa.

1983, 1984

Maldives Expeditions

“The Maldives appeared like a barrier reef, from which octopus tentacles spread to remote corners of the Old World.”

"For years I have been interested in the navigability of prehistoric types of watercraft, and my last experiment was in sailing a Sumerian type reed-ship from Iraq by way of Oman and Pakistan to Djibouti. I realize how extremely easy and natural it would be for the mariners of the early Indus Valley civilization to sail, not only to the Gulf islands and Mesopotamia, but also around the Indian sub-continent. For this reason, I have been interested in archaeology in the Maldive islands."[1] So wrote Thor Heyerdahl in a letter to the American anthropologist Clarence Maloney, one of the few academics specializing in the archipelago. Having first visited the islands in 1982, Heyerdahl found himself called back to them.

"The envelope contained a large photograph" that revealed "a masterfully carved and well preserved" large stone sculpture, an affable "faintly smiling, friendly-looking figure," with enigmatic, elongated earlobes and coiled hair held within a diminutive topknot.[2] Seated behind his expansive desk in Colla Micheri in northwest Italy, Heyerdahl was immediately struck by the figure's similarities to the *moai* scattered across Rapa Nui. Were these colossal stone figures somehow connected, he speculated? However, he immediately rejected that thought due to the enormous distance, some 10,000 miles (16,000 km), separating the Maldives islands from Rapa Nui. "Impatiently I unfolded the accompanying letter to learn where this photograph had been taken," he recalled. "The letter was indeed from Sri Lanka, but the photograph came from an atoll in the Maldives group." That absorbing letter had been sent to Heyerdahl by Bjørn Roar Bye, the director of Worldview International Foundation, who had himself received the photograph when visiting the archipelago. The puzzling head revealed within the photograph was that of "a beheaded ghost" lying in "the baking sun … a beautiful Buddha," colossal in scale and "masterfully carved from white limestone, the product of a great artist."[3]

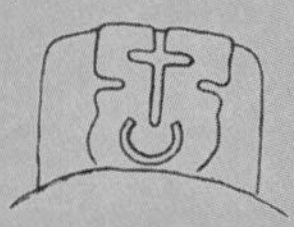

The President of the Republic of the Maldives, Maumoon Abdul Gayoom, had been entranced by the earlier Tigris voyage and invited Heyerdahl to conduct excavations on the islands. Departing at once with fellow archaeologist and friend Arne Skjølsvold, accompanied by the young Norwegian archaeologists Øystein Koch Johansen and Egil Mikkelsen, Heyerdahl arrived in February 1983. Visiting the National Museum, he examined several more stone sculptures, known as *stele*, many of which reminded him more of Mayan works from Mexico and Guatemala or pre-Inca statues from South America than any sculptual works found throughout the Indian Ocean. Where, then, had that remarkable Buddha's sculptor originated? Government archaeologists had, he wrote, "obtained a few images that were completely unlike even Buddhist art as they represented grotesque Gods with long feline teeth projecting from the mouth, and outstretched tongue and enormous ears expanded by huge circular discs in the earlobes. Clearly a Buddhist period has dominated these islands before the introduction of Moslem over 800 years ago —nevertheless, still another civilization has dominated the islands before Buddhism was introduced."[4] Buddhism notwithstanding, what other theologies may have preceded the Islamic faith present on the Maldives? Few professional archaeological excavations had occurred within the archipelago, except that undertaken by British archaeologist H.C.P. Bell (Sri Lanka's first Archaeological Commissioner) in 1922, and Heyerdahl was enthusiastic to conduct more.

He resolved to excavate upon the islands of the Addu Kandu, or Equatorial Channel, which flows between the Huvadhu Atoll and Addu Atoll in the southern Maldives. Heyerdahl had reasoned that the oldest civilizations exploring the Indian Ocean were sun worshippers who undertook celestial navigation, and conceivably pursued the equator's course. The Equatorial Channel could be, he believed, a convenient thoroughfare and a site of religious significance, conceivably containing temples constructed for sun worship.[5] Examining the mosque built when Yusuf Naib Kalegefan converted the Maldives to Islam in 1153, Heyerdahl was struck by the extraordinary craftsmanship of the carved limestone structure, the foundation of which, he suggested to have been constructed by "civilized prehistoric navigators."[6] That masterful construction paralleled, in Heyerdahl's mind, the migration cycles of reed-vessel voyaging peoples. Heyerdahl had observed similar masonry at Rapa Nui, the Incan complexes of South America, North Africa's Atlantic coast, in Asia Minor, and on the island of Bahrain in the Persian Gulf. Omnivorous in drawing apparently disparate geographies and cultures together in pursuit of a common source, he now wondered, despite the vast distances lying between Rapa Nui and the Maldives, whether contact may have somehow occurred between these two enigmatic lands.

While later examining the immaculately constructed ceremonial baths of Fua Mulaku's mosques, Heyerdahl was again struck by "a fantastic possibility": were the similar baths he had witnessed upon Peru's coastal Pacific plains somehow connected to these Maldivian examples? And was westward navigation from the Maldives archipelago toward the southern Cape of Africa, onto the South Atlantic Current, and then northwestward into the Gulf of Mexico, in fact, possible? Conventional scholarship had long dismissed voyages between southern Asia and tropical America, and so, in fact, had Heyerdahl. However, he now reimagined the archipelago as a departure site. Westward navigation from the Maldives, aided by the elements, suddenly became completely possible. Artificial earlobe elongation, practiced across Rapa Nui, Mexico, and Peru, had also occurred, he discovered, both within the Indus Valley and upon the Maldives. Such cultural parallels further suggested conceivable contact between these ancient civilizations.

Heyerdahl's expedition also examined an archaeological site at Gaaf-Gan, where, to his astonishment, he and Bjørn Bye discovered stone sculptures engraved with concentric circles, elaborate sun symbols, sunflowers, and lotus flowers, decorative symbols shared, respectively, by the ancient Egyptian, Phoenician, Mesopotamian, and Hindu civilizations. These sculptures, they believed, were evidence of the presence of Old World sun worshippers across the Maldives. Inhabitants of Gaaf-Gadu, another nearby island, regaled Heyerdahl with mythological tales of Maldivian vessels sailed by a fabled ancient people, the redin, sailing all over the Indian Ocean, as far north as Pakistan and Indonesia. Had the archipelago witnessed the confluence of these Old World cultures, Heyerdahl wondered, while serving as a strategic way station "for advanced civilizations navigating the Indian Ocean in pre-Moslem times."[7] Necessitating further excavations, Heyerdahl resolved to return to the islands the following year.

⟿

When Heyerdahl's second expedition returned to the Maldives in February 1984, they decided to undertake initial excavations at the buried "phallus temple" on the island of Nilandu, where many phalloid stones, or lingam sculptures, were discovered.[8] These once more suggested the presence of Buddhist predecessors in the islands, appearing long before the arrival of the present-day Muslim inhabitants.

"Even though there is, so far, no convincing evidence to hand stating that the Maldives were settled before the sixth century AD," expedition archaeologist Arne Skjølsvold acknowledged, there were nevertheless several indications, he and Heyerdahl believed, to substantiate such a hypothesis, including "the discovery of a Roman Republican denarius of Caius Vibius Pansa, minted in Rome in either 89 or 90 BC." Unearthed in a Buddhist stupa on Toddu island, the coin may "have circulated in the Roman Empire at any time up to AD 100" and conceivably was "included in a consignment of Roman Imperial denarii shipped out to the east. From Malabar or Sri Lanka ... [the coin] might easily have found its way via local trade networks to the Maldive Archipelago." When exactly the coin appeared on the archipelago remained unclear, however, the Buddhist stupa was believed to be older than the introduction of Islam, suggesting a similar age for the coin. Contemporary sources indicated, the expedition believed, "the Maldive Islands were known to the outside world as early as in the Roman period."[9] Despite inconclusive excavations, Skjølsvold nevertheless observed that discoveries at the stupa at Gaaf-Gan indicated the "sanctuary may date back to the first centuries AD."[10]

The expedition also visited Kudu Huvadu, where Heyerdahl encountered exceptional masonry reminiscent of Incan stonework he had encountered at Cuzco, Peru. The expedition then journeyed on to various atolls and islands, including Vilufushi, Isdoo, Dhambidu, Gan, Funadu, Gadu, and Hithadhoo, and initiated excavations at known archaeological sites, where they encountered multitudes of cowrie shells, once the archipelago's currency. Such shells were not only employed within the Indus Valley's civilization, suggesting conceivable contact between Lothal (the ancient civilization's harbor city in the Gulf of Cambay), but were also found far north, beyond the Arctic Circle, in seventh-century graves—demonstrating a possibility for interconnectedness far greater than initially considered.

Continuing onward to the Equatorial Channel islands of Gadu and Gaaf-Gan, Heyerdahl's expedition conducted excavations upon an enormous structure encompassing four ceremonial ramp approaches, oriented toward the sun and adorned with solar symbols, highlighting the conceivable presence of sun worshippers, here upon the equator.

An elaborately carved, weeping head was also discovered, reminiscent of the carved death skulls Heyerdahl had encountered at the Mayan ruins at Chichen Itza, with weeping tears symbolizing rain from the sun god in ancient Mexican and Peruvian art. "The worshippers of Allah had destroyed what the worshippers of the sun had laboriously built here," Heyerdahl declared.[11] Journeying now to the island of Vadu, the expedition unearthed additional stone sun symbols, many encompassed by concentric sun circles and carved flower petals, as well as stone fragments inscribed with hieroglyphics Heyerdahl believed to be "remarkably similar to the early Indus Valley civilization from about 1500 BC," indicating "that an early civilization had reached the Maldives as early as 3,000 years before Columbus set sail into the open ocean."[12]

Finally, the expedition moved southward to Fua Mulaku, where further excavations conducted within the ceremonial baths at the Kedere mosque revealed architecture similar to baths found at Mohenjo-Daro and Bahrain, which offered yet another connection between the Indus Valley and the Maldives archipelago. On the island of Viringili, Heyerdahl's expedition came upon an enormous, abandoned bamboo raft, about 39 by 10 feet (11.9 x 3 m), which was remarkably similar in construction to the balsa *Kon-Tiki* raft. Ostensibly originating from Burma, the raft had conceivably voyaged beyond Bangladesh, India, and Sri Lanka, about 2,000 miles (3,200 km) southward of the Maldives. The raft illustrated to Heyerdahl that seafaring Buddhists may have sailed to the Maldives, settling the archipelago long before the eventual establishment of Islam. What's more, Maldivian *dhonis*, traditional vessels now made from coconut wood, possessed, in Heyerdahl's mind, "a marked 'Egyptian' form, with the tall, arched, and incurved bow ending … in a fan-shaped papyrus blossom. This was the typical shape of the elegant reed-bundle ships shared by the world's three oldest known civilizations; in Egypt, Mesopotamia, and the Indus Valley."[13]

Despite the encouraging evidence Heyerdahl unearthed during the course of the expedition, what seafaring occurred within the Indian Ocean during the millennia before the arrival of Arab and Portuguese seafarers remained opaque. "The archipelago has a very strategic position in the middle of the sailing routes between the Near and the Far East," Skjølsvold observed, speculating that "most probably the islands have been inhabited ever since sailing craft started to cross the Indian Ocean."[14] As with Rapa Nui's three separate epochs of habitation, the Maldives archipelago, Heyerdahl believed, also experienced three successive habitations: Buddhism, Hinduism, and present-day Islam. Maldivians themselves believed that seafaring Arabs, their ancient ancestors, had voyaged to the archipelago centuries ago before introducing the Islamic faith, fanatically destroying any "evidence for the Buddhist substratum, which had been so systematically erased in the long centuries of sultanic rule."[15] Archaeologists had, Heyerdahl declared, conclusively proved that "the early Indus Valley civilization navigated as far as Bahrain, Failaka Island, and Mesopotamia. So, it would be tempting to suspect they sailed just as far in the opposite direction to reach the Maldives, Sri Lanka, and possibly, the ancient nations of Eastern Asia."[16]

⇝

After completing fieldwork along the Gulf of Cambay at Gujarat, India, Heyerdahl was now convinced that "the Hindu element in the Maldives had come from [the] north-western corner of India." However, he was adamant that the Hindus themselves were not necessarily the first sailors to voyage southward to the Maldives, suggesting instead there were antecedent sailors who, "in the days of Mesopotamian and Indus Valley seafaring had been led by the sun to the Equatorial Channel." "The lion, the bull, the lotus flower, the long-eared images, the semi-precious beads, the copper spikes, the fingerprint masonry and the classical profiles of the hawitta [temple mounds] plinths tied the pre-Muslim Maldive artists to the culture founders on the continents. One by one, or jointly, these elements had come to the Maldive atolls with seafarers from some other lands. But which lands?"[17] he wondered. Sri Lankan Buddhists and Indian Hindus appeared to have inhabited the Maldives archipelago more than two millennia ago. Whomever preceded this habitation was either expelled or absorbed. "The Maldives … now began to appear like a barrier reef," Heyerdahl declared, "from which octopus tentacles spread to remote corners of the Old World. Into the Red Sea and the Mediterranean as far as Rome. Into the Persian Gulf and beyond as far as Finland and the Arctic coast of Norway. Into the Gulf of Cambay, and around India in the opposite direction past the straits of Indonesia to distant China."[18]

However, despite how meritorious Heyerdahl's 1983–84 Maldives expedition was—and the renewed scientific interest in the archipelago he subsequently catalyzed—his characteristically cultural diffusionist hypothesis that the archipelago operated in antiquity as a nexus from which knowledgeable sailors set forth, westward, upon reed vessels, navigating as far afield as China, and his proposition that the Maldives was once inhabited by sun worshippers from the distant Indus Valley civilization failed to obtain general acceptance. One prominent detractor, the scholar, Dr. A.D.W. Forbes, declared that Heyerdahl's excavations on Gamu island, where he unearthed what he believed was a sun-worshipping temple, and his pronunciation that hieroglyphs found upon a carved coral stone resembled Indus Valley script were "premature and ill-conceived speculations" and suggested that "careful examination of the carved coral slab discovered on Vada Island indicate that it is, beyond shadow of reasonable doubt, a coral Buddha *pāduka* [footprint] … decorated with a series of *mangalas* [auspicious signs]."[19]

Heyerdahl's imaginative speculation—drawn from his apparent misidentification of Buddhist archaeological sites and artifacts—that a connection once existed between the Maldives archipelago and the Indus Valley civilization illustrates, to some extent, a tendency in his later years to engage superficially with certain areas of interest, in the process becoming unable to draw from a deep knowledge of contemporary research. It also demonstrates a confidence in his practical experiments, which supported his unwavering beliefs in cultural diffusionism and a universal interconnection facilitated by the world's vast oceans, uniting apparently disparate individuals, cultures, nations, and faiths. Encountering archaeological evidence that seemingly negated his Maldives archipelago hypotheses, Heyerdahl still favored a mythopoetic narrative, entwining the world's inhabitants symbiotically together. "The best conclusion," he allowed, "is that the ocean is and always was an open road since man began to build ships."[20]

Left: A big stone head of Buddha found on the Maldive Islands.

Right: Decorated temple wall.

Opposite (left): Part of a broken stupa.

Opposite (right): Cut stone in a temple wall, which Thor Heyerdahl interpreted as a sun symbol.

151

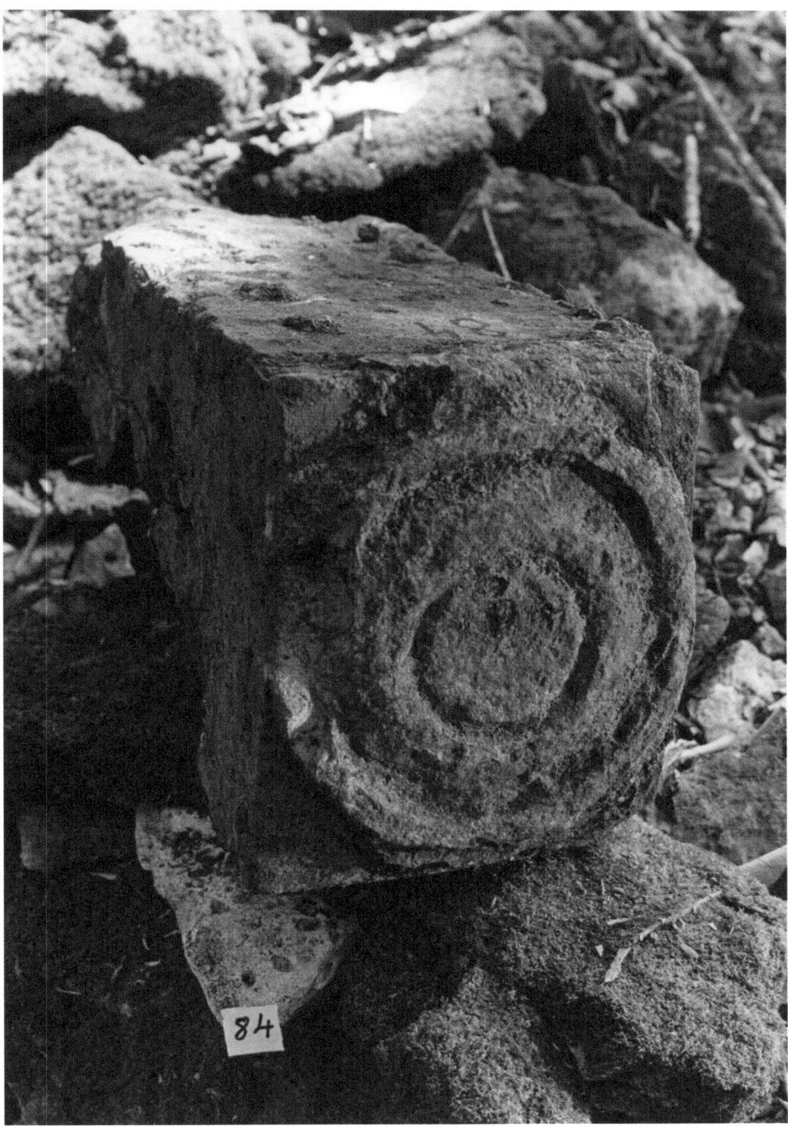
84

Top: On top of a temple mound, Maldive Islands.

Middle: Thor Heyerdahl admiring a piece of local stupa architecture on the Maldives.

Bottom: Investigating local scripts, Maldive Islands.

Opposite (top): The team of the first Maldives Expedition in 1983. From left: Mohamed Loutfi (historian working for the Maldives Department of Education), Thor Heyerdahl, Bjørn Bye, Øystein Koch Johansen (archaeologist), and Arne Skjølsvold (archaeologist).

Opposite (bottom): Locals on one of the Maldives exposing a stone foundation in 1983–84.

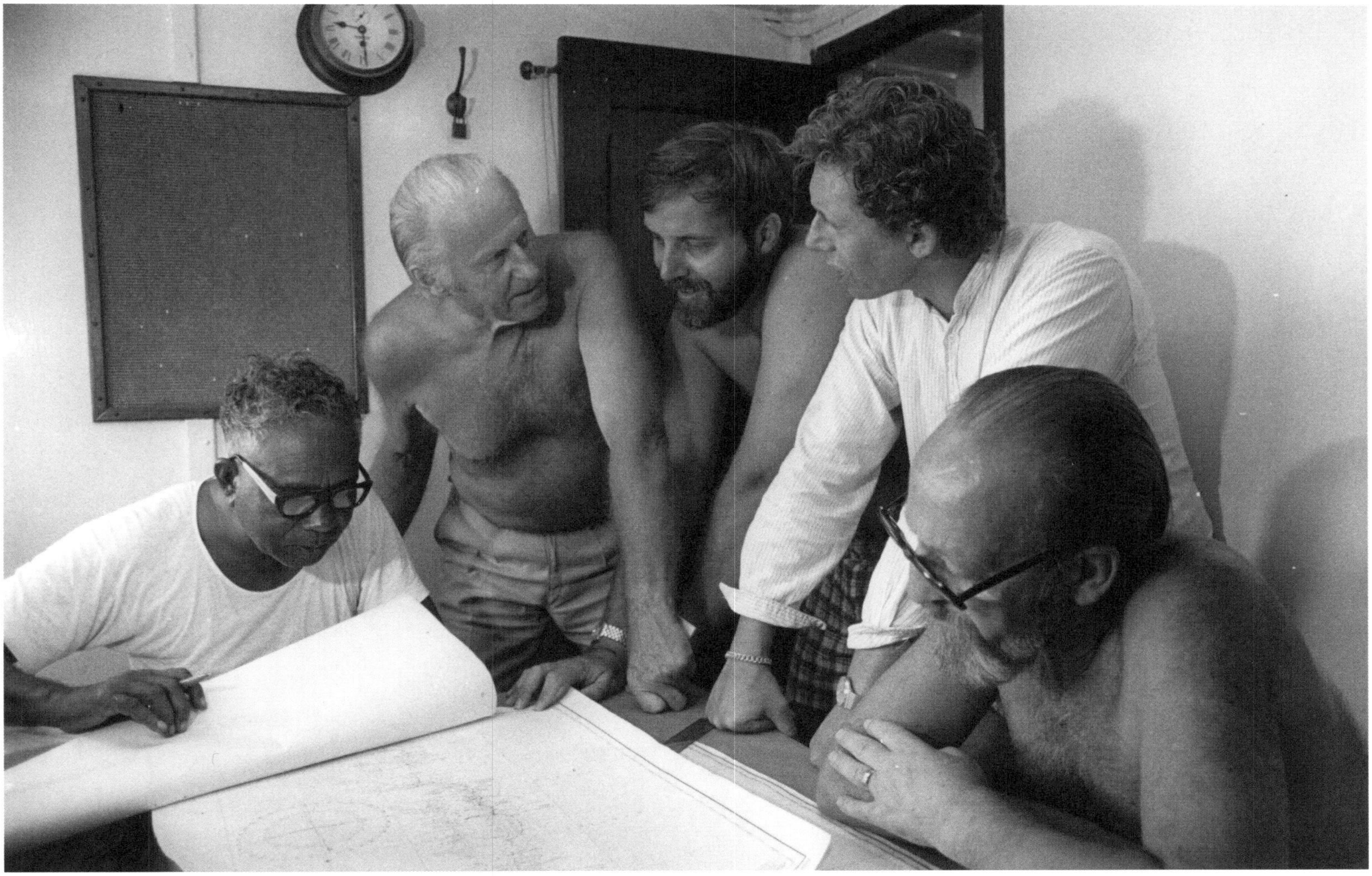

Mangrove in the
Maldive Islands.

Opposite:
Thor Heyerdahl,
Arne Skjølsvold,
and Mohamed Loutfi
walking along the
beach, Maldive
Islands.

1988~1992

Túcume Archaeological Project

"There was nothing like these strange and colossal ruins on our own familiar Earth."

"I literally felt like a visitor to another planet—there was nothing like these strange and colossal ruins on our own familiar Earth,"[1] Heyerdahl declared when first surveying the temple city of Túcume, northern Peru's vast pre-Incan archaeological complex, in October 1987. Heyerdahl had been invited to Peru earlier that year to celebrate the 40th anniversary of the 1947 Kon-Tiki expedition, and during the festivities he met Walter Alva, a local archaeologist. Alva told Heyerdahl about an amazing discovery: pyramids, long-thought to be natural hill formations, had been uncovered at an ancient site near a small village in the north of the country. Visiting this archaeological marvel months later, Heyerdahl described it as "a lifeless prehistoric city of pyramids glowing like red hills in the last rays of the sun, before the unreal vision was swallowed up in the tropical night. I knew that what I had seen would change my life. How could I free myself from this sight? Unknown people like ourselves had lived here. What would these walls enclose and these pyramids contain?"[2]

The vast, approximately 540-acre (220-ha) archaeological complex of Túcume lies upon the Saharan coastal plains of northern Peru, six degrees south of the equator, beneath the sun-baked Cerro La Raya mountain, deep within the once-fertile Lambayeque Valley, and in close proximity to the Pacific Ocean. Heyerdahl, now 74 years of age, had finally returned to the ocean that had catalyzed his remarkable Kon-Tiki expedition to complete one of his last archaeological excavations, and which would be, perhaps, the most arduous. Unable to find temporary lodging, with funds secured from the Norwegian shipping magnate and Kon-Tiki patron Fred Olsen, Heyerdahl constructed a traditional, sun-baked adobe Peruvian house, which he named Casa Kon-Tiki, at Túcume. He noted, it was "far from my own kin and my own generation," yet "the center of my world,"[3] which calls to mind his other great love, Rapa Nui, known as the Navel of the World.

Arcane Túcume encompassed 26 pyramid-shaped structures of sun-baked adobe bricks constructed from AD 1100. It was cultivated with artificial irrigation provided by colossal canals, which could facilitate navigation by balsa-wood raft both to the coast and for miles inland. Prevailing scholarly assumption held that "Peruvians in pre-Colombian times had neither the vessels nor daring to take them further than inshore fishing in the crudest of craft."[4] However, excavations at several nearby coastal Peruvian archaeological sites indicated to Heyerdahl that pre-Incan communities had, in fact, established their economy, to a significant extent, upon fishing and maritime trade. "Scholars have all too long underestimated and even ignored the maritime aspect of life along the Peruvian littoral prior to the arrival of European norms for watercraft," he declared. Notwithstanding "modern experimental ocean voyages on manned rafts made from logs of balsa wood or bundles of reeds," Heyerdahl's Kon-Tiki, Ra, and Tigris expeditions respectively, the ancient Peruvians, he believed, were dismissively mischaracterized as "a land-locked people with the most primitive forms of watercraft." Canoes remained ubiquitous upon the jungle rivers of the Inca empire, but the absence of hulled watercraft upon the Peruvian coastline illustrated, scholarly assessment held, a lack of maritime development. Heyerdahl believed, however, that "the very special coast of Peru, with endless stretches of Pacific surf breaking directly ashore upon unsheltered beaches and cliffs, called for vessels without an open, vulnerable hull,"[5] vessels inconceivable to European explorers who were acquainted with wooden-hulled seacraft. Moreover, he held that coastal populations of pre-Colonial Peru not only possessed able ocean-voyaging watercraft, but also undertook substantial voyages both northward and far westward into the vast Pacific Ocean; they possessed superior ocean-voyaging capacities that were, in fact, recorded within colonial Spanish observations.

Heyerdahl's Túcume Archaeological Project, one of many excavations undertaken at the site, both in the 19th and 20th centuries, began on 28 August 1988 at the base of the Huaca I pyramid structure. He eagerly anticipated unearthing evidence of balsa-wood raft navigation: "Túcume clearly showed that the ancient inhabitants did not ignore the ocean. Although the pyramid site was 20 km [12 miles] from the seashore … our first survey found the entire temple area littered with sea shell fragments … Excavations uncovered fish bones, fragments of fish nets, tropical *Spondylus* shell, and various marine motifs, realistic and symbolic, in pottery, wood, adobe reliefs, and wall paintings, featuring a diversity of sea creatures, diving sea birds, and anthropomorphic waves."[6] Túcume's culture centered about maritime activity—activity that was equally important as agriculture to pre-Colombian coastal inhabitants.

Heyerdahl's extensive excavations at Túcume, then the largest archaeological project in the world, continued until 1992, when Alfredo Narvaez, one of the project's lead archaeologists, was led by a local farmer (and former grave robber) to "the most impressive reed-boat illustrations ever discovered in America" on an adobe temple wall adorned with well-preserved, elaborate maritime reliefs. "Bird-headed men were sailing on board two reed boats," Heyerdahl recalled, and the boats were illustrated with cabins amidship and large numbers of oars standing in the waters. "Two mythical personages, wearing royal or ceremonial headdresses familiar from pre-Inca art, dominate all the space on each deck. All four have the heads of birds, but human arms holding the paddle shafts. In each boat one birdman has a human body and limbs, the other has a bird's body and human arms. Around the boats are fish and diving seabirds."[7]

Beneath the reed vessel itself, to Alfredo and Heyerdahl's astonishment, were several anthropomorphic waves, crested with birds' heads, while the birdmen grasped spherical objects. These objects confounded the project's American archaeologists but transfixed another expedition member, Arne Skjølsvold, who was deeply knowledgeable of Oceanic archaeology and had encountered elaborate stone reliefs of similar birdmen, crouching and clutching spherical objects, while excavating at Rapa Nui with Heyerdahl in 1955 and 1956. "Thor, those things are birdmen crouching with eggs in their hands, just like the ones on Easter Island,"[8] Skjølsvold excitedly declared on 5 March 1992. He immediately recognized that Túcume's enigmatic birdmen reliefs were exactly the same as those they had encountered on Rapa Nui several decades before, which depicted the annual birdman ceremonies and their tusk-shaped reed vessels. These Rapa Nui reed vessels were identical to those still employed along the Peruvian coastline and constructed of the same totora reeds cultivated there. This realization, along with the discovery of several double-bladed silver ceremonial paddles known across Polynesia as *ao* — along with adventurer Kitin Muñoz's remarkable demonstration of Incan designed totora reed vessels' capacity for oceangoing voyages —convinced Heyerdahl that ancient Peruvians sailed the Pacific Ocean, transplanting their culture to Rapa Nui.[i] Skjølsvold, declared the find "a great victory for Thor Heyerdahl and his theories. Without a doubt they would have to be accepted as a definite proof that Indians in prehistoric Peru was strongly maritime oriented and courageous seafarers."[9]

Deeply motivated by a desire to substantiate his Polynesian migration hypothesis, Heyerdahl's excavations at Túcume sought evidence of an enduring maritime culture, a culture that was, in fact, present, but completely unconnected to Polynesia. He wrote to his old friend Arnold Jacoby that although his finds at Túcume did not receive the attention he hoped, he continued his excavations through a strong feeling of purpose and destiny to prove his theories to the world and advance his all-encompassing belief in humanity's shared past. Heyerdahl continued, perhaps sometimes without a clear research question, to search for artifacts, because he believed what he had "immediately discovered [at Túcume] is a culture not just based on agriculture, but on fishing and long-range maritime trade."[10]

Archaeologists and ethnologists, Heyerdahl observed, "have been searching the entire Pacific in vain for the origin of this non-Polynesian cultural trait." He, however, believed he had found the origin at Túcume and the pre-Incan civilizations scattered throughout coastal Peru. Dr. Richard L. Burger, an Andean expert and professor of anthropology at Yale University, who declared Heyerdahl's Túcume hypothesis as nothing more than "idle speculation." Heyerdahl, Dr. Burger indicted, attempts "to explain the complicated civilization of the Andes by saying it was developed by outside influences ... a theory few professionals lend any credence to."

Nevertheless, Heyerdahl remained convinced that Túcume's inhabitants played a part in the settling of Polynesia. It is now largely accepted that contact occurred between Polynesians and indigenous South Americans before AD 1300, an acceptance, alongside the discovery of the DNA of South Americans found in the blood of the indigenous people on Rapa Nui, somewhat substantiating Heyerdahl's long advanced hypothesis. Túcume's excavations serve as an illustrative microcosm of Heyerdahl's belief in humanity's millennia-long entwinement by the oceans' ceaseless oscillations. And they triumphantly validated, to his mind, his-long held theory of diffusionist migration, westward from South America throughout the Pacific Ocean.

i Sonia Haoa Cardinali, who worked with Heyerdahl on his last Rapa Nui expedition, had a differing theory: that the mural depicted the moment a Polynesian double-canoe arrived on the Peruvian coast.

Øystein Koch Johansen, Thor Heyerdahl, archaeologist Daniel H. Sandweiss, and Arne Skjølsvold discussing how to proceed with the excavation at the La Raya pyramid complex, Tucumé.

Bottom: Peruvian archaeologist working at the La Raya Pyramid complex. Øystein Koch Johansen and Arne Skjølsvold are in the background, in the Temple of the Sacred Stone.

Opposite: Arne Skjølsvold inspecting archaeological investigations in Tucumé, Peru.

Left: Excavation at Tucumé, Peru, 1988–1992.

Right: Traditional Chimu anthropomorphized ceramic pot found during the excavations in Tucumé, Peru, 1988–1992.

Opposite: Building small reed boats at Lake Titicaca, Boliva/Peru.

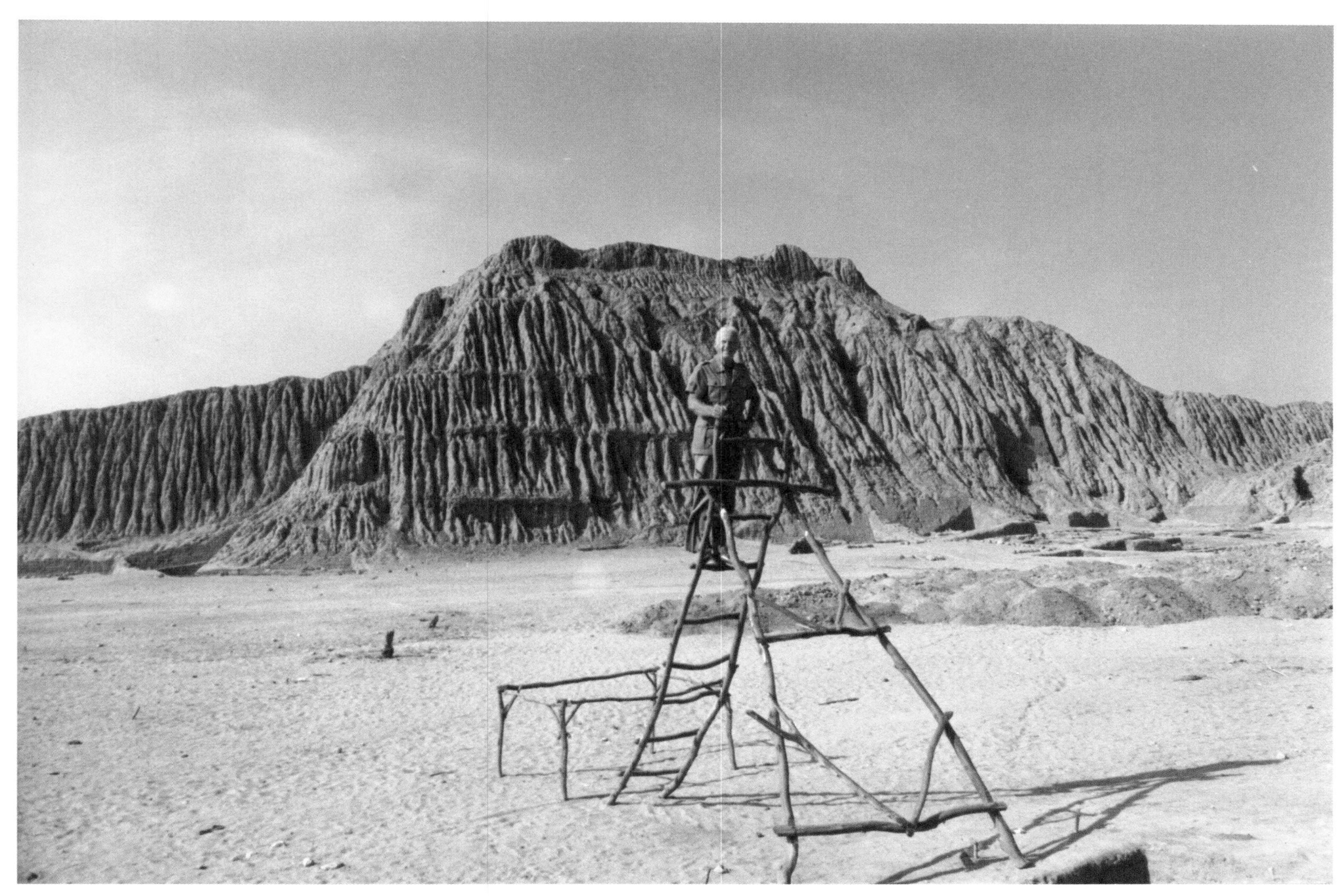

Opposite: Local fishermen using a small reed boat, known as *caballito*, in Peru.

Above: Thor Heyerdahl photographed outside Huaca I pyramid, of the La Raya Pyramid Complex, Tucumé, Peru.

Top: An approximately 2,000-year-old model of a small fishing raft of balsa, about 12⅜ in. (31.5 cm) long and 3¾ in. (9.5 cm) wide, found as grave goods in Arica, Chile. This model was part of an exchange between the Kon-Tiki Museum and Chilean culture-heritage authorities.

Middle: Five tanged arrowheads in a white quartz, from Ilo, Peru.

Bottom: Anthropomorphic stone statue, Tiawanku, Bolivia, about 9⅞ in. (25 cm) high and 3⅞ in. (9.7 cm) wide.

Opposite: Buried temple relief from archaeological excavations in Túcume, Peru, showing marine birds.

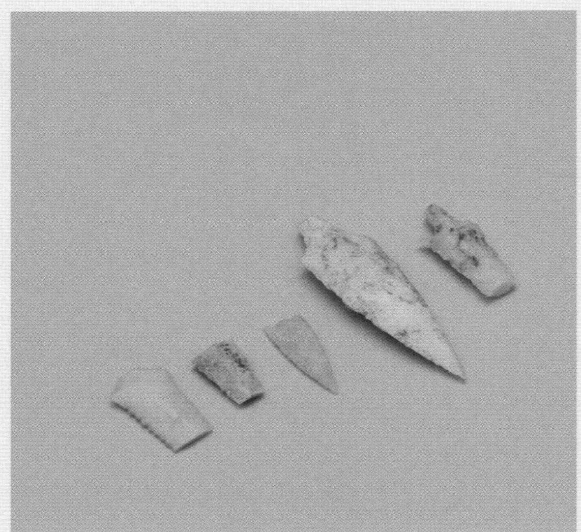

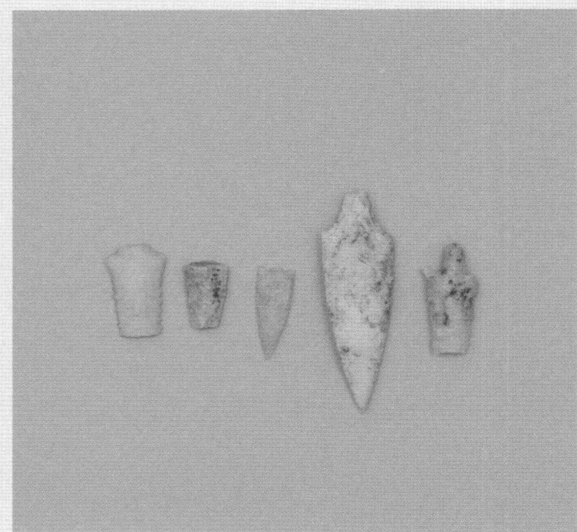

KON-TIKI
HUSET
N
A-100
CD
A-28457
N

Life, Theory, and Legacy

1990~2002

"Tucume is my greatest discovery," Heyerdahl triumphantly declared at a press conference in May 1993.[1] In talking about recent excavations at the fascinating Peruvian archaeological complex, he told a journalist in July 1991 that they, "have proven there was a highly developed maritime culture."[2] That culture, he believed, was based upon agriculture, fishing, and long-distance maritime trade. "A culture which is far older than that of the first Egyptian pharaoh must have been the basis for the spread of civilization. I hope Tucume will be able to put us on the trail of that lost culture." Regardless, Heyerdahl's hypothesis that Tucume formed part of Polynesia's cultural genesis remained unaccepted by conventional scholarship. "I don't listen to the 'know-hows,'" Heyerdahl responded, undeterred. "It is utterly illogical to think cultures developed independently without direct contact after man developed seagoing vessels about 5,000 years ago."[3]

Despite his indefatigable labors at Tucume and elsewhere, after nearly 60 years of research and expeditions, Heyerdahl was nearing the end of his life's work. Having victoriously completed reed-vessel voyages from Mesopotamia to the Indus Valley, Asia to Africa and Africa to North America, he remained convinced of the long-dismissed connection between ancient civilizations aided by our oceans. A westward voyage, aided by the elements and guided by the sun, would, he speculated, convey a reed vessel from the Indus Valley, southwestward across the Indian Ocean, past Africa's Cape of Good Hope, onto the South Atlantic trade winds and westward oscillating currents, then northward onto the North Atlantic winds into the Gulf of Mexico. Panama's isthmus, he believed, "would be the only barrier to the Pacific (and) could have been the gateway from the Old World to Peru and Easter Island."[4] "I had not only … crossed the ocean gaps from the Indus Valley to Polynesia on westward voyages in pre-European types of watercraft," Heyerdahl observed, "I had also revisited the Indian Ocean several times and found unsuspected stepping-stones bringing India closer to America for deep-sea navigators."[5] Additionally, sun worship, celestial navigation, masterful masonry, and symbolic earlobe extension convinced Heyerdahl that the cultures and regions around the Pacific Ocean were long interconnected.

Previous page: The first Kon-Tiki Museum, called the Kon-Tiki House, opened on 15 May 1950.

Nevertheless, his longstanding theory of ancient South American-Polynesian contact remained largely disputed by conventional scholarship, which asserted that the ancestors of the Polynesians, the Lapita people, a Neolithic Austronesian people, had originally voyaged eastward from Taiwan and settled remote Oceania between 1100–900 BC.

⟶

With excavations at Tucume well-established, Heyerdahl subsequently inaugurated two more fascinating expeditions. Entranced by the discovery of Tenerife's Pyramids of Güímar in 1990 and their strangely familiar appearance, Heyerdahl traveled to the island that same year to organize a Spanish-Norwegian archaeological research project to examine the six enigmatic polyhedron pyramids, terraced structures masterfully constructed from lava stone without the use of mortar. Although they were dismissed by many scholars as nothing more than stone piles amassed by indigenous Spanish farmers after discarding materials from their arable lands, Heyerdahl began excavating in the plaza located between two of the pyramids that form the central complex. The excavation yielded a series of materials from the mid-nineteenth century, ostensibly disproving construction in antiquity. Nevertheless, that same year, the researchers Juan Antonio Belmonte Avilés, Antonio Aparicio Juan and César Esteban López, from the Institute of Astrophysics of the Canary Islands, undertook a study of the archaeoastronomical characteristics of the structures. The investigations showed that the pyramids are oriented astronomically to the summer and winter solstices.

Fascinated by what Avilés, Juan, and López's excavations revealed, Heyerdahl established a permanent residence at Guimar in 1994 to continue his excavations, during which he discovered that the pyramids were constructed not of stones from nearby fields but of lava rocks quarried from farther inland, providing evidence that these pyramids were intentionally formed. Meticulously constructed stone by stone, with the stones' flat side facing out, the pyramids possessed flattened platform summits, not haphazard rock-piled peaks. Heyerdahl determined that such pyramids—which once appeared across the entire island but were gradually, systematically dismantled for the construction of new structures—were deliberately constructed by the island's original indigenous inhabitants, the Guanche, the only pre-European indigenous population in Macronesia. Fascinated by parallels he observed between Tenerife's pyramids and analogous structures found in Egypt and in pre-Columbian Mesoamerica, Heyerdahl hypothesized that the Canary Islands once formed a temporal and geographic way station on transatlantic voyages between the ancient Egypt and Maya civilizations—a hypothesis similar to the one he had proposed when exploring the Maldives. However, since then, multiple excavations undertaken at Güímar by archaeologists from the University of La Laguna and evidence published by Juan Aparicio and César Esteban López in *The Pyramids of Güímar: Myth and Reality* (2005) have revealed that although Guanche artifacts dated to between 600 and 1000 AD were discovered within a natural lava cave, the pyramidal terraced structures themselves were constructed by the 19th-century rural population, who had indeed produced these enigmatic structures while clearing cultivable land of meddlesome stones. Despite such compelling evidence, Heyerdahl's hypothesis of a possible relationship between the pyramids and the pre-Hispanic civilization of Tenerife catalyzed an enduring controversy concerning the origins of the Pyramids of Güímar among scholars for decades.

Heyerdahl's second significant undertaking during his later years advanced yet another unorthodox migration hypothesis: Scandinavia was originally populated in the first century AD by migrating peoples originating from present-day Azerbaijan in the Caucasus. This nascent, somewhat controversial, hypothesis had developed after Heyerdahl visited Gobustan, an ancient cave-dwelling site found some 30 miles (50 km) west of Baku in Azerbaijan, famed for elaborate rock carvings dated between the eighth and seventh centuries BC. Examining carved illustrations of sickle-shaped vessels containing oarsman, he was astounded to find these illustrations closely resembled rock carvings of vessels found in Norway.

Undertaking extensive research, Heyerdahl became convinced of the truth in celebrated Icelandic historian, poet, and politician Snorri Sturluson's 13th-century sagas, which tell of the Norse god Odin and the Aesir emigrating from the Don River region to Scandinavia when the Romans invaded. Heyerdahl believed that Azerbaijan was the site of the ancient, advanced civilization from whence they came, through waterways to present-day Scandinavia, traveling upon ingeniously constructed, readily transportable vessels made from animal hides. The belief in Odin's existence and emigration was first advanced by Reverend W.M.H. Milner within his 1902 book *The Royal House of Britain: An Enduring Dynasty*. "The traditions of our Scandinavian forefathers tell of a great conqueror, the hero king of Asgard—Odin,"[6] Milner declared. "He was so heroic a king, and so great a conqueror, that the superstition or reverence of after ages made a god of him … He led our forefathers across Europe. Asgard has been variously located in Armenia or on the Dniepr. In either case, his victorious march traversed Russia, Germany, Denmark, Norway, Sweden." Likewise, Heyerdahl propounded, "Snorre didn't sit down and dream this all up. In ancient times, people treated Gods and Kings as one and the same thing … I'm personally convinced that Snorre recorded oral history rather than a concocted myth."[7] King Odin, he believed, had led the Aesir northward of the Sea of Azov in Azerbaijan to Sweden about 2,000 years ago (60 BC–AD 100). Snorri said, Heyerdahl noted, "At that time when Odin lived, the Romans were conquering far and wide in the region. When Odin learned that they were coming toward the land of Aesirs, he decided that it was best for him to take his priests, chiefs, and some of his people and move to the Northern part of Europe."[8] Accompanying Roman inscriptions discovered at Gobustan were determined to have appeared between AD 84 and 97, corroborating, in Heyerdahl's mind, Sturluson's chronology of Odin's northward migration during the second half of the first century AD.

Pursuing evidence to substantiate his deeply controversial hypothesis, Heyerdahl undertook archaeological excavations at the Sea of Azov, at the mouth of the Don River, in 1999 and 2000, which would be his last archaeological expedition. It yielded ancient metal belt holders, rings, and armbands dating from AD 100–200, which he believed—in defiance of numerous archaeologists and scholars—were almost identical to Viking artifacts recovered at Gotland,

Sweden, about 800 years afterward. Additionally, between 2001 and 2002, Heyerdahl attempted to retrace King Odin's northward route as described by Sturluson. "I think it's time to look for the land that my Scandinavian ancestors came from and not merely where they subsequently went on their Viking raids and explorations,"[9] Heyerdahl declared. "They certainly did not come out from under the glaciers when the ice age ended so they must have immigrated from the south. Since their physical type is referred to as Caucasian and their very own descendant preserved an itinerary from south of the Caucasus and north of Turkey, I suspect that the present Azeri people and the Aesir of the Norse sagas have common roots and that my ancestry originated there."

Heyerdahl's speculative Azerbaijan-Scandinavia migration hypothesis was immediately and unanimously rejected by the academic and scientific community, which indicted Heyerdahl for practicing pseudo-archaeology, for his misinterpretation of Norse mythology as an objective chronicle, for the selective interpretation of research and archaeological discoveries, for lacking scientific methodology, and for a misguided reliance upon linguistic similarities he identified between Norse mythology and geographical place-names of the Black Sea region (the Pontic steppe and Caucasus). That enduring controversy was emblematic of Heyerdahl's longstanding, antagonistic relationship with the international academic community; however, it was a conflict that never dissuaded him from such imaginative hypothesizing. Although his pursuit of King Odin's northward odyssey yielded opaque conclusions and academic sanction, citizens from both nations remain entranced by Heyerdahl's archetypically imaginative, multidisciplinary hypothesizing. Regardless, as of 2022, Heyerdahl's Odin hypothesis has yet to be validated by any historian, archaeologist, or linguist.

Heyerdahl's remarkable, hypothesis-substantiating voyages around Earth, immortalized in numerous best-selling books, documentaries, and films, had transfixed enraptured audiences for more than five decades. Members of the press attending his expeditions and the various publications ensured his incandescent celebrity went far beyond

Norway's shores, a celebrity he remained wholly disinterested by but which was strategically exploited to actualize his various practicable experiments. Such daring endeavors, and the unrelentingly public life they ensured, invariably inflicted irrevocable casualties, including upon Heyerdahl's three successive marriages. Heyerdahl and his first wife, Liv Coucheron Torp, were eventually separated in December 1948 after raising two children together. Liv was an invaluable participant during their time in Fatu Hiva, assisting in recording zoological specimens and collecting ethnological artifacts. In 1949, he married Yvonne Dedekam-Simonsen, with whom he had another three children, Annette, Marian, and Helen Elsabeth. Yvonne undertook a considerable part in Heyerdahl's work, both typing up manuscripts and aiding with research, and also providing instrumental practical support in organizing expeditions, particularly the Rapa Nui and Ra projects. She was also responsible for his book contracts and licensing. The couple eventually divorced in 1969, and his final marriage was to Jacqueline Beer in 1991, to whom he stayed married until his death.

Heyerdahl's extraordinary odysseys, and the peripatetic existence they ensured, were frequently interspersed with long periods of stability enjoyed at several residences established around the world, including in Norway, Tenerife, Italy, and Peru. Colla Micheri was a magnificent 16th-century, ivy-enshrouded Italian farmhouse he acquired in 1958 that encompassed two Roman watchtowers and 85 acres (35 ha) of olive groves and orchards on mountainous terrain, with a vegetable garden and fecund vineyard, as well as chickens, goats, melodious swallows, and braying donkeys. A palpable sense of centuries of habitation pervaded the beautiful garden, and Heyerdahl's office, housed in a gabled hunting tower, commanded extraordinary panoramas over the temperate azure Mediterranean Sea as far as Corsica and across forested hills as far as the snow-enveloped Alps. Heyerdahl spent many of the subsequent decades there after purchasing the property, laboring from sunrise to sunset, six days a week, seated before an ornate, expansive oak desk beneath a domed lead-light window, with notepaper and pencil industriously authoring articles, books, and essays; organizing archaeological expeditions; and translating hieroglyphs and other ancient texts. Throughout his adult life, Heyerdahl embraced a pendulous existence, seafaring across the world's oceans for months on end, suffering privations and ceaseless horizons, courting death on innumerable occasions, yet miraculously always preserved. Then, returning to shore for long periods of rehabilitation, and the inception of transformative new hypotheses, before invariably departing, cyclically once more upon another odyssey, an endless cycle analogous perhaps of the very ocean tides Heyerdahl regularly voyaged upon.

"We have seen with our own eyes and felt in our bones that whatever splits up mankind is artificial and can be tolerated or ignored whereas whatever unites mankind is real and profound," Heyerdahl declared in an imploring 19 July 1969 telegram sent to United Nations Secretary General U Thant immediately after abandoning the papyrus vessel *Ra*. Two macrocosmic phenomena he witnessed on this voyage implacably troubled Heyerdahl's conscience: the relationship between peoples and that one between people and nature. Political factions, racial demarcations, and internecine violence was fracturing humanity, necessitating the establishment of alliances "between nations in areas where [religious-political] currents tend to drift nations apart." World federation, actualized by the United Nations, he believed, "symbolizing the ideas of building bridges and tearing down barriers, marks the only realistic road forward for man …when our common world is getting ever smaller and the national arsenals ever larger."[10] Despite enormous variances between the eight sailors on *Ra* and their ethnicities, faiths, and political ideologies, Heyerdahl believed that the largely harmonious individual interrelationships upon the reed vessel served as an illustrative microcosm for international harmony. "We feel our modest human experiment under particularly difficult conditions," he declared, "should encourage the faith of all those who believe in bringing men of all nations closer together." United, Heyerdahl wrote, humanity could vanquish "mutual problems and survive in a small world where we all have equal rights to coexist and more to gain from mutual aid than from hostility and destruction."[11] Peaceable coexistence demanded infinitely more strength and courage than violent antagonism.[12]

Heyerdahl's humanity arose from an appreciation of and interest in cultures vastly different from his native Norwegian, and a conviction that by uniting such heterogeneous cultures together, international peace could be found. Heyerdahl's fascination with non-European cultures, particularly those preserved from modernity, began in boyhood, when he first read of Greenland's Inuit people and the indigenous tribes of Africa and the Americas. Galvanized by this and his transformative encounters with the Norwegian woodsman Ola Bjørneby, he became fixated by the idea of a simple life, living at one with nature. For Heyerdahl, symbiotic interrelationships between humankind and nature encompassed harmonious interpersonal relationships between all of Earth's inhabitants. His belief that all people are the same, across geography and through time, was an ideology that presented itself early to Heyerdahl, and it was a belief he maintained his entire life. Heyerdahl's enduring emphasis on an individual's worth, regardless of ethnicity, faith, or nationality, and the universally enriching benefit of multiculturalism, preceded what we now know as globalization and was an ideology in diametric opposition to prevailing Eurocentric beliefs in the stratification of cultures according to whether they remained primitive or civilized. Dogmatic ethnocentrism, he believed, both negated non-Europeans' cultural value and catalyzed myopic narratives within which Western European empiricism determined world affairs. Heyerdahl categorically dismissed "the desperate desire of so many historians and anthropologists to reserve the first possible crossings of the Atlantic to the Spaniards and the Vikings." He wrote about an element "of religious fanaticism in the attempts by the western world to see America as a European creation, completely protected by sea until the local barbarians were found by civilized Christian pioneers." Instead, he counseled that, "we should try to be more open-minded. The art of navigation, literacy, even the symbol of the cross and the religion we carried to America, we had first obtained from Asia."[13]

Heyerdahl's expeditions were themselves emblematic of his enduring faith in the transformative capacity of intercultural dialogue, believing microcosmic individual exchanges held the capacity for macrocosmic, peaceable enrichment of world affairs. Enlisting expedition members from across all faiths, nations, ethnicities, and political affiliations, Heyerdahl sincerely believed that these individuals would symbolically align to achieve common aspirations, and artificial superimpositions of sectarianism and national opposition upon individuals, which establish conflict and sustain antagonism, would therefore be revealed as destructive fallacies. His sustained advocacy for the United Nations as the centre of world government, and his incendiary political agitations for world peace, including the destruction of *Tigris* and his petitioning of national governments illustrate such a belief. Heyerdahl believed that international cooperation, including nuclear disarmament and the eradication of national territories, was the key to preserving humankind's existence and protecting against Earth's environmental devastation.

Heyerdahl's environmentalism was a multidimensional affair that evolved over the course of his many expeditions and peripatetic encounters. Deeply influenced again by Bjørneby's nature-centered philosophy and his exemplary human-nature symbiosis, Heyerdahl's transformative expedition to Fatu Hiva in 1937 also developed his nascent biophilia into an enduring ideology recognizing humankind's extraordinary capacity for destruction and the need for nature's preservation. However, instead of actualizing Milton's paradigm of *Paradise Lost*, rejecting technology and embracing Luddism, Heyerdahl's environmentalism encompassed practical application. He believed that antagonistic humanity was simultaneously courting nuclear holocaust and waging an environmental war against a shared world, fracturing that fragile symbiosis between *Homo sapiens* and Mother Nature and subsequently threatening the annihilation of all Earth's inhabitants. "While our … planet soars through the universe," he wrote in his essay "Our Silent Enemy," humanity endeavors to develop, stockpile, and release "all the explosives … all the poisons … the human [mind] can possibly contrive to eradicate … [all] biological life." Heyerdahl believed that the "modern venoms we carelessly throw away" and the pollutions that accumulate silently are distributed among all nations by Earth's rotation, cyclical air, and ocean currents.[14]

Sailing westward across the North Atlantic Ocean, Heyerdahl's *Ra* and *Ra II* had witnessed the ocean's degradation by oil, hydrocarbons, pesticides, industrial chemicals, and other devastating contaminants. Inundated by inorganic flotsam, wildlife-entangling jetsam, and industrial refuse, his environmentalism became galvanized into sustained political agitation. After *Ra's* 1969 voyage, an expedition that was never intended to draw biological or ecological conclusions from oceanic observations, Heyerdahl presented an alarming report of Atlantic Ocean contamination to the United Nations through a letter that became much publicized throughout the world. Further investigation, commissioned by Secretary General U Thant, was undertaken during *Ra II's* successful 1970 voyage. Heyerdahl went on to present his findings to the Oslo Convention in 1972 and to the United States Congress, enacting real legislative change in Norway and landing himself an advocacy role for the Norwegian Department of Foreign Affairs. Heyerdahl's discovery of Atlantic Ocean degradation, had, he declared, "more impact than the voyage of *Ra* itself. People could hardly believe that the open seas were polluted. I myself thought [that] was impossible. How could [insignificant] Man pollute the whole, gigantic ocean?"[15]

Acknowledging in 1971, "the effect of pelagic pollution upon the chemical and biological factors guiding the life functions of plankton and other microorganisms," and that "pollution observed must inevitably reduce light penetration and hence photosynthesis by phyto-plankton on which virtually all other life in the ocean depends," Heyerdahl's apolitical report emphasized "the alarming fact that the Atlantic Ocean is becoming seriously polluted, [and] a continued indiscriminate use of the world's oceans as an international dumping ground for imperishable human refuse may have irreparable effects on the productivity and very survival of plant and animal species."[16]

Industrialized humanity had produced materials undesirable to Mother Nature: that were "indestructible substances which fall outside the functional life cycle of evolution … in the ecological world. Modern synthetics [plastics, pesticides], and other chlorinated hydrocarbons, are eternally dead and non-transferable." With the oceans serving as the cesspool for the world's now-polluted fields, lakes, and rivers, towns, cities, and industries, humanity was rapidly annihilating Earth's "only indispensable purification system." Heyerdahl was one of the first to recognize that the ocean's ceaseless movement spread these pollutants across the world, devastating oxygen-producing plankton, marine, and coastal life, and eventually entering humankind's food and water supply. "The spice that one nation adds to the soup, all of us have to taste." He cautioned, "we must never forget that we are part of a … symbiosis of biological species ranging from the oxygen-producing plankton of the sea and forests of the land to the food-producing soil and water." Humanity's survival necessitates the protection of nature's complex ecosystem to sustain an "equilibrium between the multitude of biological species." Only the restoration of this essential equilibrium could prevent a holocaust of all Earth's species. "Man represents the crown of a family tree with all its roots in the ocean," Heyerdahl wrote. Earth's ecosystem is that tree, and "we draw all our sap from the rest of the tree as long as it keeps its roots and branches. Man, the top shoot, is a vulnerable part of an ecological entity, totally incapable of independent survival."[17] Life would "be impossible both now and in the future without life in the ocean."[18]

Heyerdahl's environmentalism was not limited to oceanic degradation–deforestation also plagued the explorer's consciousness. "Man came into existence somewhere in the forest as a genuine child of the virgin sylva," yet "man, and not any of the innumerable beasts of prey, giant reptiles, parasites or pests … began afflicting lasting wounds to the mother forest which had given him his very existence."[19] Only modern-day conservation endeavors, restoration of the ecological balance undone by wholesale monoculture, and preservation of Earth's forests will prevent their complete devastation and restore humanity's symbiotic, life-sustaining relationship with nature.

Heyerdahl's solution for the problems facing our natural world was again based on his recognition of the fallacy of the claims of respective nations on territory, both on land and sea. He frequently analogized Earth's oceans to one large lake: "A dead ocean [is] a dead planet," he declared, "and it makes no difference whether we live in Switzerland or on the Riviera."[20] He had assumed that industry, or political leadership, would address world environmental concerns. In later life, however, becoming more knowledgeable about ocean degradation through the marine research conducted by his son, Thor Jr., he advocated for individual political action at the Norwegian Institute of Marine Research, through his work with One World, Green Cross, WWF, and Worldview International Foundation. The hour had come "for every man in the street to demand … something be done—we must preserve our environment, whether water or land or air." Individual political action also required conscientious education of, and active participation by, a new generation of engaged environmentalists. "Young blood and fresh [minds]—open eyes and new thoughts—must be injected into an old global civilization which, according to the declarations of all experts, is about to destroy the environment and itself."[21] While still possessing time to preserve Earth, "our children," he declared in 1982, should be informed that humanity has "nowhere to escape, nowhere to emigrate, no alternative but to work together intelligently and effectively in safeguarding the perpetual rotation of the hands of the global clockwork. We cannot [continue interfering] with the biological cogwheels and changing the surface features of our planet eternally without affecting the intricate performance of the clock."[22]

Appealing for environmental protections, Heyerdahl recognized the absolute necessity of an international alliance, transcending faith, geography, nationality, and ideology, to preserve all life on Earth. "Whether we are Hindus, Buddhists, Jews, Christians, Moslems, or Darwinists … we all agree that man was created by an ecosystem which functioned with nature's own law of balance until mankind entered and took the lead as masters of creation."[23] Humankind was now at a decisive juncture, having long erroneously equated civilization and modern industrialization with enlightened progress. "[Our] planet is not designed as a home for man alone. Our extended family which grew up on this planet before us, comprises all species … planted as tiny seeds to grow up, enjoy a limited lifetime on Earth and multiply to survive eternally as a species …. We have all inherited life from our common ancestors, the single-celled plankton that began the evolution of all life on Earth." Recognizing that humankind depended entirely upon the ocean for survival and evolution, authoring the future required drawing from our known shared past. Heyerdahl implored every individual to "reach an open hand to fellow humans everywhere, and whenever you can, use both hands to protect nature. All members of mankind's extended family were here before us to give us living conditions. We all need them … to survive together forever."[24]

→»»

Despite his invaluable archaeological excavations and research, Heyerdahl remained largely committed to advancing his migration hypotheses, emphasizing ethnographic enquiry and his own individual environmental efforts rather than sustained legislative agitation. Nevertheless, environmentalism remained central to his enduring belief in an essential symbiosis between humankind and nature. And, despite regularly traveling across the world, Heyerdahl's self-sustaining life at his Italian residence at Colla Michieri was also emblematic of his nature-centered ideology, with a vegetable garden, orchards, and an olive grove providing the household's necessities—a household without a telephone or vehicle, with transport provided by mule. Embracing pastoral village life, unchanged by either modernity or millennia's passage and necessitating only minimal toll upon Earth's resources while preserving time-honored agricultural practices and symbiotic husbandry, he continued in his reverence for nature: "If I was ever going to pray to anything it would be the sun and the full moon, as symbols of nature."[25]

And it was here, at Colla Micheri, with pine trees soughing over the Ligurian Peninsula, suffusing harmoniously with the scent of sun-baked Italian soil, coupled with the saline breath of Heyerdahl's beloved Mediterranean Sea, he finally lay, now 87 years old, refusing food, water, and medication after being diagnosed with a brain tumor several days before.[i] Surrounded by the entire Heyerdahl kinfolk and gazing meditatively at a child's wooden diorama of Noah's Ark (itself a Sumerian reed vessel) he had constructed many years ago, he took his last breath on 18 April 2002, and embarked upon a final unfathomable voyage across the uncharted *mare incognitum* ("unknown sea") to that vast *terra incognita* ("unexplored territory") only death inhabits. "The sea I would like to see is the one I saw in 1947 when I crossed 4,300 miles [7,000 km] of the Pacific Ocean from Peru to the Tuamotu Islands in Polynesia with the balsa raft *Kon-Tiki*," Heyerdahl had declared within an elegiac, mediative essay. "Or better still the one seen by the Phoenicians, the Vikings and Columbus when man did no more harm to the marine environment than the whales and fish and plankton that abounded in the sparkling water. Future generations will never see such an ocean unless the present generation begins to understand what the ocean really is, and take steps to prevent its destruction."[26]

i Heyerdahl had once revealed that his desired passage from our earthly plain was to travel back to Peru, construct another balsa-wood raft that accommodated just one solitary argonaut, have it furnished with fresh produce and the finest red wine, then cast forth, alone, sailing away into the sunset of oblivion.

Top: Knut M. Haugland, Thor Heyerdahl, Herman Watzinger, President Truman, unknown, Erik Hesselberg, and Torstein Raaby in the garden of the White House, Washington, unfolding the American flag that flew on the *Kon-Tiki* raft.

Top right: Thor Heyerdahl showing Queen Elizabeth II around the Kon-Tiki Museum in 1955.

Opposite (top): Thor Heyerdahl looking at small stone figurines (cave stones) from Rapa Nui in the basement of the Kon-Tiki Museum in 1956.

Opposite (bottom): Josephine Baker and Knut M. Haugland, crewmember of the Kon-Tiki expedition and director of the Kon-Tiki Museum, onboard the Kon-Tiki raft, 1954.

Opposite: Arnold Jacoby and Thor Heyerdahl walking along the old Roman road leading into the town square at Colla Micheri, in the early 1960s.

Top: Thor Heyerdahl in his study, located in an old hunting tower, in Colla Micheri, Italy.

Bottom: Thor Heyerdahl Jr. (playing ukulele) and Bjørn (Bamse) Heyerdahl playing Polynesian songs while their sister Annette listens, in the house of Thor and Yvonne Heyerdahl in 1956–58.

Top: Thor Heyerdahl at the 7th International Congress of Anthropological and Ethnological Sciences in Moscow in 1964.

Bottom: Arne Skjølsvold and Captain de Broek, who sailed the ship that took the Franco-Belgian Expedition to Rapa Nui in 1934, visits the Kon-Tiki Museum.

Opposite: Annette Heyerdahl, Yvonne Heyerdahl, and Thor Heyerdahl celebrating the 20th anniversary of the Kon-Tiki expedition on an island in the Oslo fjord.

A ceremony in the office of the United Nations Secretary General Kurt Waldheim, during the awarding of the third International Pahlavi Environmental Award to Thor Heyerdahl and Mohammad El-Kassas. (from left: Thor Heyerdahl, unknown, Kurt Waldheim, Mohammad El-Kassas).

The International Pahlavi Environment Prize
1978
Thor Heyerdahl
Field Of The Environment

Volcanic eruption in the Hawaiian Islands.

Opposite:
The Dalai Lama and Thor Heyerdahl.

Right: Thor Heyerdahl worked well into old age, completing excavations and research all over the world.

“The essence is the same today as in the days of the Pharaohs, it is the same for someone from the Congo as it is for someone from Norway, in Alaska as in the Sahara. And it is symbolized by nature itself. By the magic rays of the sun, the mystery of the moonlight, the splendor of the flowers, the solid power of the mountains, the purity of the spring water, the abundant diversity of wildlife, and the love and charm of the human couple. It is a bottomless source from which we can fetch. And we are allowed to fetch as much as we want. Not only do we have permission to use this source, we have a moral duty to do so. We have attempted this once before, but with flawed prerequisites. It took us a long step forward, we have learned a lot from our South Sea adventure. More than we realize ourselves, I believe. We have become more humble, have learned that it is more than the outer physical nature that creates happiness and harmony, we have learned that a paradise is not found on this Earth, but that it can be wonderful and full of possibilities despite this fact."

Heyerdahl, T. (3 June 1944), letter to Liv Heyerdahl.

Revisiting Thor Heyerdahl's Oceanic Migration Hypotheses

Atholl Anderson
Oceanic Archaeologist

In developing his ideas about Polynesian origins, Thor Heyerdahl mined a rich vein of romantic diffusionism from the works of Edward Tregear, Percy Smith, John MacMillan Brown, and other Oceanic ethnologists from 1880–1930. They envisaged almost effortless voyages that populated Polynesia with Eurasian migrants who were described as "Aryan" in origin and language, with some traveling through North America and others moving to and from South America. Heyerdahl's subscription to these ideas, although they had long been dismissed peremptorily by anthropologists, coloured the scholarly evaluation of his fieldwork projects, despite them being based on practical scientific method and in collaboration with archaeologists and other specialists. His research on long-distance maritime migration and an Amerindian role in Polynesian colonization was unorthodox but produced substantial conclusions, and it is worthwhile to consider how it might be assessed today.

Maritime Migration

Heyerdahl's long-distance voyages across the Atlantic (*Ra* and *Ra II*) and the Arabian Sea (*Tigris*) demonstrated the seafaring capability of reed-bundle rafts but not much else. There is circumstantial but debated evidence of travel in the tropical transatlantic and trans-Indian oceans, but because substantial wooden boats existed in the Mediterranean and Persian Gulf by the third millennium BC, before colonization of either the Canary Islands or the Maldives, voyaging on bundle rafts to them and beyond is a largely redundant proposition.

Conversely, the balsa-log raft *Kon-Tiki* was a transparently decisive experiment[i]. Heyerdahl had observed, and many Oceanic scholars have chosen to ignore, that there is a long history of balsa rafting on the Andean coast. The rafts were 18 to 33 feet (6–11 m) long, could sail several long passages before refitting, had a cargo capacity of 11 to 33 tons (10–30 tonnes), and possessed good windward ability with dagger boards and cotton sails. There are archaeological indications that, since 500 BC, there have been offshore passages of up to 3,000 miles (5,000 km) between Mexico and Peru. *Kon-Tiki* inspired 20 subsequent rafting expeditions and computer simulated drifting, all of which show that rafting from Ecuador and Peru to Polynesia was eminently feasible. It was thought that the powerful Humboldt Current could push rafts north into the Galápagos Islands, where Heyerdahl found sites with Amerindian pottery, and later research showing no prehistoric habitation there is consistent with the strong sailing capability of the rafts.

Heyerdahl's voyaging argument was almost universally rejected by archaeologists. Academic opinion

i So much so that it has been adopted as a rhetorical type: "Kon-Tiki experiments"; Novick, A., Currie A., McQueen E., and N. Brouwer (2020), *Philosophy of Science* 87: 213-236.

held that Polynesian canoes had been capable of sailing to and from South America and, therefore, the few items of Polynesian culture that had indisputable American origins, notably the *kumara* or sweet potato, had more probably been transferred in Polynesian excursions. In other words, contact between Polynesia and South America was made west to east, not east to west. It has been difficult to document this contention. Polynesian canoe and raft voyages using modern versions of traditional sailing rigs have failed to reach South America. If they had been rigged with the inferred sails of the Polynesian colonization era, then success would have been even less likely.

It is unsurprising, therefore, that evidence considered important in supporting the idea of Polynesian landfalls in South America is now plainly in question. Statistical analysis of Amerindian and Polynesian types of hand clubs shows no pre-European relationship; in Chile, Polynesian DNA is absent in the Mocha Island burials showing the "Polynesian" skeletal traits, and the Pre-Columbian "chicken" bones from El Arenal appear to have been from the native tinamou (Nothoprocta perdicaria). The case for Hawaiians reaching California is, likewise, archaeologically dubious and its linguistic basis has been dismantled. The Polynesian voyaging hypothesis is now much less reasonable as an explanation of South American contact than Heyerdahl's hypothesis of Amerindian balsa rafts sailing into Polynesia.

Amerindian Pacific Migration

Heyerdahl asserted that Andean migrants from the Tiwanakan culture (AD 400–1100) brought monumental architecture to Rapa Nui. His argument, however, has been contradicted by the unique occurrence of Polynesian artifacts and Pacific rat bones in the oldest Rapa Nui sites, which have now been radiocarbon dated to 1150–1280, and exclusive Polynesian habitation is now widely accepted. Nevertheless, recent developments provide support for Heyerdahl's hypothesis of Amerindian migration.

The famous Ahu Tahiri (Ahu Vinapu 1), probably built 1300–1500, has construction characteristics also found in the Incan period of 1400–1532: precisely fitted rectangular or trapezoidal blocks laid in 'quasi-courses'; curvature in plan with rounded corners (which can be noted in regional Incan building); convex curvature to block faces and chamfering on joint lines with some blocks having corner cutouts fitted with shaped inserts. Both the block thickness and wall batter (the slope of the wall) are also within Inca ranges.

Birdman figures on Rapa Nui, in general, have long, hooked beaks, circular eyes with a visible pupil, and limbs with five-digit fingers and toes. Many are depicted face-to-face in pairs that are joined at the feet, hands, or beak, and some hold a round object in their hands, possibly a ceremonial egg. Their age is uncertain, but 86 percent of them are at Orongo, where the earliest houses date to the 16th century. Paired figures closest in form to the Rapa Nui examples can be found mainly in the Manteño-Guancavilca culture of coastal Ecuador, dating to 1100–1530.

Rapa Nui *tupa* are circular stone towers with an internal cavity reached by a narrow passage. There is uncertainty about their purpose, but some contain human remains and historical evidence suggests a mortuary function. These *tupa* have not been dated, but they are similar in construction to early forms of *chullpa*, dating to 1100–1450, which can be found in the northern Andes. These were tombs for communal aboveground burial and they served as sites of ancestor veneration. It is plausible that the *tupa* reflect the Andean form and functions as well as their name.

The probability that these cultural similarities, in both form and age, represent actual Amerindian habitation on Rapa Nui is indicated persuasively by genetic research on East Polynesian human DNA. The admixture of Amerindian and Polynesian DNA found on the Society, Marquesas, Tuamotu, and Gambier islands from about 1200, and on Rapa Nui from about 1380 supports earlier genetic research indicating an Amerindian influx 1300–1500. Amerindian arrival on Rapa Nui might have occurred as a separate dispersal and archaeological data suggest that, from about the 15th century, megalithic *ahu* construction dispersed westward to French Polynesia.

Because the Rapa Nui items are not matched unequivocally elsewhere in East Polynesia, and they closely resemble cognate forms in late prehistoric Ecuador and Peru, it is implausible that they developed independently on the Polynesian island nearest to an existing source. It is also improbable that multiple, intricate resemblances in material culture were reproduced on Rapa Nui by recalling fleeting observations in South America. Therefore, when compared to propositions of convergent development or stylistic adoption, the remarkable concordance of Rapa Nui art and architecture with contemporary Andean parallels favors the cultural transference hypothesis advocated by Heyerdahl.

Looking Forward

Ancient tropical-oceanic migration is actively under investigation in the Indian Ocean, less so in the Atlantic, while possible migration between the Americas and Oceania continues to revolve around an impediment in the research of the southeast Pacific. Since at least 1870, both South American and Polynesian archaeologists had preferred to keep their research domains apart, and Heyerdahl's more peculiar beliefs only reinforced that territorial circumscription. Infrequent Polynesian return voyages to South America have been accepted, but Amerindian dispersal into the Pacific with settlement on Rapa Nui has been viewed from both perspectives as subversive. Consequently, collaboration on the systematic sampling and quantitative analyses of archaeological collections, radiocarbon databases, historical linguistics, and other material needed to establish the extent, if any, of direct cultural transmission between South America and East Polynesia has happened relatively seldom and never with the diversity and scale that is needed.

We need to get over the territorial issues and collaborate in multidisciplinary research aimed at elucidating the kinds, extent, timing, and agencies of pre-European connectivity across the southeast Pacific. In his academically untutored way, that was part of what Heyerdahl was trying to do and, in retrospect, it appears that he made a more important contribution to the broad objective than he has been given credit for.

Epilogue

Thor Heyerdahl, Changemaker

Sylvia Earle Oceanographer

During his lifetime, Thor Heyerdahl significantly contributed to answering the questions that have inspired humanity for as long as we have existed: Who are we? Where did we come from? And where might we be going? While his lifelong passion was unraveling puzzles about human connections, Heyerdahl was also mindful that humans are a part of nature. More than most of his scientific colleagues, he recognized and cared about how the environment determines human success and failure and questioned "common knowledge" with uncommon willingness to prove or disprove dogmatic concepts, putting himself at the cutting edge of learning.

Heyerdahl helped document the greatest era of change in the history of civilization, his life spanning the latter part of the Holocene epoch and the start of a new epoch, the Anthropocene, marked by the impact of human industrialization, destruction of wilderness, and fallout from nuclear detonations. Until then, it seemed that nothing that humans could do could alter the habitability of Earth. Air, water, land, and wildlife were treated as limitless "natural resources" to be used or consumed to foster human prosperity. During the early part of the Holocene, only a few thousand humans existed. As a young man, Heyerdahl was one of about two billion. That number doubled by 1980 and it has since doubled again. Supporting our needs and desires is putting unprecedented pressure on the natural systems that underpin our existence. About 90 percent of the fish consumed by humans are at a fraction of their former abundance and coral reefs, mangroves, seagrass meadows, and kelp forests have been reduced by about half. Heyerdahl wrote about the pristine nature of the sea while aboard the *Kon-Tiki* in 1947, and how in a few decades, aboard *Ra II*, he witnessed tar balls, oil slicks, and an avalanche of refuse sweeping the ocean.

I first met Heyerdahl in the 1970s. He was curious about my findings as a scientist and "aquanaut" under the sea compared to his observations from the surface. We shared the wonder of the recent first images from the moon, which made it clear that Earth is mostly blue and that boundaries imposed by humans tend to disappear when viewed from high above, under, or on the sea. Heyerdahl demonstrated that the sea has not only been a formidable barrier over the ages but also a well-traveled network of aquatic highways, connecting people over vast distances. His brilliant accounts, laced with wonder, scientific insights, and humor, take readers into the unknown, traveling with him and his multinational crew. Compassion and respect for life in the sea develops, as it becomes clear how all living things are connected to the ocean. While defining ancient pathways traveled by humans, he simultaneously gathered vital insights about other high-seas voyagers, from sharks, whales, turtles, dolphins, squid, and birds to legions of planktonic creatures. If the ocean is in trouble, so are we. It is, and we are. But Heyerdahl remained optimistic that the 21st century could be the turning point from decline to recovery as the dire consequences of conflict and complacency come into focus.

We met many more times over the years. In the 1980s, I joined Heyerdahl and Sir Peter Scott on a mission to win support for a moratorium on commercially killing whales. And in the 1990s, I was with Heyerdahl at Japan's Osaka Aquarium when I had my first glimpse of a whale shark. Heyerdahl described an encounter with one twice her size during the Kon-Tiki expedition. At the time, little was known about their generally gentle nature and the black and white images of the encounter were among the first ever recorded. The last time I spoke with Heyerdahl was at an Explorers Club event celebrating the accomplishments of 20th century scientists and explorers. Among them, a certain tall, thoughtful Norwegian loomed large for his decades of heroic efforts to understand the past as the vital prelude to an enduring future for all of life on Earth.

Thor Heyerdahl's most important legacy may be as a champion for nature, inspiring others to see the significance of the living ocean to everything we care about: health, prosperity, security, and most of all, the existence of life itself. Late in his life, he composed a message to his children and to all the children to come, asking for forgiveness for what we, their predecessors, have done to diminish their chance for success. He seeks their help to "Heal the system we have wounded. All that walk and crawl and swim and fly are members of our extended family." Thank you, Thor Heyerdahl, for your inspired leadership, and especially for your message of hope that we can and will find an enduring place for ourselves within the wild, mostly blue, systems that sustain us.

Endnotes

GENESIS

Prologue
1 Jacoby A. (1967) *Señor Kon Tiki*, p. 64.
2 Jacoby A. (1967) *Señor Kon Tiki*, p. 29.

HEYERDAHL'S NORWEGIAN BOYHOOD
1 Jacoby A. (1967) *Señor Kon Tiki*, p. 29.
2 Heyerdahl T. (3 June 1944) letter to Liv Heyerdahl.
3 Heyerdahl T. (1927-28) school essay book.
4 Heyerdahl T. (1996) *Green was the Earth on the Seventh Day*, p. 29.
5 Jacoby A. (1967) *Señor Kon Tiki*, p. 31.
6 15 Heyerdahl T. (1996) *Green was the Earth on the Seventh Day*, p. 28.
7 Heyerdahl T. (1996) *Green was the Earth on the Seventh Day*, p. 31.
8 Heyerdahl T. (1996) *Green was the Earth on the Seventh Day*, p. 31.
9 Heyerdahl T. (1974) *Fatu-Hiva: Back to Nature*, p. 9.
10 Heyerdahl T. (1996) *Green was the Earth on the Seventh Day*, p. 36.
11 Heyerdahl T. (1974) *Fatu-Hiva: Back to Nature*, p. 12.
12 Heyerdahl T. (1996) *Green was the Earth on the Seventh Day*, p. 38.

REVELATION
1 Heyerdahl T. (1996) *Green was the Earth on the Seventh Day*, p. 39.
2 Heyerdahl T. (1996) *Green was the Earth on the Seventh Day*, p. 42.
3 Heyerdahl T. (1996) *Green was the Earth on the Seventh Day*, pp. 58-59.
4 Heyerdahl T. (1974) *Fatu-Hiva: Back to Nature*, p. 33.
5 Heyerdahl T. (1974) *Fatu-Hiva: Back to Nature*, p. 35.
6 Heyerdahl T. (1974) *Fatu-Hiva: Back to Nature*, p. 38.
7 Heyerdahl T. (1974) *Fatu-Hiva: Back to Nature*, p. 38.
8 Heyerdahl T. (1996) *Green was the Earth on the Seventh Day*, p. 70.
9 Heyerdahl T. (1974) *Fatu-Hiva: Back to Nature*, p. 45.
10 Heyerdahl T. (1996) *Green was the Earth on the Seventh Day*, p. 71.
11 Heyerdahl T. (1974) *Fatu-Hiva: Back to Nature*, p. 47.
12 Heyerdahl T. (1974) *Fatu-Hiva: Back to Nature*, p. 54.
13 Heyerdahl T. (1974) *Fatu-Hiva: Back to Nature*, p. 71.
14 Heyerdahl T. (1974) *Fatu-Hiva: Back to Nature*, p. 55.
15 Heyerdahl T. (1996) *Green was the Earth on the Seventh Day*, p. 83.
16 Heyerdahl T. (1996) *Green was the Earth on the Seventh Day*, p. 153.
17 Heyerdahl T. (1974) *Fatu-Hiva: Back to Nature*, p. 165.
18 Heyerdahl T. (1974) *Fatu-Hiva: Back to Nature*, p. 166.
19 Heyerdahl T. (1974) *Fatu-Hiva: Back to Nature*, p. 147.
20 Heyerdahl T. (1996) *Green was the Earth on the Seventh Day*, p. 160.
21 Heyerdahl T. (8 June 1937) letter to his parents in law.
22 Heyerdahl T. (1996) *Green was the Earth on the Seventh Day*, pp. 159-160

HYPOTHESIS
1 Heyerdahl T. (1974) *Fatu-Hiva: Back to Nature*, p. 216.
2 Heyerdahl T. (1948) *Kon-Tiki: By Raft Across the South Seas*, p. 11.
3 Heyerdahl T. (1974) *Fatu-Hiva: Back to Nature*, p. 218.
4 Heyerdahl T. (1974) *Fatu-Hiva: Back to Nature*, p. 234.
5 Heyerdahl T. (1974) *Fatu-Hiva: Back to Nature*, p. 227.
6 Heyerdahl T. (1974) *Fatu-Hiva: Back to Nature*, p. 233.
7 Heyerdahl T. (1974) *Fatu-Hiva: Back to Nature*, p. 229.
8 Heyerdahl T. (1974) *Fatu-Hiva: Back to Nature*, p. 266.
9 Heyerdahl T. (1974) *Fatu-Hiva: Back to Nature*, p. 13.
10 Heyerdahl T. (1974) *Fatu-Hiva: Back to Nature*, pp. 263-265.
11 Heyerdahl T. (1974) *Fatu-Hiva: Back to Nature*, p. 264.

RESOLUTION
1 Heyerdahl T. (1948) *Kon-Tiki: By Raft Across the South Seas*, p. 22.
2 Heyerdahl T. (1948) *Kon-Tiki: By Raft Across the South Seas*, p. 22.
3 Heyerdahl T. (1948) *Kon-Tiki: By Raft Across the South Seas*, p. 14
4 Heyerdahl T. (1948) *Kon-Tiki: By Raft Across the South Seas*, p. 18.
5 Heyerdahl T. (1946) "Polynesia and America; A Study of Prehistoric Relations."
6 Heyerdahl T. (1996) *Green was the Earth on the Seventh Day*, p. 259.
7 Heyerdahl T. (27 August 1944) letter to Liv Heyerdahl.
8 Heyerdahl T. (1948) *Kon-Tiki: By Raft Across the South Seas*, p. 23.
9 Heyerdahl T. (1948) *Kon-Tiki: By Raft Across the South Seas*, p. 25.

UNCEASING VOYAGES

KON-TIKI EXPEDITION
1 Heyerdahl T. (1948) *Kon-Tiki: By Raft Across the South Seas*, pp. 30-31.
2 Heyerdahl T. (1948) *Kon-Tiki: By Raft Across the South Seas*, pp. 38-39.
3 Heyerdahl T. (1948) *Kon-Tiki: By Raft Across the South Seas*, pp. 57-58.
4 Heyerdahl T. (1948) *Kon-Tiki: By Raft Across the South Seas*, p. 73.
5 Heyerdahl T. (1948) *Kon-Tiki: By Raft Across the South Seas*, pp. 79-80.
6 Heyerdahl T. (1948) *Kon-Tiki: By Raft Across the South Seas*, p. 83.
7 Heyerdahl T. (1948) *Kon-Tiki: By Raft Across the South Seas*, p. 89.
8 Heyerdahl T. (1948) *Kon-Tiki: By Raft Across the South Seas*, p. 94.
9 Heyerdahl T. (1948) *Kon-Tiki: By Raft Across the South Seas*, pp. 94-98.
10 Heyerdahl T. (1948) *Kon-Tiki: By Raft Across the South Seas*, p. 113.
11 Heyerdahl T. (1948) *Kon-Tiki: By Raft Across the South Seas*, p. 120.
12 Heyerdahl T. (1948) *Kon-Tiki: By Raft Across the South Seas*, pp. 129-130.
13 Heyerdahl T. (1948) *Kon-Tiki: By Raft Across the South Seas*, p. 143.
14 Heyerdahl T. (1948) *Kon-Tiki: By Raft Across the South Seas*, pp. 153-154.
15 Heyerdahl T. (1948) *Kon-Tiki: By Raft Across the South Seas*, p. 184.
16 Heyerdahl T. (1948) *Kon-Tiki: By Raft Across the South Seas*, pp. 182-183.
17 Heyerdahl T. (1948) *Kon-Tiki: By Raft Across the South Seas*, p. 184.
18 Heyerdahl T. (1948) *Kon-Tiki: By Raft Across the South Seas*, p. 236.
19 Heyerdahl T. (1948) *Kon-Tiki: By Raft Across the South Seas*, p. 237.
20 Heyerdahl T. (1948) *Kon-Tiki: By Raft Across the South Seas*, p. 198.
21 Heyerdahl T. (1948) *Kon-Tiki: By Raft Across the South Seas*, p. 202.
22 Heyerdahl T. (1948) *Kon-Tiki: By Raft Across the South Seas*, p. 204.
23 Heyerdahl T. (1948) *Kon-Tiki: By Raft Across the South Seas*, p. 206.
24 Heyerdahl T. (1948) *Kon-Tiki: By Raft Across the South Seas*, p. 207.
25 Heyerdahl T. (1948) *Kon-Tiki: By Raft Across the South Seas*, p. 241.
26 Heyerdahl T. (1948) *Kon-Tiki: By Raft Across the South Seas*, p. 256.
27 Heyerdahl T. (1948) *Kon-Tiki: By Raft Across the South Seas*, pp. 266-267.
28 Heyerdahl T. (1948) *Kon-Tiki: By Raft Across the South Seas*, p. 284.
29 Heyerdahl T. (1948) *Kon-Tiki: By Raft Across the South Seas*, p. 288.
30 Heyerdahl T. (1948) *Kon-Tiki: By Raft Across the South Seas*, p. 299.
31 Heyerdahl T. (1948) *Kon-Tiki: By Raft Across the South Seas*, p. 299.
32 Heyerdahl T. (1948) *Kon-Tiki: By Raft Across the South Seas*, pp. 300-302.
33 Heyerdahl T. (1948) *Kon-Tiki: By Raft Across the South Seas*, pp. 303-304.
34 Heyerdahl T. (1948) *Kon-Tiki: By Raft Across the South Seas*, pp. 307-312.
35 Heyerdahl T. (1948) *Kon-Tiki: By Raft Across the South Seas*, p. 313.
36 Heyerdahl T. (1950) Kon-Tiki [documentary transcript].
37 Heyerdahl T. (1948) *Kon-Tiki: By Raft Across the South Seas*, p. 314.
38 Heyerdahl T. (1948) *Kon-Tiki: By Raft Across the South Seas*, p. 372.
39 Heyerdahl T. (1948) *Kon-Tiki: By Raft Across the South Seas*, p. 373.
40 Heyerdahl T. (1948) *Kon-Tiki: By Raft Across the South Seas*, p. 375.
41 Sir Buck P. (1945) *An Introduction to Polynesian Anthropology*, p. ii.
42 Heyerdahl T. (1952) *American Indians in the Pacific*, p. 72.
43 Heyerdahl T. (1952) *American Indians in the Pacific*, p. 349.
44 Ekholm G. (1954) "Review: American Indians in the Pacific." *Geographical Review*, 44(2) p. 308.
45 Linton R. (1954) "Review: American Indians in the Pacific." *American Anthropologist*, New Series, 56(1): p. 123.
46 Norbeck E. (1953) "Review: American Indians in the Pacific." *American Antiquity*.

GALÁPAGOS EXPEDITION
1 Heyerdahl T. (1954) "Preliminary Report on the Discovery of Archaeology in the Galápagos Islands," p. 689.
2 Heyerdahl T. (1954) "Preliminary Report on the Discovery of Archaeology in the Galápagos Islands," pp. 688-689.
3 Heyerdahl T. (1954) "Preliminary Report on the Discovery of Archaeology in the Galápagos Islands," p. 692
4 Heyerdahl T. (1954) "Preliminary Report on the Discovery of Archaeology in the Galápagos Islands," p. 694.
5 Heyerdahl T. (1954) "Preliminary Report on the Discovery of Archaeology in the Galápagos Islands," p. 697.

EASTER ISLAND EXPEDITIONS
1 Heyerdahl T. (1958) *Aku-Aku: The Secret of Easter Island*, p.15.
2 Heyerdahl T. (1958) *Aku-Aku: The Secret of Easter Island*, p.16.
3 Heyerdahl T. (1958) *Aku-Aku: The Secret of Easter Island*, p.20.
4 Heyerdahl T. (1958) *Aku-Aku: The Secret of Easter Island*, p. 26.
5 Heyerdahl T. (1958) *Aku-Aku: The Secret of Easter Island*, p.22.
6 Heyerdahl T. (1958) *Aku-Aku: The Secret of Easter Island*, p.26.
7 Heyerdahl T. (1958) *Aku-Aku: The Secret of Easter Island*, p. 15.
8 Roggeveen J. (1722) Ship logs of 1722 voyage of Jacob Roggeveen (6 April).
9 Heyerdahl T. (1958) *Aku-Aku: The Secret of Easter Island*, p.26.
10 Heyerdahl T. (1958) *Aku-Aku: The Secret of Easter Island*, p. 26.
11 Heyerdahl T. (1958) *Aku-Aku: The Secret of Easter Island*, p. 55.
12 Heyerdahl T. (1958) *Aku-Aku: The Secret of Easter Island*, p. 47.
13 Heyerdahl T. (1958) *Aku-Aku: The Secret of Easter Island*, p. 38.
14 Heyerdahl T. (1958) *Aku-Aku: The Secret of Easter Island*, p. 67.
15 Heyerdahl T. (1958) *Aku-Aku: The Secret of Easter Island*, p. 74.
16 Heyerdahl T. (1958) *Aku-Aku: The Secret of Easter Island*, p. 86.
17 Heyerdahl T. (1958) *Aku-Aku: The Secret of Easter Island*, p. 86.
18 Heyerdahl T. (1958) *Aku-Aku: The Secret of Easter Island*, p. 88.
19 Heyerdahl T. (1958) *Aku-Aku: The Secret of Easter Island*, p. 92.
20 Heyerdahl T. (1958) *Aku-Aku: The Secret of Easter Island*, pp. 92-93.
21 Heyerdahl T. (1958) *Aku-Aku: The Secret of Easter Island*, p. 103.
22 Heyerdahl T. (1958) *Aku-Aku: The Secret of Easter Island*, p. 105
23 Heyerdahl T. (1958) *Aku-Aku: The Secret of Easter Island*, p. 105.
24 Heyerdahl T. (1958) *Aku-Aku: The Secret of Easter Island*, p. 113.
25 Heyerdahl T. (1958) *Aku-Aku: The Secret of Easter Island*, p. 129.
26 Heyerdahl T. (1958) *Aku-Aku: The Secret of Easter Island*, p. 131.
27 Heyerdahl T. (1958) *Aku-Aku: The Secret of Easter Island*, p. 134.
28 Heyerdahl T. (1958) *Aku-Aku: The Secret of Easter Island*, pp. 150-151.

29 Heyerdahl T. (1958) *Aku-Aku: The Secret of Easter Island*, pp. 181-182.
30 Heyerdahl T. (1958) Aku-Aku: The Secret of Easter Island, p. 220.
31 Heyerdahl T. (1989) *Easter Island: Mystery Solved*, p. 7.
32 Heyerdahl T. (1958) *Aku-Aku: The Secret of Easter Island*, p. 372.
33 Heyerdahl T. (1958) *Aku-Aku: The Secret of Easter Island*, p. 324.
34 Heyerdahl T. (1958) *Aku-Aku: The Secret of Easter Island*, p. 331.
35 Heyerdahl T. (1958) *Aku-Aku: The Secret of Easter Island*, p. 332.
36 Heyerdahl T. (1958) *Aku-Aku: The Secret of Easter Island*, pp. 327-328.
37 Heyerdahl T. (1958) *Aku-Aku: The Secret of Easter Island*, p.340.
38 Heyerdahl T. (1958) *Aku-Aku: The Secret of Easter Island*, p. 347.
39 Heyerdahl T. (1958) *Aku-Aku: The Secret of Easter Island*, p., 349.
40 Heyerdahl T. (1958) *Aku-Aku: The Secret of Easter Island*, pp. 372-373.
41 Heyerdahl T. (1958) *Aku-Aku: The Secret of Easter Island*, p.354.
42 Heyerdahl T. (1958) *Aku-Aku: The Secret of Easter Island*, pp. 372-373.
43 Heyerdahl T. (1989) *Easter Island: Mystery Solved*, p. 215.
44 Heyerdahl T. (1989) *Easter Island: Mystery Solved*, pp. 220-221.
45 Heyerdahl T. (1989) *Easter Island: Mystery Solved*, p. 215.
46 Heyerdahl T. (1989) *Easter Island: Mystery Solved*, p.226.
47 Heyerdahl T. (1989) *Easter Island: Mystery Solved*, p. 227.
48 Heyerdahl T. (1989) *Easter Island: Mystery Solved*, p. 245.
49 Heyerdahl T. (1989) *Easter Island: Mystery Solved*, p. 245.

RA & RA II EXPEDITIONS
1 Heyerdahl T. (1972) *The Ra Expeditions*, p. 15.
2 Heyerdahl T. (1972) *The Ra Expeditions*, p. 34.
3 Heyerdahl T. (1972) *The Ra Expeditions*, p. 32.
4 Boas F. (1925) "America and the Old World," *International Congress of Americanists*, vol 21, no. 2.
5 Heyerdahl T. (1972) *The Ra Expeditions*, p. 46.
6 Heyerdahl T. (1972) *The Ra Expeditions*, p. 47.
7 Heyerdahl T. (1972) *The Ra Expeditions*, p. 21.
8 Heyerdahl T. (1972) *The Ra Expeditions*, p. 23.
9 Heyerdahl T. (1972) *The Ra Expeditions*, p. 25.
10 Heyerdahl T. (1972) *The Ra Expeditions*, p. 26-27.
11 Heyerdahl T. (1972) *The Ra Expeditions*, p. 31.
12 Heyerdahl T. (1972) *The Ra Expeditions*, p.21.
13 Heyerdahl T. (1972) *The Ra Expeditions*, p. 16.
14 Heyerdahl T. (1972) *The Ra Expeditions*, p. 18.
15 Heyerdahl T. (1972) *The Ra Expeditions*, p. 72.
16 Heyerdahl T. (1972) *The Ra Expeditions*, p. 67.
17 Heyerdahl T. (1972) *The Ra Expeditions*, p. 69.
18 Heyerdahl T. (1972) *The Ra Expeditions*, p. 72.
19 Heyerdahl T. (1972) *The Ra Expeditions*, p. 75.
20 Heyerdahl T. (1972) *The Ra Expeditions*, p. 76.
21 Heyerdahl T. (1972) *The Ra Expeditions*, p. 87.
22 Heyerdahl T. (1972) *The Ra Expeditions*, p. 88.
23 Heyerdahl T. (1972) *The Ra Expeditions*, p. 91.
24 Heyerdahl T. (1972) *The Ra Expeditions*, p. 120.
25 Heyerdahl T. (1972) *The Ra Expeditions*, p. 123.
26 Heyerdahl T. (1972) *The Ra Expeditions*, p. 126.
27 Heyerdahl T. (1972) *The Ra Expeditions*, p. 163.
28 Heyerdahl T. (1972) *The Ra Expeditions*, p. 181.
29 Heyerdahl T. (1972) *The Ra Expeditions*, p. 190.
30 Heyerdahl T. (1972) *The Ra Expeditions*, p. 189.
31 Heyerdahl T. (1972) *The Ra Expeditions*, p. 206.
32 Heyerdahl T. (1972) *The Ra Expeditions*, p. 216.
33 Heyerdahl T. (1972) *The Ra Expeditions*, p. 217.
34 Heyerdahl T. (1972) *The Ra Expeditions*, p. 206.
35 Heyerdahl T. (1972) *The Ra Expeditions*, p. 182.
36 Heyerdahl T. (1972) *The Ra Expeditions*, p. 210.
37 Heyerdahl T. (1972) *The Ra Expeditions*, p. 232.
38 Heyerdahl T. (1972) *The Ra Expeditions*, p. 232.
39 Heyerdahl T. (1972) *The Ra Expeditions*, p. 226.
40 Heyerdahl T. (1972) *The Ra Expeditions*, p. 225.
41 Heyerdahl T. (1972) *The Ra Expeditions*, p. 347.
42 Heyerdahl T. (1972) *The Ra Expeditions*, p. 252.
43 Heyerdahl T. (1972) *The Ra Expeditions*, p. 259.
44 Heyerdahl T. (1972) *The Ra Expeditions*, p. 261.
45 Heyerdahl T. (1972) *The Ra Expeditions*, p. 291.
46 Heyerdahl T. (1972) *The Ra Expeditions*, p. 294.
47 Heyerdahl T. (1972) *The Ra Expeditions*, p. 309.
48 Heyerdahl T. (1972) *The Ra Expeditions*, p. 310.
49 Heyerdahl T. (1972) *The Ra Expeditions*, p. 311.
50 Heyerdahl T. (1972) *The Ra Expeditions*, p. 312.
51 Heyerdahl T. (1972) *The Ra Expeditions*, p. 313.
52 Heyerdahl T. (1972) *The Ra Expeditions*, p. 314.
53 Heyerdahl T. (1972) *The Ra Expeditions*, p. 314.
54 Heyerdahl T. (1972) *The Ra Expeditions*, p. 317.
55 Heyerdahl T. (1972) *The Ra Expeditions*, p. 323.
56 Heyerdahl T. (1972) *The Ra Expeditions*, p. 324.
57 Heyerdahl T. (1972) *The Ra Expeditions*, p. 325.
58 Heyerdahl T. (1972), *The Ra Expeditions*, p. 334.
59 Heyerdahl T. (1972), *The Ra Expeditions*, p. 335.
60 Heyerdahl T. (1972), *The Ra Expeditions*, p. 337.
61 Heyerdahl T. (1972), *The Ra Expeditions*, p. 359.
62 Heyerdahl T. (1972), *The Ra Expeditions*, p. 360.
63 Heyerdahl T. (1972), *The Ra Expeditions*, p. 361.
64 Heyerdahl T. (1972), *The Ra Expeditions*, p. 362.
65 Heyerdahl T. (1972), *The Ra Expeditions*, p. 363.
66 Heyerdahl T. (1972), *The Ra Expeditions*, p. 365.

TIGRIS EXPEDITION
1 Bibby, G. (22 August 1971) "The Ra Expeditions," *New York Times*, p. 21.
2 Heyerdahl T. (1982) *The Tigris Expedition: In Search of Our Beginnings*, p. 14.
3 Heyerdahl T. (1982) *The Tigris Expedition: In Search of Our Beginnings*, p. 3.
4 Heyerdahl T. (1982) *The Tigris Expedition: In Search of Our Beginnings*, p. 4.
5 Heyerdahl T. (1982) *The Tigris Expedition: In Search of Our Beginnings*, p. 6.
6 Heyerdahl T. (1982) *The Tigris Expedition: In Search of Our Beginnings*, p. 6.
7 Heyerdahl T. (1982) *The Tigris Expedition: In Search of Our Beginnings*, p. 5.
8 Heyerdahl T. (1982) *The Tigris Expedition: In Search of Our Beginnings*, p. 9.
9 Heyerdahl T. (1982) *The Tigris Expedition: In Search of Our Beginnings*, p. 18
10 Heyerdahl T. (1982) *The Tigris Expedition: In Search of Our Beginnings*, p. 36.
11 Heyerdahl T. (1982) *The Tigris Expedition: In Search of Our Beginnings*, p. 42.
12 Heyerdahl T. (1982) *The Tigris Expedition: In Search of Our Beginnings*, p. 43.
13 Heyerdahl T. (1982) *The Tigris Expedition: In Search of Our Beginnings*, p. 51.
14 Heyerdahl T. (1982) *The Tigris Expedition: In Search of Our Beginnings*, p. 72.
15 Heyerdahl T. (1982) *The Tigris Expedition: In Search of Our Beginnings*, p. 75.
16 Heyerdahl T. (1982) *The Tigris Expedition: In Search of Our Beginnings*, p. 73.
17 Heyerdahl T. (1982) *The Tigris Expedition: In Search of Our Beginnings*, p. 60.
18 Heyerdahl T. (1982) *The Tigris Expedition: In Search of Our Beginnings*, p. 67.
19 Heyerdahl T. (1982) *The Tigris Expedition: In Search of Our Beginnings*, p. 68.
20 Heyerdahl T. (1982) *The Tigris Expedition: In Search of Our Beginnings*, p. 78.
21 Heyerdahl T. (1982) *The Tigris Expedition: In Search of Our Beginnings*, p. 82.
22 Heyerdahl T. (1982) *The Tigris Expedition: In Search of Our Beginnings*, p. 83.
23 Heyerdahl T. (1982) *The Tigris Expedition: In Search of Our Beginnings*, p. 87.
24 Heyerdahl T. (1982) *The Tigris Expedition: In Search of Our Beginnings*, p. 111.
25 Heyerdahl T. (1982) *The Tigris Expedition: In Search of Our Beginnings*, p. 131.
26 Heyerdahl T. (1982) *The Tigris Expedition: In Search of Our Beginnings*, p. 134.
27 Heyerdahl T. (1982) *The Tigris Expedition: In Search of Our Beginnings*, p. 136.
28 Heyerdahl T. (1982) *The Tigris Expedition: In Search of Our Beginnings*, p. 164.
29 Heyerdahl T. (1982) *The Tigris Expedition: In Search of Our Beginnings*, p. 178.
30 Heyerdahl T. (1982) *The Tigris Expedition: In Search of Our Beginnings*, p. 179.
31 Heyerdahl T. (1982) *The Tigris Expedition: In Search of Our Beginnings*, p. 186.
32 Heyerdahl T. (1982) *The Tigris Expedition: In Search of Our Beginnings*, p. 211.
33 Heyerdahl T. (1982) *The Tigris Expedition: In Search of Our Beginnings*, p. 216.
34 Heyerdahl T. (1982) *The Tigris Expedition: In Search of Our Beginnings*, p. 264.
35 Heyerdahl T. (1982) *The Tigris Expedition: In Search of Our Beginnings*, p. 280.
36 Heyerdahl T. (1982) *The Tigris Expedition: In Search of Our Beginnings*, p. 286.
37 Heyerdahl T. (1982) *The Tigris Expedition: In Search of Our Beginnings*, p. 288.
38 Heyerdahl T. (1982) *The Tigris Expedition: In Search of Our Beginnings*, p. 310.
39 Heyerdahl T. (1982) *The Tigris Expedition: In Search of Our Beginnings*, p. 311.
40 Heyerdahl T. (1982) *The Tigris Expedition: In Search of Our Beginnings*, p. 326.
41 Heyerdahl T. (1982) *The Tigris Expedition: In Search of Our Beginnings*, p. 333.
42 Heyerdahl T. (1982) *The Tigris Expedition: In Search of Our Beginnings*, p. 334.
43 Heyerdahl T. (1982) *The Tigris Expedition: In Search of Our Beginnings*, pp. 336-37.

MALDIVES EXPEDITIONS
1 Heyerdahl T. (21 December 1983) letter to Clarence Maloney.
2 Heyerdahl T. (1987) *The Maldive Mystery*, p. 6.
3 Heyerdahl T. (1987) *The Maldive Mystery*, pp. 15.
4 Heyerdahl T. (1983-84) interview with Neil Hollander.
5 Heyerdahl T. (1987) *The Maldive Mystery*, p. 22.
6 Heyerdahl T. (1987) *The Maldive Mystery*, p.55.
7 Heyerdahl T. (1987) *The Maldive Mystery*, p.171.
8 Heyerdahl T. (1987) *The Maldive Mystery*, pp. 117-123.
9 *The Kon-Tiki Museum Occasional Papers, Archaeological Test-Excavations on The Maldive Islands*, Volume 2, Oslo, 1991, pp.66, 67.
10 *The Kon-Tiki Museum Occasional Papers, Archaeological Test-Excavations on The Maldive Islands*, Volume 2, Oslo, 1991, p. 70.
11 Heyerdahl T. (1987) *The Maldive Mystery*, p. 166.
12 Heyerdahl T. (1983-84) interview with Neil Hollander.
13 Heyerdahl T. (1987) *The Maldive Mystery*, p. 218.
14 Skjølsvold A. (1991) *Archaeological Test-Excavations on the Maldive Islands*, Vol. 2, p. 201.
15 Heyerdahl T. (1987) *The Maldive Mystery*, p. 199
16 Heyerdahl T. (1987) *The Maldive Mystery*, p. 16.
17 Heyerdahl T. (1987) *The Maldive Mystery*, p. 238.
18 Heyerdahl T. (1987) *The Maldive Mystery*, p. 308.
19 Forbes, Andrew D. W. (1987) "The Pre-Islamic Archeology of the Maldive Islands," *Bulletin de l'École française d'Extrême-Orient*, Vol. 76, pp. 281-288
20 Heyerdahl T. (1987) *The Maldive Mystery*, p. 308.

TÚCUME ARCHAEOLOGICAL PROJECT

1 Heyerdahl T. (1995) *Pyramids of Túcume*, pp. 38-39.
2 Heyerdahl T. (1995) *Pyramids of Túcume*, p. 42.
3 Heyerdahl T. (1998) *Green was the Earth on the Seventh Day*, p. 16.
4 Heyerdahl T. (1995) *Pyramids of Túcume*, p. 15.
5 Heyerdahl T. (1995) *Pyramids of Túcume*, p. 37.
6 Heyerdahl T. (1995) *Pyramids of Túcume*, p. 201.
7 Heyerdahl T. (1995) *Pyramids of Túcume*, pp. 224,225, and 226.
8 Kvam, R. (2013) *Thor Heyerdahl: Mannen og mytene* [The man and the myths], p. 266
9 Skjølsvold A. (15 April 1992) "Thor Heyerdahl har gjort sensasjonelle funn i Peru", *Aftenposten*.
10 Heyerdahl T. (1991) in interview with Gary Marx, "Beyond Kon-Tiki," *Chicago Tribune*.

VOYAGE'S END

LIFE, THEORY, AND LEGACY

1 Heyerdahl T. (1993) Press announcement, Kon-Tiki Museum.
2 Heyerdahl T. (1991) in "Heyerdahl, scorned by many scientists, digs for vindication in Peru's pyramids," *Baltimore Sun*.
3 Heyerdahl T. (1991) in "Heyerdahl, scorned by many scientists, digs for vindication in Peru's pyramids," *Baltimore Sun*.
4 Heyerdahl T. (1989) *Aku-Aku: The Secret of Easter Island*, p. 216.
5 Heyerdahl T. (1989) *Aku-Aku: The Secret of Easter Island*, p. 216.
6 Milner, W.M.H. (1902) *The Royal House of Britain: An Enduring Dynasty*, pp. 31-32.
7 Heyerdahl T. (29 November 2001) press conference launch for The Hunt for Odin.
8 Heyerdahl T. (2000) "Scandinavian Ancestry: Tracing Roots to Azerbaijan", *Azerbaijan International*.
9 Heyerdahl T. (1995) "The Azerbaijan Connection: Challenging Euro-Centric Theories of Migration", *Azerbaijan International* (3.1).
10 Heyerdahl T. (19 July 1969) telegram sent to United Nations Secretary General U Thant after abandoning Ra.
11 Heyerdahl T. (23 July 1969) telegram sent to United Nations Secretary General U Thant after abandoning Ra.
12 Heyerdahl T. (13 January 1971) address to Egyptian government at Cairo.
13 Heyerdahl T. (1982) *The Tigris Expedition: In Search of Our Beginnings*, p. 280.
14 Heyerdahl T. (10 November 1971) "Our Silent Enemy."
15 Heyerdahl T. (1978) report to the United Nations, joint winners of the 1978 Pahlavi prize.
16 Heyerdahl T. (1971) "Atlantic Ocean Pollution Observed" report, p. 167.
17 Heyerdahl T. (1982) reporting the news.
18 Heyerdahl T. (6 July 1972) "How Vulnerable is the Ocean."
19 Heyerdahl T. (1975)"Forestry in a World of Limited Resources."
20 Heyerdahl T. (1980) "The Ocean is a Lake."
21 Heyerdahl T. (1974) speech to Aberdeen youth orchestra.
22 Heyerdahl T. (1983) "Craftsmanship and Progress."
23 Heyerdahl T. (1985) at the Right Livelihood Award.
24 Heyerdahl T. (30 September 1995) speech at the opening of the Nordic United World College.
25 Heyerdahl T. (12 July 1944) letter to Liv Heyerdahl.
26 Heyerdahl T (February 1975) "The Sea I Would Like to See," written at Colla Micheri.

All letters, interviews and other miscellaneous papers are held in the Kon-Tiki Museum Archive, Oslo.

Bibliographies

GENESIS, UNCEASING VOYAGES, VOYAGE'S END

This book was made possible by the special access granted to us of the letters, journals and papers of The Kon-Tiki Museum Archive.

- Andersson A. (2010) *A Hero for the Atomic Age: Thor Heyerdahl and the Kon-Tiki Expedition.* Peter Lang, Oxford.
- Boas, F. (1925) *America and the Old World, international congress of Americanists,* vol 21, no.2
- Boas, F. (1930) Karl Von Den Steinen. *Science,* 71(1827).
- Buck, P. H. (1945) *An Introduction to Polynesian Anthropology.* Bernice P. Bishop Musuem, Honolulu.
- Cook, K. (2015). "Ke Ao a me Ka Pō: Postmillennial Thought and Native Hawaiian Foreign Mission Work." *American Quarterly,* 67 (3), pp. 887-912.
- Fischer S.R. (1997) *Rongorongo: The Easter Island Script: History, Traditions, Texts.* Clarendon Press, Oxford.
- Golson, J., Groves, M., Parsonson, G. S., Dening, G. M., Bechtol, C. O., Heyen, G. H., Hilder, B., Maude, & Key, N. (1962) Memoir No. 34. Polynesian Navigation. A Symposium on Andrew Sharp's Theory of Accidental Voyages [Part 1]. *The Journal of the Polynesian Society,* 71(3), pp. 1-viii.
- Herman D. (September 2014) "How the voyage of the Kon-Tiki misled the world about navigating the Pacific." *Smithsonian Magazine.*
- Heyerdahl, T. (1958) *Aku-aku: The Secret of Easter Island.* Allen and Unwin, London.
- Heyerdahl, T. (1952) *American Indians in the Pacific: The theory behind the Kon-Tiki expedition.* Allen and Unwin, London.
- Heyerdahl, T. (1978) *Early Man and the Ocean: The beginning of navigation and sea born civilization.* George Allen & Unwin Ltd, London.
- Heyerdahl, T. (1989) *Easter Island: Mystery Solved.* Random House, New York.
- Heyerdahl, T. (1974) *Fatu-Hiva: Back to Nature.* George Allen & Unwin Ltd, London.
- Heyerdahl, T. (1996). *Green was the Earth on the Seventh Day.* Random House, New York.
- Heyerdahl, T. (2000). *In the Footsteps of Adam: A memoir of an extraordinary life.* Little Brown and Company, London.
- Heyerdahl, T. (trans. Lyon F.H.) (1950). *The Kon-Tiki Expedition: By Raft Across the South Seas.* Allen and Unwin, London.
- Heyerdahl, T. (1986) *The Maldive Mystery.* George Allen & Unwin Ltd, London.
- Heyerdahl, T. (1955) "Preliminary report on the discovery of archaeology in the Galápagos Islands." *Anais do XXXI Congreso Internacional de Americanistas,* São Paulo, pp. 685-697.
- Heyerdahl, T., Sandweiss, D. H., and Narváez, A. (1995), *Pyramids of Túcume:*
- *The quest for Peru's forgotten city.* New York: Thames and Hudson.
- Heyerdahl, T. (1970) *The Ra Expeditions.* George Allen & Unwin Ltd, London.
- Heyerdahl, T. and Ferdon, E. (eds.) (1961) "Reports of the Norwegian Archaeological Expedition to Easter Island and the East Pacific. Volume 1. Archaeology of Easter Island." *Monographs of the School of American research and the Kon-Tiki Museum,* Number 24, Part 1. Forum Publishing House, Stockholm.
- Heyerdahl, T. (1968) *Sea Routes to Polynesia: American Indians and early Asiatics in the Pacific.* George Allen & Unwin Ltd, London.
- Heyerdahl, T. (1979) *The Tigris Expedition: In Search of our Beginnings.* George Allen & Unwin Ltd, London.
- Heyerdahl, T. (1941) "Turning Back Time in the South Seas." *National Geographic,* Vol. 79, pp. 109-136.
- Jacoby, A. (1968) *Señor Kon-Tiki: The biography of Thor Heyerdahl.* Allen and Unwin, London.
- Kluckhohn, C. (1958) *Ralph Linton 1893-1953: A biographical memoir.* National Academy of Sciences, Washington D.C.
- Linton, A. and Wagley C. (1971) *Ralph Linton: Leaders of Modern Anthropology.* Columbia University Press, New York City.
- Linton, R. (1924). "The Degeneration of human figures used in Polynesian decorative art." *The Journal of the Polynesian Society* 33, 4(132), pp. 321-324.
- Linton R. (1926). "Ethnology of Polynesia and Micronesia." *Guide (Field Museum of Natural History)* 6, pp. 1-191.
- Melander V. (2020) "Coming of the White Bearded Men: The origin and development of Thor Heyerdahl's Kon-Tiki Theory. PhD Thesis." The Australian National University, Canberra.
- Melander V. (2019) "David's Weapon of Mass Destruction: The Reception of Thor Heyerdahl's 'Kon-Tiki Theory'." *Bulletin of the History of Archaeology,* 29(1), pp. 6.
- Morris, N.J. (1979) "Hawaiian Missionaries in the Marquesas." *Hawaiian Journal of History,* 13, pp. 46-58.
- Oliver, D. L. (1974) *Boats and Travel in Ancient Tahitian Society.* University of Hawai'i Press, pp. 194-219.
- Osmond, M., Ross, M., Pawley A. and Osmond, M. (2007) "Navigation and the Heavens." *The Lexicon of Proto Oceanic: The culture and environment of ancestral Oceanic society: 2 The Physical Environment,* pp. 155-192. ANU Press, Canberra.
- Steinen, K. (trans. Langridge M., ed. Terrell, J.) (1988) "Von den Steinman's Marquesan Myths." *Journal of Pacific History and Target Oceania,* Canberra.
- Van Tilburg, J. (2003) *Among Stone Giants: The life of Katherine Routledge and her remarkable expedition to Easter Island.* Scribner, London.
- Van Tilburg, J. (2014) "Lost and Found: Hoa Hakananai'a and the Orongo 'Doorpost'. *The Journal of the Polynesian Society* 123(4), pp. 383-97.

REVISITING THOR HEYERDAHL'S OCEANIC MIGRATION HYPOTHESES

- Anderson A. (2021) "Returning to the hypothesis of Amerindian settlement on Rapa Nui (Easter Island)." *Journal of the Polynesian Society* 130, pp. 245-256.
- Anderson A. (2022) "Ex Oriente Lux: Amerindian seafaring and Easter Island. Contact revisited." In Rull V. and C. Stevenson C. (eds), "The Prehistory of Rapa Nui (Easter Island), *Developments in Paleoenvironmental Research* 22.
- Anderson A., Camens A., Clark G., and S. Haberle (2018) "Investigating pre-modern colonization of the Indian Ocean: the remote islands enigma." In Seetah, K. (ed) *Connecting Continents: Archaeology and history in the Indian Ocean.* Ohio University Press, Athens, pp. 30-67.
- Anderson A., Stothert K., Martinsson-Wallin H., Wallin P., Flett I., Haberle H., Heijnis, H. and Rhodes E. (2016) "Reconsidering Precolumbian Human Colonization in the Galápagos Islands, Republic of Ecuador." *Latin American Antiquity* 27, pp. 169-183.
- Anderson, A. (2022) "An historical analysis of waka unua and the Māori sail." *Journal of the Polynesian Society* 131, pp. 33-70.
- Buhring, K. (2020) "The archaeology of trans-pacific interactions: evaluating cultural transmission between Polynesia and South America." PhD thesis, University of Auckland.
- Callaghan, R., Montenegro, A. and Fitzpatrick, S. (2022) "The effects of intra- and interannual wind and current variation on sailing raft travel along the Pacific coast of the Americas." In Beekman C. Beekman and McEwan C. (eds) *Waves of Influence: Pacific maritime networks.* Dumbarton Oaks, Washington, DC, pp. 93-120.
- DiNapoli R., Rieth T., Lipo C. and Hunt T. (2020) "Tempo of '"collapse'": A model-based approach to the case of Rapa Nui (Easter Island)." In *Journal of Archaeological Science* 116, pp. 1-13.
- Golson, J. (1965) "Thor Heyerdahl and the Prehistory of Easter Island." Oceania 36, pp. 38-83.
- Green, R. (2001) "Commentary on the sailing raft, the sweet potato and the South American connection." *Rapa Nui Journal* 15, p. 69-77.
- Holton, G. (2004) "Heyerdahl's Kon Tiki theory and the denial of the indigenous past." *Anthropological Forum* 14, pp. 163-81.
- Traditional rigs in Howe, K. (ed) (2006) *Vaka Moana: Voyages of the Ancestors.* Bateman, Auckland.
- Ioannidis A. G., Blanco-Portillo J., Sandoval K., Hagelberg E., Miquel-Poblete J. F., Moreno-Mayar, J. V., Rodriguez J.E. et al. (2020) "Native American gene flow into Polynesia predating Easter Island settlement." *Nature* 583, pp. 572-77.
- Jett, S. (2017) *Ancient Ocean Crossings: Reconsidering the case for contacts with the Pre-Columbian Americas.* University of Alabama Press.
- Jones, T., Storey A., Matisoo-Smith, E., and Press Ramirez-Aliaga J. (eds) (2011) *Polynesians in America: pre-Columbian contacts with the New World.* Altamira, Lanham.
- MacMillan, Brown J. (1924) *The Riddle of the Pacific.* Fisher Unwin, London.
- Martinsson-Wallin H., Wallin P., Anderson A., and Solsvik R. (2013) "Chronogeographic Variation in Initial East Polynesian Construction of Monumental Ceremonial Sites." *The Journal of Island and Coastal Archaeology,* 8, 405-421.
- Melander, V. (2020) "The Coming of the White Bearded Men: The origin and development of Thor Heyerdahl's Kon-Tiki theory,". PhD thesis, Australian National University, Canberra.
- Meroz, Y. (2013) "The Plank Canoe of Southern California: not a Polynesian Import, but a local innovation." In Sylak-Glassman J. and Spence J. (eds) "Structure and contact in Languages of the Americas." *Survey of Californian and other Indian Languages* 15, 103-188.
- Montenegro A., Avis C., and Weaver A. (2008) "Modeling the prehistoric arrival of the sweet potato in Polynesia." *Journal of Archaeological Science* 35, 355-67.
- Nair, S. and Protzen J.P. (2015) "The Inka built environment." In Shimada I. (ed) *The Inka Empire: A Multidisciplinary Approach.* University of Texas Press, Austin, pp. 215-31.
- Sandweiss, D. and Reid D. (2016) "Negotiated subjugation: Maritime trade and the incorporation of Chincha into the Inca empire." *Journal of Island and Coastal Archaeology* 11, pp. 311-25.
- Sorrenson, M. (1979), *Maori Origins and migrations: The genesis of some Pakeha myths and legends.* Aucklan University Press, Auckland.
- Stanish, C. (2012) "Above-ground tombs in the circum-Titicaca basin." In Vranich, A. Vranich, Klarich E., and Stanish C. (eds) *Advances in Titicaca Basin Archaeology III.* University of Michigan, Ann Arbor, pp. 203-20.
- Tregear, E. (1885) *The Aryan Maori.* Government Printer, Wellington.
- Wallin P. (2020) "Native South Americans reached Polynesia early." *Nature* 583, pp. 524-25.

Chronology, 1914–2012

6 October 1914 | Born in Larvik, Norway, the only child of Thor and Alison Heyerdahl.

1933 | Starts attendance at University of Oslo, specializing in zoology and geography.

1933 | Meets Liv Coucheron Torp.

Christmas Eve 1936 | Marries Liv Coucheron Torp (two sons, divorces 1947).

Christmas Day 1936 | Travels to Fatu Hiva in the Marquesas Islands, where they collect specimens and Heyerdahl first considers theories of how Polynesia was populated, finding evidence that links the islands to South America.

1938 | Returns to Norway, settling near Lillehammer.

1938 | *In Search of Paradise* published in Norway without fanfare (many decades later, he publishes it in English as *Fatu-Hiva: Back to Nature*).

1939–40 | Moves to British Columbia, Canada, to study the Kwakiutl First Nation, looking for links between Polynesians and Pacific Northwest Coast indigenous peoples.

1940 | Pacific migration hypothesis made public for the first time, reported by the *Vancouver Sun*.

9 April 1940 | German troops enter major Norwegian ports and occupy Norway.

Spring 1940 | Stuck in Canada on his visitor visa with his young family and in debt, Heyerdahl manages to secure a work permit and is employed for a year by the Consolidated Mining and Smelting Company in the Rocky Mountains.

Winter 1941 | Quits his laborer job and travels to Baltimore, Maryland, for a prospective job.

7 December 1941 | Japanese forces bomb Pearl Harbor, Hawaii.

December 1941 | Contacts the Norwegian Embassy in the United States and enlists in the Norwegian Army. His family returns to Tadanac, British Columbia. Sells his entire Marquesas collection to the Brooklyn Museum in New York.

1942 | Attends training camp as a private in Lunenburg, Nova Scotia, then sent to radio school training in Toronto, Canada, at the "Little Norway" camp established by Norwegian airmen who escaped the invasion.

1942 | Selected, as one of eight men from Lunenburg, to join a special operations unit of the Norwegian Air Force called "I-Group." Relocated to a specialized radio training camp near Huntsville, Ontario, where Liv and the boys join him.

1 September 1943 | Arrives in London with I-Group and is assigned a post in Scotland.

6 June 1944 | D-Day allied invasion of Europe. Heyerdahl, now promoted to sergeant, moves with I-Group to a British unit, where they transmit and receive coded messages.

September 1944 | I-Group is dissolved. Heyerdahl is reissued to "52" Special Operations training unit for parachutists and saboteurs.

Late 1944 | Travels to the Norwegian frontier in Kirkenes.

25 October 1944 | Red army occupies Kirkenes in northern Norway. Heyerdahl leaves for a mission in Finnmark, Norway.

26 December 1944 | Becomes a lieutenant. En route to England from Finnmark, Heyerdahl serves as second-in-command of a small Norwegian unit.

6 February 1945 | Goes to London and is appointed to set up a radio training school in Kallax, Sweden.

1945 | Ceasefire announced; war ends.

August/September 1945 | Returns to Norway, settling in Lillehammer with Liv and his family. Begins work on *Polynesia and America, A Study of Prehistoric Relations*, the manuscript for what will become *American Indians in the Pacific*.

28 April 1947 | *Kon-Tiki* raft leaves Callao, Peru, aiming to sail to Polynesia. The raft, constructed out of balsa wood, takes its name from a legendary seafaring sun king who appears in both Inca and Polynesian mythologies.

7 August 1947 | *Kon-Tiki* runs aground on Raroia Reef in the Tuamotu Archipelago after traveling 101 days on the Pacific Ocean.

7 November 1948 | *The Kon-Tiki Expedition* is published in English and in later years is translated into 84 languages.

1949 | Marries his second wife Yvonne Dedekam-Simonsen (three daughters, divorced in 1969).

1950 | The *Kon-Tiki Expedition* movie is released.

1950 | The Kon-Tiki Museum opens in Oslo, Norway, as a private museum dedicated to preserving vessels, artifacts, and documents related to Heyerdahl's expeditions.

1951 | *Kon-Tiki* movie wins an Oscar for best documentary.

12 August 1952 | *American Indians in the Pacific: The Theory Behind the Kon-Tiki Expedition* published in London, Chicago, and Stockholm. A culmination of 20 years of independent research on Pacific migration theory, it was the only book expressly written for an academic readership.

1953 | Travels to Galápagos to conduct the first archaeological expedition. Heyerdahl and his team uncover pre-Inca objects.

1955 | *Galápagos* documentary released.

1955–56 | Travels to Rapa Nui to study *moai* statues.

1958 | *Aku-Aku: The Secret of Easter Island* published.

1960 | *Aku-Aku* documentary released.

1962 | Travels to Russia to lecture at the Soviet Academy of Science, one of the first Westerners to do so during the height of the Cold War.

1968 | Heyerdahl tours pyramids in Egypt and witnesses ancient depictions of sailors in papyrus boats, which will eventually inform the *Tigris* expedition.

1969 | *Ra* vessel launched from Safi, Morocco. Constructed in Egypt, the vessel was meant to reach Barbados, but the mission is aborted after eight weeks due to the raft nearly sinking.

1969 | Sends his first letter to the United Nations on ocean pollution observed during the original Ra expedition.

1970 | *Ra II* launched from Safi just ten months after the ill-fated original Ra expedition. Vessel is constructed by indigenous Aymara craftsmen and successfully completes its journey to Barbados after 57 days.

January 1971 | *Ra II* voyage featured as the cover story in *National Geographic*.

1971 | *The Ra Expeditions* published.

1972 | *The Ra Expeditions* (or *Ra*) documentary released, directed by Heyerdahl and Lennart Ehrenborg. Nominated for an Academy Award for Best Documentary Feature.

1973 | Presents a report on oceanic pollution at the United Nations third Conference on the Law of the Sea.

1976 | Goes to Iraq to study reed boats.

1977 | Construction of the *Tigris* reed boat in Iraq, setting sail the same year from Shatt-al-Arab. The vessel reaches Pakistan and finally Djibouti after 143 days.

3 April 1978 | *Tigris* burned outside the port at Djibouti as a protest against war.

1979 | *Tigris* published in Norwegian, with the English edition following five years later.

August 1981 | First visit to the Soviet Republic of Azerbaijan to see petroglyphs at Gobustan and research origins of Scandinavian peoples in the Caucasus region, pre-Viking times.

1982 | Heyerdahl receives a letter with a picture of stone statues from the Maldives.

1983 | First Maldives expedition, conducting the first archaeological digs since 1922.

1984 | Second Maldives expedition.

1988–92 | Archaeological excavations at the La Raya pyramid complex near Túcume, Peru.

1986–88 | Easter Island expedition to test how *moai* statues were moved around the island.

1986 | *The Maldive Mystery* published.

1989 | *Easter Island: The Mystery Solved* published.

1991 | Marries his third wife, French actress Jacqueline Beer.

1993 | *Pyramids of Túcume: The Quest for Peru's Forgotten City* published.

1998 | Visits Iceland on invitation by the President, where he stumbles upon a copy of Snorri Sturluson's old Norse sagas that sets him on an investigation into Nordic ancestry.

1999 | Travels to the Shaki-Gabala region and village of Nij in Azerbaijan, searching for further evidence on an early Caucasus peoples led by Odin to Scandinavia.

1999 | *No Borders* published. Co-authored with Per Lillieström on the theory of Vikings originating in the Caucasus region. Heyerdahl is famously known for saying: "Borders? I have never seen one. But I have heard they exist in the minds of some people."

September 2000 | Visits Azerbaijan for the last time with his wife, Jacqueline Beer, to meet the indigenous Udi people of the Gabala region, for further research into ancestral links between Caucasus and Scandinavian peoples. Presents at the Academy of Sciences in Baku.

2000 | Begins excavations in Azov, Russia, to further investigate links between Scandinavia and the Caucasus.

2001 | *The Search for Odin: On the Trail of our Past* published in Norwegian, co-authored with Per Lillieström.

18 April 2002 | Dies at the age of 87 at his home in Colla Micheri, Italy.

2011 | Conference on Heyerdahl's Odin theory in Azerbaijan, organized by the University of Oslo and University of Azerbaijan.

May 2011 | Heyerdahl's archives included in UNESCO's Memory of the World Register, which not only recognizes Heyerdahl's personage but the importance of the material as documents of "places that soon after would face modernization and globalization processes."

2012 | *Kon-Tiki* book published in Azerbaijan.

2012 | New *Kon-Tiki* movie released. Nominated for an Academy Award for Best Foreign Language Film. Also nominated for a Golden Globe.

About the Museum and Archive

Thor Heyerdahl is one of history's most famous explorers. He completed world-renowned ocean voyages and undertook important archaeological excavations, through which he championed his deep passion for both the environment and world peace. The Kon-Tiki Museum exhibits objects from Heyerdahl's world-famous expeditions, including the original *Kon-Tiki* raft, and the papyrus boat *Ra II*.

The Thor Heyerdahl Archive provides a unique insight into Heyerdahl's life through photographs, films, manuscripts, and documents of historical, artistic, and cultural value. His expeditions and books were a source of inspiration for generations of adventurers, scientists, and people all around the globe. The document archive contains Heyerdahl's original book manuscripts, papers, and speeches from 1947 to the end of his life. Correspondence and notes associated with organizing his world-famous expeditions, his research into prehistoric voyaging and contacts between cultures, and his fight against pollution of the ocean and a world with fewer borders makes up the rest of the archive.

The archive is administered by the Kon-Tiki Museum and the National Library of Norway in Oslo and is part of the Memory of the World, UNESCO's list of immaterial cultural heritage.

Contributors

Atholl Anderson PhD, ScD (Cambridge) is Emeritus-Professor of Prehistory at the Australian National University and a Fellow of the Royal Society of New Zealand, the Australian Academy of the Humanities, and the Society of Antiquaries, London. An oceanic archaeologist, he has worked on island prehistory and palaeoecology across the Indo-Pacific region from the Galápagos to Madagascar, and particularly in Polynesia.

Sonia Haoa Cardinali is a Rapanui archaeologist with the Mata Ki Te Rangi Foundation and coordinator of the island's national monuments. She has an honorary doctorate in philosophy from Uppsala University.

Sylvia A. Earle is Explorer in Residence at the National Geographic Society, Founder of Mission Blue, Founder of Deep Ocean Exploration and Research, a Founding Ocean Elder, Honorary Chair of the Advisory Council for the Harte Research Institute, and former Chief Scientist of NOAA. Author of more than 230 publications, leader of more than 100 expeditions with years at sea and thousands of hours underwater, she has received 33 honorary doctorates, been named *Time Magazine's* first Hero for the Planet and a Living Legend by the Library of Congress. Her more than 150 honors include the Netherlands Order of the Golden Ark, the Princess of Asturias Prize for Concord, the TED Prize, the Tallberg Global Leadership Prize, the Explorers Club Medal, Royal Geographic Society's Patron's Medal, and the National Geographic's Hubbard Medal.

Kingston Trinder is a nonfiction author and publisher originally from New Zealand. His work includes the novel *Milk Tooth* (2012), and several fine art monographs: *Old Glory* (2016), *Chromatic Reflection* (2016), *An Atlas of Rare & Familiar Colour* (2017), *Who is Michael Jang?* (2019), *John Cage: a Mycological Foray* (2020), and and *Talk Soon* (2021). He holds a graduate degree in cultural anthropology (Material & Visual Culture) from UCL.

Image Credits

A number of individuals took or provided images on each of the expeditions, and in many cases they are unknown. Lead photographers are listed below.

Fatu Hiva, 1936–37: Thor Heyerdahl and Liv Heyerdahl.
Bella Coola, 1939–40: Thor Heyerdahl and Liv Heyerdahl.
Kon-Tiki Expedition, 1947: Thor Heyerdahl, Erik Hesselberg, Bengt Danielsson.
Galápagos Expedition, 1952–53: Thor Heyerdahl and Per Høst.
Easter Island Expedition, 1955–56: Erling J. Schjerven (expedition photographer), Arne Skjølsvold, Magnar Hille, Ingvald Olsen.
Ra Expedition, 1969: Carlo Mauri.
Ra II Expedition, 1970: Carlo Mauri and Kei Ohara.
Tigris Expedition, 1977–78: Norris Brock, Carlo Mauri, Gerhmán Carrlassco.
Maldives Expedition, 1983 and 1984: Bengt Jonson and Åke Karlsson (both from SeBra Film).
Easter Island Expedition 1986–88: Bengt Jonson, Anders Berg, Åke Karlsson, Johnny Steen (all three from SeBra Film), Walter Leonardi.
Túcume Expedition: Helene Elisabeth Heyerdahl and others unknown.
Kon-Tiki Museum artifacts: Sissel Bjørkan Bukkemoen.

Index

TEXTS BY:
Kingston Trinder

ADDITIONAL TEXTS BY:
Atholl Anderson, Sylvia Earle,
Sonia Haoa Cardinali

EDITORIAL DIRECTOR:
Pascale Georgiev

MANAGING EDITOR:
Lucy Kingett

RESEARCH ASSISTANT:
Josephine Minhinnett

COPY-EDITORS:
Nancy Wallace and
Theresa Bebbington

PROOFREADER:
Lindsay Kaubi

INDEXER:
Annette Musker

DESIGN:
Alizée Freudenthal

DESIGN ASSISTANT:
Emma Singleton

PHOTO EDITOR:
Marina Vitaglione

ILLUSTRATION P.4-5:
Espen Friberg

Produced in collaboration
with The Kon-Tiki Museum.

The publisher would like to thank Reidar Solsvik for his invaluable contributions to the book.

With thanks to the Ontario Arts Council.

PUBLISHED BY:
Atelier Éditions
Los Angeles, USA
www.atelier-editions.com

DISTRIBUTED BY:
ARTBOOK | D.A.P.
75 Broad Street, suite 630
New York, New York 10004
artbook.com

First edition of 3,000

Printed in Italy on 100% ecological paper from sustainable forests
978-1-954957-99-2